THE WILD REGION IN LIFE-HISTORY

Northwestern University

Studies in Phenomenology

and

Existential Philosophy

THE WILD REGION IN LIFE-HISTORY

László Tengelyi

Translated from the German
by Géza Kállay with the author

Northwestern University Press
Evanston, Illinois

Northwestern University Press
Evanston, Illinois 60208-4170

Printed in the United States of America

10 9 8 7 6 5 4 3 2 1

ISBN 0-8101-1871-8 (cloth)
ISBN 0-8101-1661-8 (paper)

Library of Congress Cataloging-in-Publication Data

Tengelyi, László.
[Zwitterbegriff Lebensgeschichte. English]
The wild region in life-history / László Tengelyi; translated from the German by Géza Kállay with the author.
p. cm.
Includes bibliographical references (p. 207) and index.
ISBN 0-8101-1871-8—ISBN 0-8101-1661-8
1. Self (Philosophy) 2. Identity (Psychology) I. Title.
BD438.5 .T4613 2002
126—dc21 2002012764

The paper used in this publication meets the minimum requirements of the American National Standard for Information Sciences—Permanence of Paper for Printed Library Materials, ANSI Z39.48–1992.

Contents

Preface

The investigations resumed in this book outline a phenomenological approach to some main topics of theoretical philosophy, like meaning, sense, temporality, unity of life, narrative history, self-identity, and intersubjectivity, as well as to an ethics of alterity. Their point of departure is a critical examination of what is commonly referred to as "the narrative view of the self," which tends to put an equal sign between life-history and personal identity. While challenging this position, what is going to be revealed is the hidden area of a rarely noticed, often discarded, and sometimes even repressed sense formation in life-history; it will be shown that while this area does nurture the narratives designed to convey a determinate and definitively fixed meaning upon one's self, it is not, however, exhausted by them. It is this hidden area which is described, with an expression taken from the later Merleau-Ponty, as *the "wild region" in life-history.*

Different domains belong to this wild region. The broadest of them is constituted by *experience,* which, properly understood, turns out to be nothing other than the emergence of a new sense in conflict with previous expectations. A closely related domain may be designated as the *unconscious*—a concept which (as Husserl and also some of his successors realized) has a phenomenological scope and pertinence just as much as it has possible applications in the field of psychoanalysis. Further instances belonging to the wild region are *operative language* and *creative expression,* in the sense Merleau-Ponty assigned to these terms. Operative language and creative expression, constantly remaining in touch with experience, give rise to a surplus of sense irreducible to experience but equally irreducible to the ready-made, fixed, institutionalized meanings they make use of. An area which partly overlaps with the hitherto mentioned domains is formed by critical situations and events apt to provoke *unforeseen alterations* in life-history. The irruption of primal impressions into the temporality of experience may serve as a formally generalized model for the study of such sudden changes. Yet, upon closer examination, the domain of radical turns in life-history proves to be inseparable from another wide area, which encompasses all kinds of *alterity in experience:* from the otherness one's own body may be said to involve, to the alien alterity one is confronted with in his or her encounter with another human being. Finally, not even the *immediate ethical consequences* of this encounter transcend the wild region in life-history: on the contrary, they include, as one can show with Levinas, a whole range of elementary claims and ties which precede duty, law, justice, and obligation, without, however, being integrated into a moral order of aims and goals.

The present text—with the exception of the first chapter and some parts of the last chapter—is a strongly abridged, slightly reshaped—and, I hope, even amended—version of a more voluminous book which was published in German with the title *Der Zwitterbegriff Lebensgeschichte* (Wilhelm Fink Publishing House, Munique, 1998). I wrote the German text while I was doing research in Germany for two years. I would like to express my gratitude to the Alexander von Humboldt Foundation for their grant during this period and for their generous assistance in the publication of the German original.

Various influences left their traces on the inquiries summarized in the German book. It was a special privilege that the two greatest thinkers in contemporary German phenomenology, Professor Klaus Held (Wuppertal) and Professor Bernhard Waldenfels (Bochum) were willing to accept the task of directing my work during my stay in Germany. Without the manifold inspiration I took from their courses, their works, and our numerous discussions, I would never have been able to write this book.

The first to convince me of the pertinence of both Husserlian and French phenomenology was, however, Professor Rudolf Bernet (Leuven). It was more than twelve years ago (in the academic year of 1988–89) that a ten-month-long stay, generously granted by the Hungarian Soros-Foundation, provided me with the opportunity of getting the first impressions of Professor Bernet's acute and precise ways of practicing phenomenological analysis at university lectures and in his written studies. The effect of this encounter has only been even more corroborated by the philosophical discussions and friendly conversations I have repeatedly had with him ever since.

The entirely original version of phenomenology developed by Professor Marc Richir (Brussels, Paris) in a whole series of profound works has had a stronger impact on the method of my investigations than I have been able to acknowledge in my considerations specifically devoted to his ideas. This impact is probably even more perceptible in the English version of the book, which carries some traces of the period I spent in France partly as a guest professor at the University of Poitiers, partly as an associate researcher at the Maison des Sciences de l'Homme in Paris. While expressing my gratitude to the Ministry of Education and Scientific Research of France, to the University of Poitiers, to the Andrew W. Mellon Foundation, and to the Maison des Sciences de l'Homme, I should like to emphasize that, among other benefits, the guest professorship and the research I could do in France made it possible for me to discuss some of my topics with Professor Richir personally, as well as to discuss some of his topics with my French students.

I am very grateful to all of these excellent scholars for their unfailing attention and encouragement. At the same time, I would like to express my special thanks to Professor Géza Kállay (Budapest), the cotranslator of this book. The English version could never have been finished without his expertise and care. A considerable part of the book is in his translation, and he took upon himself the painstaking task of correcting the remaining part as well. Thus, the final formulation of the text carries everywhere traces of his hand. It is not only for linguistic precision and stylistic sensibility but also for philosophical clarity that I am grateful to him.

Our work was generously supported by the Hungarian Soros Foundation. We both should like to express our gratitude for this support.

Yet, nothing would have become of my whole venture had Professor David Michael Levin, the editor of this book, not taken matters into his hands with great expertise, tact, patience, and care. I owe special thanks to him not only for proofreading the whole book but also for his excellent suggestions both during his stay in Budapest in 1994 and over the period the manuscript took its final shape.

The first chapter of the present book as well as some parts of the last chapter have specifically been prepared with the English edition in mind. While working on them, I have been relying upon some studies I wrote after the publication of the German original. These studies are the following:

"Sinn und Bedeutung in phänomenologischer Sicht," *Internationale Zeitschrift für Philosophie* 1 (1998): 64–73. (Serbian translation: "Smisao i znacenje iz fenomenoloskog ugla," *Filozofski Godisnjak* 10 [1997]: 251–59.)

"Die Erfahrung und ihr Ausdruck." In *Das Phänomen und die Sprache.* Edited by J. Trinks. Vienna: Turia and Kant, 1998, pp. 24–37.

"Schwierigkeiten mit Husserls Begriff der kategorialen Anschauung." Paper read at the Congress of the German Society for Phenomenology (September 23 and 26, 1998, Leuven, Belgium). Forthcoming in a collective volume edited by Antje Kapust and Rudolf Bernet.

"Erfahrung und Ausdruck." In *Philosophia Hungaria.* Edited by W. Hogrebe. Würzburg: Königshausen and Neumann, 2001, pp. 219–28.

"L'expérience et son expression catégoriale." In *Studia Universitatis Babeş—Bólyai, Philosophia* 44, 1–2 (1999), Cluj, 2001.

"A tapasztalat és a valóság" ("Experience and Reality"). In *Filozófia az ezredfordulón.* Edited by J. Nyíri. Budapest: Áron Publishing House, 2000.

"Erfahren, Handeln, Erzählen." Paper read at the Conference *Möglichkeiten und Grenzen der Narration* (April 12–16, 2000, Otterthal, Austria). Forthcoming in a collective volume edited by J. Trinks.

"Gesetz und Begehren in der Ethik von Levinas." *Der Anspruch des Anderen. Perspektiven phänomenologischer Ethik.* Edited by B. Waldenfels and I. Därmann. Munique: W. Fink, 1998, pp. 165–75.

"Gesetzesanspruch und wilde Verantwortung." In *Hermeneutik des Selbst—Im Zeichen des Anderen.* Edited by B. Liebsch. Freiburg and Munique: K. Alber, 1999, pp. 260–72.

Paris, January 2001

Prelude: Self-Identity and Life-History

The time we live in is interwoven with stories. Our place in the world, before we reach self-awareness—or, I dare claim, even before we are born—is assigned by family stories. The stories we thus inherit are, in turn, supplemented by the ever-changing story of our own, which will not come to rest even at the moment of our death. What effects us from the outside, and what we ourselves do, think, imagine, or experience, we relate about ourselves and about one another to others; we relate it: we recount it to *an other,* again and again, in *another* way. Our recountings, from time to time, reach back to previous recountings, and then they start all over again: this is the way they try to encircle and enmesh the fleeing events. What we consciously pass over in silence and what we unconsciously avoid lives in the shadow of the already recounted and of that which still remains to be told.

However, we encounter a question here. In his novel *The Magic Mountain,* Thomas Mann reflects on the recountability of time. He asks himself: "Can one tell—that is to say, narrate—time, time itself, as such, for its own sake?"[1] Thus, it is a "time novel"—in the sense of a "tale about time"[2]—a *Zeitroman,* which raises the fundamental question of not only every time novel but of every life-history as well.

The "hermetical magic,"[3] which, according to Mann's text, pertains to all recountings, liberates the novel to play an ironic game with the fundamental question. The novel offers a term as an answer, which implies that a life-history is permeated with a mysterious unity. The term is *destiny* (*Schicksal*).

Destiny is mentioned by Hans Castorp in his great debate with Mynheer Peeperkorn. What Castorp performs around this word is significant: first he lets it drop, then he returns to it, indicating that it is still on his mind, and then he turns to something else again. It is only much later that he is willing to explain what he meant by destiny:

> For love of her [that is, of Clawdia Chauchat], in defiance of Herr Settembrini, I declared myself for the principle of unreason, the *spiritual*

> principle of disease, under whose aegis I had already, in reality, stood for a long time back, and I remained up here, I no longer know precisely how long [. . .].[4]

"For a long time back" (*von langer Hand und jeher schon*): this expression makes it clearer what we should mean by destiny. To realize the *hidden unity* this expression attributes to life will not go without our astonishment.

The idea of destiny will, undoubtedly, offer an answer to the fundamental question of all life stories, including time novels: although time, "time itself, as such, for its own sake" cannot be narrated, we are able to recount time woven into destiny.

However, this answer remains within the realm of the ironic game. What should we think of Hans Castorp's destiny if the last lines of the novel relate that although he may very well have stood under the aegis of the spiritual principle of disease for a long time back, he did not, eventually, remain on the magic mountain?

In his novel called *Doctor Faustus,* Thomas Mann uses *destiny* or *sending* (*Schicksal*) to characterize the times around the outbreak of the First World War. On this occasion, the term is used by Serenus Zeitblom, who, by looking back on those years from the time of the Second World War, recounts what he was once thoroughly enthusiastic about. So what was once said, gets retold, and retold in another way. The words once uttered in ecstasy sound like "an ancient, pagan chant," "a tragic mythological, musical-dramatic motif."[5] This is enough to cast a somewhat poetic shadow over the concept of destiny.

The term *Schicksal* (destiny, fate) has been branded as "usurpatory concept," too, and by no lesser a thinker than Immanuel Kant.[6] However natural it may sound that time can only be recounted when it is woven into destiny, this may very well become misleading as well, since it creates the impression that we might find a mysterious and hidden unity where, on the contrary, we may witness to the effect of various diverse ingredients, the conflict of opposing factors.

That it is diverse ingredients which come into play here cannot be emphasized enough, since there is a deep-seated ambiguity at the bottom of the concept of life-history: it may mean the immediate experience of a life in its totality, as well as our recounted—or recountable—story, our reflected history.

Dilthey, who was the first to ask how the events of a life are connected with each other, did not distinguish between these two possible interpretations.[7] In his investigations, the task assigned to the concept of the "connectedness of life" or "cohesion of life events"—*Zusammenhang des Lebens*—was to reconcile such diverse concepts as "vividness" and "meaning," or "force" and "sense."[8] Phenomenology, however, did not hesitate to take the first option: a life-history was interpreted as lived experience, always already carrying a sense it gains from the temporal unity it is endowed with—without this unity even the possibility of narrating stories would be defunct. Both Edmund Husserl's concept of life-history, and the conception of historicity Martin Heidegger put forward in *Being and Time,* bear the unmistakable characteristics of such an approach.

The second option has been taken by the recent theory of "narrative identity." The gist of this approach might be formulated in the following way: *who we are shows itself in the history of our life.* It was Alasdair MacIntyre who constructed a detailed conception of "narrative selfhood" for the first time. Paul Ricoeur's investigations of the relationship between time and narrative yielded a more refined version, originally independently of MacIntyre. Further proponents of the theory include such eminent philosophers as David Carr and Charles Taylor.

The idea of a narrative selfhood may serve as a starting point to articulate the ambiguity inherent in the concept of the history of a life we encountered above. It will turn out, however, that this ambiguity generates problems the theory of narrative identity is unable to meet. This critical insight will require a return to the phenomenological analysis of the history of a life. If, however, the use of the "usurpatory" concept of destiny is to be avoided, we will have to rely on a radically renewed version of phenomenology.

I. Self-Identity as Narrated Life Story

The theory of narrative identity revolves around two main tenets. The first claims that our personal identity—or selfhood—consists in the unity of the history of our life. The second major claim adds that the unity of the history of our life is structured as the unity of the narrated stories is structured. To investigate the profound sense of the above theses, we may follow the refined version of the theory proposed by Ricoeur, whose connection of life-history with self-identity serves a dual purpose.

1. Two Aims of the Theory of Narrative Identity

The first aim is to distinguish between the identity of the self and the identity or sameness that pertains to substantial entities, which remain, during a more or less long period, permanent and recognizable, even while their states or some of their properties change. Here Ricoeur tries to meet a requirement formulated by such early phenomenologists as Husserl, Scheler, and Heidegger, who insisted on a sharp distinction between the identity of the self and the identity and permanence of substantial entities.[9] That entities remain identical with themselves—that they remain "the same"—is a fact settled, in each case, by a spectator from the outside. If we happen to be policemen or work for a court of justice, it will be the "personal identity" of people we will have to establish in an analogous way. In such a case, identity will have to be considered as a relation between the present and the past self of a person, different from ourselves; the procedure will involve the perspective of the outsider, in fact it will be carried out from a third-person perspective. However, this perspective will not be of much use once we try to interpret the identity we attribute to ourselves, since here identity is a relation we cannot observe externally, but it is one we have to establish from within: here we ourselves relate to ourselves. In other words, here we have to take a first-person perspective. Ricoeur shows how the philosophical notion of "personal identity," as it has been used since John Locke's time, is heavy with inextricable perplexities and confusions. These justify the introduction of the term "selfhood." In clarifying this concept, Ricoeur makes use of two Latin terms: he distinguishes between sameness in the sense of *ipse,* and in the sense of *idem.* The corresponding French expressions carrying the same contrast are *ipséité* (selfhood) and *mêmeté* (sameness). The point of this opposition is to underscore that we may remain *ourselves* without remaining *the same as we were:* sameness is by no means implied by selfhood, *ipséité* does not presuppose that which we designate by *mêmeté* in French. Thus, the identity of the self—in contrast with the identity of substantial entities—does not require that our being should have a hard core which remains intact amidst the flow of perpetual transitions; it is neither the permanence of our bodily features, nor the constancy of our character, nor the stability of our convictions that make us identical with ourselves. What is required as a necessary condition of *ipseity* is, according to Ricoeur's claim, that all changes we undergo in the course of our lives should be insertable into the framework of a meaningful story. It is this claim that is carried by the motto that selfhood or *ipseity* is a narrative identity.

The narrative view of selfhood has, as mentioned above, a further purpose, too: it wishes to connect *ipseity* with alterity. Here Ricoeur tries to meet a requirement formulated, this time, by Emmanuel Levinas: Ricoeur wishes to show how alterity gets woven into our *ipseity,* how "the intrigue of the Other within the Same" is possible.[10] This task is formulated as early as the title of one of Ricoeur's most important books: *Oneself as Another.*

The narrative view of selfhood has no difficulty in meeting the first requirement specified above: dissociated from sameness on the one hand, and assimilated to the unity of the history of a life on the other, *ipseity* has sufficiently been separated from the identity and permanence of substantial entities. As far as the second requirement is concerned, the chances of the theory of narrative identity are no less promising: the unity of a life-history will undoubtedly tolerate alterity, it will by no means discard alteration, and it will even invite the variety of relationships with other people.

However, the ambiguity that lies in the very concept of the history of a life gives rise to a difficulty which has divided the proponents of the theory into two opposing camps. The question is as follows: is our selfhood constituted in the complex of our recounted stories? Or should we rather suppose in the background of these stories the temporal unity—or even totality—of lived experience, as constitutive of destiny?

Ricoeur's answer appears to be rather straightforward: "We consider life to be identical with the stories we tell about it."[11] Ricoeur's view, however, is more complex, as it unfolds in the debate he has with the original version of the theory, formulated by MacIntyre.

2. Structural Differences between Life and Narrative

In his famous book *After Virtue,* MacIntyre argues that neither a single action nor the whole of a life could become the subject matter of narration if it were not in itself an *enacted narrative.* According to him, the history of a life is "an enacted dramatic narrative in which the characters are also authors."[12] This conception is opposed to a theory of historiography expounded by Hayden White and Louis O. Mink. Mink's famous thesis, *Stories are not lived but told,* is challenged by a counterthesis: *Stories are lived before they are told.*[13]

However, this claim will provoke, as MacIntyre admits himself, a whole legion of objections which have to do with the difference between the respective structures of a life story and of a narrative. (1) A narrative has an author; but is one really the author of the history of one's own life? (2) A narrative has a beginning and an ending; but is our life rounded off with such closures as well? This is highly doubtful, even in the face of the undeniable facts of birth and death, since the years of our early childhood will fade into oblivion and it is only in the narratives of the survivors that our death becomes a part of the history of our life. (3) Further, could not a single life-history become the subject matter of several authentic narratives? Clearly, different narratives can be told of one and the same life-history, so different ones may belong, at least in certain cases, to such multifarious genres as hagiography or tragedy. (4) Even further, a single history of a life can indeed be made the subject matter of a narrative, but is there such a thing as a single history of a life? Is it not so that a history of a life is inserted, from the outset, into a web of various other life-histories, intertwined with one another? (5) Finally, narration is a retrospective act, looking back, and thus focused, on the past, while in the actual course of our life we interpret ourselves—as Heidegger or Jean-Paul Sartre argued, or, if nothing else than our everyday experience has taught us—in the light of our future possibilities: the very notion of an action has a prospective order.

As Ricoeur admits, MacIntyre is not only fully aware of these objections but he has powerful arguments to meet them one by one as well. In *Oneself as Another,* Ricoeur explicitly summarizes the position MacIntyre takes in *After Virtue.* We may draw upon this summary all the more, since Ricoeur's version is a slightly modified and a particularly sophisticated one, presented here in the form of a series of further questions: (1) as far as our existence is concerned, we are certainly not the authors of our life stories, yet as regards its sense or meaning, should we not consider ourselves as at least coauthors? That we are "co-authors of our own narratives" is emphasized by MacIntyre as well, but it is Ricoeur who adds the distinction between "existence" on the one hand and the "sense of a life-story" on the other. (2) Do we not take full advantage of the closures provided by narrative genres in the shaping of our life stories when, for example, we try to give a respectable weight to our new undertakings, or when we try to fix, at least with a relative permanence, some of our necessarily provisional goals? (3) Is it not an indispensable feature of the unity characteristic of our life stories that we are always able to provide more than one authentic story about ourselves and that we, accordingly, keep leaving various possibilities open for ourselves? (4) Do not such ancient forms of narratives as, e.g., embedding one story into another (as in "chest-of-drawers tales") help to orient ourselves amidst the entanglements of intertwined life-histories? (5) It is easy to see, finally, that the retrospective nature of narratives is by no means incompatible with the fact that among the recounted events in the past tense we find plans, expectations, and anticipations. Thus, is it not the case that both historiographic and fictive narratives display the same double dimension of "experiential space" and "the horizon of expectations," characteristic of real life stories? It cannot be emphasized enough that the retrospective character of a story is not the perspective of its characters but of the standpoint the "voice of the narrative" requires.

3. Controversial Points in the Theory of Narrative Identity

These answers clearly indicate that there is no unbridgeable gap between life and narrative—this is fully acknowledged by the exponents of either view. Divergence starts with respect to the consequences one might draw from the above insights. For MacIntyre, the convergence between lived experience and storytelling is a proof for the thesis that "we live out narratives in our lives." Ricoeur disagrees; he claims that the various structures of narratives are applied to, or even projected onto, the heterogeneous body of lived experience; our lives get organized according to the inherent forms of the stories we are familiar with. Instead of considering life as an "enacted narrative," he takes it to be "an unstable mixture of fabulation and actual experience."[14] So, unlike MacIntyre, he does not have to suppose a hidden unity where, according to his claim, there is rather a cooperation of diverse factors.

Ricoeur's version is undoubtedly more sophisticated than MacIntyre's, containing delicate nuances which cannot right now be accounted for. Nevertheless, it is far from being flawless: a theory of *ipseity* that does not shrink from reducing self-identity to "an unstable mixture of fabulation and actual experience" indeed cannot lay any claim to unquestionable self-evidence. Even if we suppose that the structural patterns of fictive history become active participants in organizing our lived experience, we can hardly claim that our selfhood or self-identity would be a mere product of our storytelling activity. Ricoeur himself warns us of this view by maintaining that "we attempt to *discover* and not simply impose from outside the narrative identity which constitutes us."[15] However, it is obviously impossible to discover what in no way exists. Thus, one is compelled to suggest that the ground of selfhood is to be sought not in the unity of a narrated life story, or in life as a complex of told stories, but in life as a totality of lived experiences, in the time structure of the life we "actually went through."

This difficulty may prompt us to look for a way that leads us back from the theory of narrative identity to phenomenology.

II. Dispossessed Sense in Life-History

Exploring the relationship between life-history and self-identity, we may largely rely on the approaches of such early phenomenologists as Husserl and Heidegger. Husserl's *Cartesian Meditations* come up with two major tenets, both linking his later philosophy with our present concerns. According to the first, *the phenomenology of the ego's self-constitution coincides with phenomenology as a whole;* according to the second, *the ego constitutes himself in, so to speak, the unity of a "history."*[16] In his manuscripts left behind, Husserl—even if between quotation marks—also uses the expression "history of a life."[17] Thus, in his later works, a close connection can be detected between self-constitution and life-history. At the same time Heidegger, in *Being and Time,* takes Dilthey's question concerning the "connectedness of life" as a point of departure to clarify the respective concepts of historicity and destiny. These considerations deserve to be taken into account in any inquiry into the relationship between life-history and self-identity.

However, it would not entirely be appropriate to connect the present investigation directly or uncritically either with Husserl's or with Heidegger's approach, since they both assign a *solipsistic structure* to the notion of time, which is at the root of their interpretations of life-history, historicity, and destiny. This is evidently true of Husserl, who considers "life time" to be a *Selbstzeit* (time of the self),[18] disabling himself—as he himself admits—by this very conception to account for what he calls the "alterity of the Other." And this is true of Heidegger as well, who is undoubtedly aware of the fact that an impenetrable facticity and alterity belongs to human existence by necessity, but nevertheless attributes an original historicity—in the sense of a peculiar sort of temporalization—only to those who are able to transmute all unchosen, uncontrollable, or even indomitable factors of their life-histories—birth, ancestry, bodily features, intellectual abilities, unintended incidences of any kind, and so forth—into elements of their own self-identities, assuming, thereby, all facticity as a piece of their proper destinies, and thus capable of appropriating all alterity.

That is why both Husserl's and Heidegger's approaches to time obstruct our quest for finding a relationship between self-identity and alterity in life-history. We cannot rely on a ready-made philosophical method worked out in all details; consequently, when a return from the theory of narrative identity to phenomenology is thus proposed, our task will precisely be to modify the initiatives taken by Husserl and Heidegger, and to elaborate a new version of phenomenology, trying to meet the requirements we are confronted with when examining the intricate relationship between self-identity and alterity in the history of a life.

In regards to Ricoeur's view above, it was contended that we are coauthors of our life-history with respect to its *meaning* or its *sense,* rather than to its "real manifestation," or to the actual course of our existence. Everything depends, however, on the exact way this idea is interpreted. The first possibility is to view our narratives as lending *sense* to our lives:

one is tempted to think that sense is bestowed upon life precisely—and exclusively—by the narratives that are told about it. This idea of an exclusive sense bestowal—the Husserlian *Sinngebung*—by storytelling is, however, hardly compatible with Ricoeur's remark that "we attempt to *discover* and not simply impose from the outside the narrative identity which constitutes us." It would equally be premature to jump to the opposite conclusion and say with MacIntyre that our lived experience is nothing but an "enacted narrative." In fact, the very notion of "enacted narratives" originates in a deceptive illusion. This is the first point we have to make; afterward, we can return to the question of sense bestowal.

1. The Illusion of "A Life Narrating Itself"

Once more, we may draw upon a novel by Mann, who, in *Joseph and His Brothers,* plays an ironic game with the idea of "a life narrating itself." There is perhaps no narrator who could get away from the impression "that before the story was first told, it had to tell itself with an exactitude of which life alone is master, and to attain which a narrator has no hope or prospect at all."[19] Still, this impression is nothing but a fugitive mirage. The remarks of Mann allow us to reconstruct the process in which this mirage is generated. The first step is to notice that several authentic stories may be told of one and the same life. As noted already, this observation, considered in isolation, could easily be adduced as an argument precisely *against* the identification of the actual experience of a life with a narrated story. Yet, this fact is easily overlooked on account of the recognition that the same life may be depicted by different narratives with different degrees of "exactitude": they can be more or less *detailed* and can be "faithful to reality" in various ways. It is this that may give rise to the impression that narrated texts only *approximate* the actual experience of a life, which, in turn, is the "original text" (*Urtext*).[20] This impression, however, is a result of an almost imperceptible but by no means harmless "method of limits." We envisage a whole series of more and more precise narratives, and we end up identifying the real course of a life with the *most precise* one. Here we fall victim to an illusion that can be analyzed in Kantian terms: what is in fact a *regulative* principle of narration is mistaken for a *constitutive* principle of life. So the hidden evenness and the mysterious unity which flares up as an unattainable ideal before the storyteller is taken to be a particular and organic feature of real life experience itself. No wonder, then, that the mirage of a life narrating itself gives rise to a metaphysics of destiny.

2. Dissociation of Life and Narrative

If we reject not only MacIntyre's idea of "enacted narratives" but also Ricoeur's thesis, according to which the identity of the self is nothing more than an unstable mixture of fabulation and actual experience, we are confronted with a serious dilemma. On the one hand, we cannot deny that there are more or less precise and more or less authentic narratives, because otherwise we could not claim to *discover* the identity that constitutes us by telling stories about our lives; but, on the other hand, we do not know how to measure exactitude and authenticity after the discovery that life itself cannot, except for playful irony, be considered as an "original text" to which narratives should correspond, or which they should approximate.

A way out of this dilemma may, nevertheless, be found if we abandon the external stance, from which, in the above considerations, we regarded the relationship between life and narrative, and take an internal point of view instead, examining the question of exactitude and authenticity as it *actually arises in our own life-histories.* Ricoeur himself comes close to this decisive step when he claims, with respect to psychoanalytic therapy, that "the history of a life is constituted by a series of rectifications applied to preceding narrations."[21] The question of exactitude and authenticity takes an entirely new shape if we stop envisaging, *in abstracto,* a series of narratives referring to one and the same life-history and return to our own life-histories, in order to examine, *in concreto,* the critical situations (some "stances of crisis") that compel us to rectify the narratives which we earlier held to be precise and authentic.

The difference between the structure of a life and the structure of a narrative becomes nowhere so clear as in such critical situations. Here the aforementioned divergences are rendered even more prominent and take almost the form of "chasms." Without adhering to the order of the previous exposition, our task is now to reconsider these divergences.

We may begin, this time, with the difference that was specified above as the last one: (5) narratives undoubtedly have a retrospective character, but in the interludes of rectifying previously accepted stories, even the slightest modification can initiate a fresh start or even create, so to speak, a *new beginning.* In this exceptional moment, storytelling shares the prospective character of life itself: recounting and expectant initiative can by no means be opposed because in such situations constructing and recounting a reshaped narrative does not only mean to give a retrospective account of past experiences but precisely take a prospective initiative as well. (3) The possibility of grasping one and the same life-history by a plurality of authentic narratives manifests itself nowhere so incontestably than in a situation that confronts us with alternative roads to take, i.e., where we may choose between various courses of action. (2) In the intermediary interval, in which we are driven to suspend the validity of narratives that we ourselves have considered as precise and authentic, the lines leading back to the beginnings of our life-histories, as well as those pointing forth to their ends, are suddenly blurred. Therefore, in such moments it is particularly evident to what extent the actual experience of a life is devoid of the closures characteristic of literary forms. (4) In a critical situation it turns out at once that the narratives by the means of which we fixed the identity of ourselves—for ourselves as well as for others—have to be revised and rectified. As a consequence, we often find ourselves divided against ourselves. It is not an exaggeration to speak of a *split of the self* with respect to such a situation. That our life-histories are intertwined with those of others, and that our identity is forever bound up with alterity, are nowhere more self-evident and nowhere prove to be so clearly an unmistakable fact than in this very moment, when we have nothing else but our relationships with others to rely on in order to restore our broken self-understanding. (1) In the critical situation we are considering here, there is a special emphasis on the assertion that we are only "coauthors" of our lives, even as far as its sense is concerned. For in such situations, the sense bestowed upon the actions and upon the events of our lives in the narratives told by ourselves and by others is all of a sudden dispelled, dissipated, disintegrated, and it is not in our power to suddenly replace the "old" sense by the sense of freely invented stories. It is not as a result of *our* initiative that a new sense emerges here. On the contrary: here our activity is reduced to discovering a spontaneously emerging sense. These considerations urge us to distinguish the phenomenon of a spontaneous emergence of sense—of a *Sinnbildung*—in the history of a life, from all the sense bestowal—*Sinngebung*—by a subject.

Before going further, it will be useful to illustrate this distinction by some examples. If we select our examples from literature, the reader will be more in a position to put our statements to the test.

3. The Arrogance of Coldness and the Alchemy of the Beautiful

In Mann's *Doktor Faustus*, Serenus Zeitblom presents the letter which Adrian Leverkühn, at a turning point of his young years, sent to his music master, Wendell Kretschmar. Kretschmar replies, and the ensuing correspondence persuades Leverkühn to break with theology and to choose the career of a composer instead. At the beginning, however, this decision cannot be regarded as unproblematic or unambiguous. Adrian is induced by the crisis he lives through to formulate a serious judgment upon himself:

> I fear, dear and beloved friend and master, I am a lost soul, a black sheep; I have no warmth. As the Gode Boke hath it, they shall be cursed and spewed out of the mouth who are neither cold nor warm but lukewarm. Lukewarm I should not call myself. I am cold out of all question; but in my judgment of myself I would pray to dissent from the taste of that Power whose it is to apportion blessing and cursing.[22]

Adrian tells why he entered into the service of theology: he wished to humiliate himself, to bend his backbone, to *punish the arrogance of his coldness.* It is still this very wish by which he is prevented from changing his course of life and from embracing the career of a musician: he is convinced that those not having any warmth or robust naïveté in themselves are incapable of the illusionism, witchcraft, black magic, artistic trickery, imposture, or, in a word, of the alchemy of the beautiful which, he thinks, is nevertheless a necessary ingredient of music. We remember the famous description which even Adorno, the great connoisseur of music, could not identify—to Mann's great astonishment[23]—as the prelude of the third act of Wagner's *Meistersinger:*

> the cellos intone, by themselves, a pensive, melancholy theme, which questions the folly of the world, the wherefore of all struggle and striving, pursuing and plaguing—all highly expressive and decorously philosophical [. . .].[24]

Finally, Leverkühn says:

> Why does almost everything seem to me like its own parody? Why must I think that almost all, no, all the methods and conventions of art *are good for parody only?*[25]

What is the answer to this desperate, self-tormenting question? "Affectation, Adri," says Kretschmar, and he makes clear what we ourselves were struck by when reading Adrian's letter: his pupil wants to elude art with reference to properties which are precisely required by it,[26] and, at the bottom of his heart, he is himself aware of this fact. Kretschmar adds:

> Art needed just his sort today—and the joke, the hypocritical, hide-and-seek joke, was that Adrian knew it perfectly well.[27]

Leverkühn's words say more than they are meant to. The story he constructs in order to grasp his previous conduct is close to reality; its authenticity is beyond any doubt; it is, as a scornful summary, a veritable confession. Yet, it rather conceals than discloses the real causes and effective circumstances of the crisis he goes through. The only reason why these causes and circumstances still become perceptible is that his meaning turns bit by bit into its opposite. Kretschmar has an easy job: he has but to grasp this twist of Adrian's meaning. The arrogance of coldness is undoubtedly incompatible with the alchemy of the beautiful. But does not the broken spell of the beautiful illusion give rise to the claim of a less ostentatious, more ascetic, but, at the same time, more solid and truthful art? What else does this art in its break with illusion making need than precisely the arrogance of coldness that despises all trickery and imposture? Who knows all this better than the writer of the letter himself? Kretschmar's judgment is consequently well founded: here apprehensive concern and self-torment are nothing else than "affectation" and a "hypocritical, hide-and-seek joke." However, it would be a mistake to hold it to be a deliberate dodge, a perfidy contrived in bad faith. The meaning of Adrian's letter gets detached from the intention of the writer, and enters a career of its own. It becomes Kretschmar's task to grasp and to articulate this meaning, emerging of itself—a meaning that cannot be reduced to any meaning bestowal by a subject.

4. The "Florentine Masterpiece"

Would it not be an ungenerous restriction if we limited the validity of what has been said about the spontaneous emergence of sense in life-history just to *critical* situations? It will not be pointless to consider another example, which seems to lend itself to some generalization as well.

Marcel Proust discerns the almost imperceptible transitions that gradually turn Swann into a slave of love and jealousy. The process Proust depicts is so unambiguous, irresistible, and continuous that it does not allow for any *critical* situation. Still, there are turning points in the story. We know what importance is attached to the moment when the little phrase of Vinteuil's sonata is played for the first time. The resemblance Swann discovers between Odette and Botticelli's Zipporah is no less important. The fresco of the Sixtus Chapel of Florence is endowed with a new sense, which is enforced and corroborated also by language; eventually, this sense spreads over the bodily appearance of Odette, resuscitating a desire that could not be maintained by a tired face and a not entirely perfect skin. Proust says:

> The words "Florentine painting" were invaluable to Swann. They enabled him (gave him, as it were, a legal title) to introduce the image of Odette into a world of dreams and fancies which, until then, she had been debarred from entering, and where she assumed a new and nobler form. And whereas the mere sight of her in the flesh, by perpetually reviving his misgivings as to the quality of her face, her figure, the whole of her beauty, used to cool the ardor of his love, those misgivings were swept away and that love confirmed now that he could re-erect his estimate of her on the sure foundations of his aesthetic principles; while the kiss, the bodily surrender which would have seemed natural and but moderately attractive, had they been granted him by a creature of somewhat withered flesh and sluggish blood, coming, as now they came, to crown his adoration of a masterpiece in a gallery, must, it seemed, prove as exquisite as they would be supernatural.[28]

The expression "Florentine masterpiece" is indeed a *parole magique*, a magical word: it projects a new sense onto a "withered flesh" (*chair abîmée*), and generates thereby a desire that did not awaken by itself.

5. Spontaneous Emergence and Retroactive Fixation of Sense

Our examples show that life-history is characterized by the spontaneous formation of a sense which is by no means at our disposal, which is, in fact, totally beyond our control. In its unavailability, this sense cannot be traced back to any sense bestowal by a subject: in this way it is a *dispossessed* sense.

Ricoeur says that life is "a tissue of narrated histories."[29] But in the critical situations that constrains us to rectify the stories held to be precise and authentic by ourselves, and, even in the steady flow of life, whenever an image, a word, a face, or a shape gets endowed with a new sense, this tissue becomes threadbare: we catch sight of an ungovernable and uncontrollable process which results in the spontaneous emergence of a dispossessed sense.

For sure, we attempt to articulate—and thereby to *fix*—this sense retrospectively or, better still, retroactively by telling rectified—reshaped, modified or entirely renewed—stories. Thus, we try to get hold of what is beyond our scope and control. Owing to this endeavor, we succeed in most cases in preserving the identity of ourselves, or at least we manage to recuperate it after the interlude of a crisis. But nothing warrants the success of our continual efforts to fix retroactively the spontaneously emerged senses in our lives. On the contrary: experience shows that the process of sense formation repeatedly escapes from our grasp, challenging over and over again even our rectified stories and breaking up, from time to time, the supposedly hard core of our identity.

This observation points to a difficulty which proves to be insurmountable for the theory of narrative identity in each of its versions. A sense in the making, illustrated by the above examples, cannot be characterized "as an unstable mixture of fabulation and actual experience" (because it can by no means be considered as a mere product of narrative fabulation, even if it can be fixed—retrospectively or retroactively—by narrated histories; and because it can by no means be considered as an immediate object of lived experience, even if it is undoubtedly a formative factor of the reality of a life). Nor can a sense in the making be viewed as a piece of evidence testifying to the idea of "a life narrating itself" (because the tissue of narrated histories, whenever it occurs, rather becomes threadbare).

Based on the above considerations, we may draw the conclusion that *life-history* and *self-identity* cannot be taken as concepts having the same meaning. What Heidegger designates as *Jemeinigkeit* in the German original of *Being and Time,* is certainly an indubitable fact: indeed, nobody can live any other life than his or her own. One may be tempted to infer from this to the inseparability of life-history and self-identity. Admittedly, the inference is perfectly sound in a certain sense: the two concepts do belong together. However, from the above discussion it also seems to follow that here *inseparability* does not amount to *interchangeability.* If we consider life-history as a region where a *spontaneous formation* of sense takes place, and we further conceive of self-identity as something which is at stake in every attempt at a *retroactive fixation* of a spontaneously emerged sense, the difference of the two concepts becomes unmistakably clear, even if it remains true that they belong inseparably together.

Here we find ourselves challenged by a new task: we have to specify the conceptual scheme that enables us to grasp the relationship between a spontaneous formation and a retroactive fixation of sense.

6. Diacritical Phenomenology

Mann mentions that once he read the correspondence of Leverkühn and Kretschmar in a close circle of friends, and Adorno, the "Hegelian" philosopher, who was also present, was taken by the *dialectical* character of this passage.[30] In the previous discussion, I myself used an expression which may evoke the tradition of dialectical thinking: I said that the meaning of Leverkühn's letter "turned into its opposite." The above characterization of the relationship between a spontaneous formation and a retroactive fixation of sense may have left the same impression in the reader. It may be added that Ricoeur, when analyzing the relationship between time and narrative, remains, undoubtedly, close to Hegel himself.

Yet, the experience of the spontaneous emergence of a sense, which does not allow for any definitive fixation, keeps us away from the dialectical path. This "disruption" exhibits such a novelty that dialectical thinking, with its ready-made conceptual schemes, cannot live up to the task of giving an adequate account of it.

That is why we made use of a new conceptual scheme above. We followed, indeed, a procedure that led us first, to dissociate lived experience and narrative fabulation from each other; second, to distinguish the spontaneous sense formation not only from all sense bestowal by a subject but also from all retroactive sense fixation; and finally, to discern life-history and self-identity. It will be useful to bring, retrospectively, the two main characteristics of this procedure into focus.

The first characteristic is the *recourse to lived experience.* Instead of analyzing *in abstracto* the conceptual elements just mentioned, we considered them in the light of vital (critical, crisis-stricken) situations that permitted us to examine their relationships *in concreto.* In each case, it was such a situation which revealed the difference of those conceptual elements which otherwise prove to be inseparable. The procedure of discerning and dissociating otherwise inseparable conceptual elements does not coincide, as was argued, with the dialectical method, either. It differs from it already by the fact that, far from remaining content with a purely conceptual analysis, it has recourse to vital and crisis-stricken situations in which "actual" phenomena show up, and lived experience is readily available.

The second main feature of our procedure consists in the *specific interpretation of the difference* it reveals. We detached life-history from self-identity by establishing a difference between a spontaneously emerging and a retroactively fixed sense. It may once more be emphasized that we have no reason to consider this difference as the germ of a dialectical opposition or contradiction. It may be regarded rather as a *diacritical difference.* This term refers to the relationship to be found between opposing elements in language which constitute it as a *system,* the system Ferdinand de Saussure called *langue* as opposed to *parole;* the system of differences on which the cohesion of meaningful expressions is based.

If we characterize the procedure we have followed in distinguishing between life-history and self-identity as a *diacritical method,* we attach ourselves to an initiative taken, or at least suggested, by the later Maurice Merleau-Ponty in his last works.

The idea of an *emploi du diacritique*[31] could hardly have been conceived of if Merleau-Ponty had not recognized—very early—the philosophical significance of both Saussurean linguistics and Claude Lévi-Strauss's ethnological structuralism. But every "use of the diacritical" does not, in itself, commit us to structuralism as a philosophical stance. Merleau-Ponty speaks of a "diacritical system" of perception, as well as of intersubjectivity,[32] but it is not simply a structural analysis of these systems which he insists on. He attributes an even greater importance to a question which everybody has to put *in the first-person singular* and which concerns, to use the first-person singular indeed, "my being set up on a universal diacritical system."[33] If it is true that the specific difference of a phenomenological approach from other approaches consists in its reliance on an experience that finds its proper expression in the first-person singular, then this very question unmistakably suggests that the "use of the diacritical" indicates, in the later Merleau-Ponty, a *phenomenological* way of thinking.

This statement is correct only if *phenomenology* is taken in a somewhat unusual sense. According to the interpretation accepted even today, this method of philosophical investigation does not rely on the conviction that we can find a corresponding intuition to every conceptual element of our thinking. If the word *phenomenology* were taken in this sense, the diacritical method could not be called a phenomenological one, since a diacritical distinction takes place whenever the difference of two things that were originally held to be identical is *subsequently* revealed. (That was the structure of the above line of thought, which resulted in the dissociation of actual experience and the narrated history of a life.) It follows, however, that a diacritical difference becomes manifest only with a temporal shift, with a phase delay, and therefore it cannot be, at least in the initial state, *exhibited* intuitively (as early phenomenology would require), even if it can very well be subsequently *exposed.*

My purpose in insisting on the phenomenological character of the diacritical method is not so much to emphasize, once more, that philosophical investigations are not to be based simply upon conceptual analysis and that they have rather to be anchored in the consideration of vital (critical) situations, in which phenomena *show up,* and lived experiences are *available.* Nor is it merely to stress that the diacritical method is concerned with processes of sense formation. This feature of my approach is not, in itself, at odds with the conception of early phenomenology; the only characteristic of early phenomenology that was contested in the above argumentation is the position that all formations of sense originate in a sense bestowal by the subject. The very introduction of the diacritical method requires that the assessment of the accomplishments and the limits of our activity of sense bestowal should be founded upon the distinction between *spontaneous sense formation* and *retroactive sense fixation*. This distinction, however, implies not only the very fact of a spontaneous sense formation that reaches far beyond the scope of the subject's sense-bestowing activity, but, in addition, it presupposes a "diacritical *system*," resulting from the differential coherence or, in other words, the oppositional interdependence of spontaneously emerging shreds of sense at every moment. My main aim in insisting on the *phenomenological* character of the diacritical method is to underscore that this diacritical system is not to be considered from the outside, but—in accordance with Merleau-Ponty's question cited above—it is precisely "my being set on this diacritical system" that has to be inquired into. This inquiry may indeed be characterized as a phenomenological one because—in contrast with all kinds of structural analyses—it puts a diacritical system in the light of an *experience* that finds its proper expression in the *first-person singular*.

However, the last part of these methodological considerations anticipates what still has to be explained. A diacritical system resulting from the interrelations of the spontaneously emerged shreds of sense has already been included in our approach. But it still has to be shown how such a system is generated and reorganized. A phenomenological approach thus requires the adoption of an internal point of view, allowing for an experience that finds its proper expression in the first-person singular.

7. Accepted and Discarded Shreds of Sense

Let us envisage a situation in which a new sense emerges for us, as for the young Leverkühn, when he is about to change his profession, or for Swann, when he discovers the features of Botticelli's Zephora on the face of Odette. We immediately see that the new sense emerges *unexpectedly* in such a situation: it thwarts preceding expectations, and thereby it opens up a *new beginning* in life-history (unless it encounters insurmountable opposition).

Retrospectively, however, we may easily detect some precursory life events that have already signaled, foreshadowed, or foreboded, the recently emerged sense. (Here we may think of Swann and Odette: for instance, is the little phrase of Vinteuil's sonata not such a precursor of the experience hinted at by the expression "Florentine masterpiece"? As far as Leverkühn and the career of a composer is concerned, we stumble upon a whole series of premonitory signs, from the suspicious experiments of the father, who never stops "speculating in the elements," to the exercises in fugato prescribed by Kretschmar, and so on.) The retrospective discovery of such anticipations integrates the recently emerged sense with some earlier life events, which are thus taken to be its precursors. That is why such a retrospection can serve as a starting point for a retroactive sense fixation. For to fix a sense is precisely to insert it into a sequence that, "in reality," can only be discovered afterward. But a spontaneously emerging sense could not create a new beginning in life-history if it did not contain at least some ingredients that do not lend themselves to the retroactive constitution of such a sequence. These recalcitrant shreds of sense, which threaten to break the subsequently established order and coherence of life events, fall victim to the retroactive sense fixation: they are put aside, dismissed, sometimes even repressed; they are, in any case, not accounted for by the rectified narratives that are designed to draw the lessons from the earlier crisis. However, the discarded shreds of sense do not disappear without leaving some trace behind; on the contrary, they often reemerge, sometimes bringing about a decisive, almost fateful turn. It is peculiar to a great writer to indicate the avatars of a sense in the making, although they are, strictly speaking, hardly even recountable. Let us consider the example of Botticelli's fresco. What is at stake here amounts to much more than the animation of Swann's passion for Odette by its fusion with the "adoration of a masterpiece in a gallery." This is only the first meaning of the expression "Florentine masterpiece"—a meaning explicitly intended, it seems, by the text. But the reader soon discerns another meaning, which, being only suggested and not expressly revealed, is all the more sinister. Swann's attachment to art and creation is gradually transfused into his not easily awakened desire. We know that he is elaborating a study on the painting of Vermeer without, however, finishing it. The upshot is that he finds himself deprived of the last refuge in which he could take shelter against the feeling he is more and more possessed with. We may also consider Leverkühn's letter once more. Are there no hints in it that make it doubtful if he really abandons theology when choosing the career of a composer? Is he really going to break with what he was exclusively attracted by in theology, namely with the *Apostate* and the *apostasy,* which, as we are told, is itself "an act of faith": "everything happens in God, most of all the falling from Him"?[34] This eruptive utterance remains without resonance in Kretschmar's reply, but we know that Adrian's destiny finds an emblematic expression in it.

These examples show clearly that a sense in the making is always a multiple and fluctuant sense, containing, in itself, some refractory shreds, which are discarded by the retroactive fixation of sense without, however, being prevented thereby from exerting an underground influence. From this observation, several conclusions may be drawn. First, we may claim that a spontaneously emerging sense is accompanied by *a continuous formation of a surplus.* Second, it may be added that this process cannot be regarded as an accumulation of any well-defined and accomplished ingredients of sense, but it must be interpreted rather as a *proliferation of some inchoate, fluctuant, and indeterminate shreds of sense.*[35] Third, it may be asserted that, at every moment, these germs of sense are integrated into a *diacritical system* by their differential interrelations with each other, as well as with the already fixed sense. Finally, we may reply to Merleau-Ponty's question by pointing out that the reason why we are not in a position to consider the totality of these differential interrelations from the outside (why, in other words, we find ourselves always already *included* in this diacritical system) is that we adhere, from the outset, to *some* meaningful sequences of life events, and whenever we see ourselves constrained to abandon or modify them, we single out, once again, *some* of the inchoate and fluctuant shreds of sense, discarding at the same time all others, in order to construct and fix another meaningful sequence of the same life events.

8. Life-History and Destiny

Once discarded shreds of sense may, as it has been said, reemerge, they might sometimes bring about a decisive, almost fateful turn. It is as if the reemergence of the discarded shreds of sense could reveal a mysterious and hidden unity where in reality we perceive only the effect of various diverse ingredients, the conflict of opposing factors. Unexpectedly reemerging shreds of sense are undoubtedly apt to evoke a sentiment expressed by the words "for a long time back" (*von langer Hand und jeher*). All of a sudden, we get the impression of being driven by hidden forces in a determinate direction which points—even amidst events that happen to us almost entirely without our contribution—at the unmistakable identity of ourselves, as though we had nothing else to do than to let these forces pursue their unswerving course, so that we may find relief and comfort after so many doubts and concerns.

However, it is not difficult to see that this conception of self-identity as a destiny is nothing more than a delusive mirage again. The illusion of a hidden unity is dissipated as soon as the once discarded but later on reemerging shreds of sense are recognized as parts of a whole system—or rather, a proliferating multiplicity—of heterogeneous sense formations. Regarded from this point of view, *destiny* proves indeed to be, in Kant's words, a "usurpatory concept." For how is this concept generated? We are struck by the repeated occurrence of an inchoate shred of sense, and, astonished by the coincidence, we cannot avoid interpreting this return of the same as an unambiguous manifestation of the identity of ourselves; however, thereby we convey the delusive appearance of predetermination, definitiveness, and unity to what is in itself irremediably fluctuant, indeterminate, and polysemous.

In *Being and Time,* when Heidegger undertakes to restate the idea of destiny within the framework of a phenomenological inquiry, he embarks upon a venture with a doubtful outcome. He is certainly aware that human existence is continuously confronted by events that are never entirely within its reach and scope, since these events transcend the limits of the power of existence. Yet he thinks that what proves to be in this way indomitable, uncontrollable, and ungovernable in our lives can nevertheless not only be suffered as an affliction, but also assumed as a proper destiny in firm resolution and thereby be transmuted into an ingredient of self-identity. However clearly here Heidegger dissents from Husserlian phenomenology, which does not admit the existence of any impenetrable facticity that could set a limit to our activity of sense bestowal, Heidegger all the same shares one of the main assumptions of Husserl's claim: he conceives, just as Husserl, of life-history as of the *domain of the constitution of self-identity.* The above considerations show, however, that this assumption is far from being self-evident. The previous inquiry into our being, based on a diacritical system of accepted and discarded shreds of sense, enables us to distinguish between two spheres within the wide range of life-history: a broad region, in which the spontaneous emergence of sense takes place—we may call this region the "phenomenological field"—and, within this very region, the narrow domain of a retroactive fixation of sense, which stands in the service of the constitution of self-identity. The previous discussion equally entitles us to characterize what has just been called the "phenomenological field" in a way different from Husserl's or Heidegger's approach: not as the domain of the subject's self-constitution, nor as the sphere of an existentially interpreted destiny, but as a *no-man's-land* that gives room to the avatars of a dispossessed—or as Merleau-Ponty would put it, "wild"[36]—sense.

To reject the notion of destiny as a "usurpatory concept" does by no means amount, however, to refusing the idea that there are critical situations, decisive incidences, and, as it were, "fateful" or "destinal" events in life-history. We should not forget that the repeated occurrence of a discarded shred of sense usually gives rise to *astonishment.* This phenomenon asks for an explanation, even if we reject the notion of destiny. This notion was based on the assumption that the astonishment provoked by the return of "the same" in life-history was related to the coincidence in the repetition as an unmistakable sign of a hidden unity, considered, in its turn, as the main guarantee of self-identity. This assumption is, however, far from being without problems. There is another reason for being astonished here. As it has been said, a new sense always emerges *unexpectedly*, because it balks previous expectations. This is true even when no repetition takes place. We may, therefore, maintain that it is not the mysterious return of the same, but rather the *emergence of a dispossessed sense*, to which the phenomenon of astonishment is related. It may be added that the supposition of a hidden unity in life-history is attached to this astonishment rather as a reassuring belief.

Here two conceptions of the history of a life are opposed to each other. The first revolves around the profound but obscure notion of destiny; the second is based on the plain concept of a radical turn in this life-history. The first presupposes that life-history, as the vehicle of self-identity, is a closed totality in which impenetrable facticity and alterity can be transmuted into *ipseity*. The concept of a radical turn in life-history refers, by contrast, to events characterized by an irrevocable alterity that provoke the split of the self. The real core of the otherwise preposterous notion of destiny is contained in this latter concept.

9. Self-Identity and Singularity

As it has been pointed out, diacritical phenomenology differs from the structural analysis of a system formed by differential interdependencies by its recourse to an experience which finds its proper expression in the first-person singular. It should not, however, be believed that if one takes such an experience as a point of departure, one remains necessarily a "captive of the cogito," as Claude Lévi-Strauss puts it, or commits oneself, definitively, to the "anthropological configuration of modern philosophy," as Michel Foucault maintains.[37] For here the first-person singular does not refer to a personal ego with particular characteristics, experiences, and ways of behavior. Nor does it indicate a transcendental ego, whose formal marks would fit anybody—and therefore nobody in particular. What finds its expression in the first-person singular here is in reality nothing more than *a difference between oneself and another;* it is founded on the remarkable fact that no change, however profound and comprehensive it may be, can transform me into another than *myself,* although it can make me, of course, other than *I was.* This difference between oneself and another does not rest on any personal characteristics; it is, therefore, not *substantive* but merely *positional.* For it is evident that we do not remain ourselves because we differ from others by our particular personalities but, inversely, we differ from others because it is impossible for us not to remain *ourselves,* even if our particular personalities may not show any really distinctive features.

Should we claim that the *identity of ourselves* is preserved even if we do not remain the same as we were? This statement expresses one of the most fundamental observations that gave rise to the theory of narrative identity. But this statement, although not untenable, is seriously misleading. It is not untenable because it may be construed as equivalent to the self-evident assertion according to which we remain *ourselves* even if we do not remain the same as we were. But it is seriously misleading indeed, because it contains the ambiguous expression "identity of ourselves." Even if we take this expression to refer to a *narrative* identity, it will depend upon some particularities which are irreducible to the purely positional fact that we remain *ourselves,* even if we do not remain the same as we were. But is it not quite doubtful whether we really preserve the identity of ourselves—in the sense of an identity depending upon personal features—in the course of all alterations affecting us during the span of our lives? Is it not possible that our convictions, our moral particularities, and our intellectual abilities, at least in some cases, undergo so profound—and sometimes even so sudden—a change that makes us *others* than we were? Could not such a change turn us into somebody *else?* We are undoubtedly inclined to reply that we can never become *as much* others as not to remain *ourselves.* It should not, however, escape us that this apparently evident but in reality quite delusive reply rests on the confusion of the identity of ourselves with the purely positional fact that we do remain *ourselves* even if we do not remain the *same* as we were.

By these considerations, we are led to distinguish between two senses of *being ourselves.* The theory of narrative identity is certainly not entirely unjustified: we may indeed accept the tenet that the unity of a narrated history is the basis of what we may keep on calling "self-identity" or "*ipseity.*" But we must add that self-identity, in this sense of the word, is neither the main source, nor an indispensable condition of our *singularity,* i.e., our *irreplaceable unicity.* It is our singularity that finds its expression in the purely positional fact that we remain *ourselves* even if we do not remain the same as we were.

This distinction between self-identity and singularity, inspired by Levinas, is comparable to the Kantian opposition between the ego as a *transcendental subject* and the ego as an *empirical object.* In both cases, a purely positional basis of being oneself is indicated; a basis, which, in other words, is independent of all personal characteristics. However, the Kantian and the Levinasian distinctions do not coincide. The discrepancy between them is a consequence of the divergent nature of the difference designed in the two cases to determine the position of the self. Kant exclusively relies on the opposition between the subject and the object. The weak point of this approach is that it cannot account for the difference between the self in question from any other self, because the opposition of the subject to the object applies to any *other* subject, as well as to myself. That is why the transcendental subject has to be considered as an indeterminate and purely formal "X" that has nothing to do with oneself's irreplaceable unicity. This is not the case with the concept of singularity, as it is considered from a Levinasian perspective. For this concept is founded on an insurmountable though purely positional difference between oneself and another. Our irreplaceable unicity is based on the position each of us takes, as Merleau-Ponty might put it, within the "diacritical system of intersubjectivity." We could also say—borrowing this time an expression from Levinas—that it is the "intrigue of the Other in the Same" which assigns a singularity to each of us.

It is not by chance that the word *intrigue* is used in the above expression. This word refers to the *drama* life gives to narrate, while there is no narrative capable of exhausting and entirely absorbing this drama. This dramatic dimension does not coincide with the *epic* dimension of narrative fabulation or emplotment. A dramatic intrigue is in every case a consequence of the fact that oneself is *different* from any other, while oneself is grasped only *as* another by the notion of narrative identity.

To sum up, the theory of narrative identity may be charged with a certain confusion of *self-identity* and *singularity*. However, this confusion may be the result of an illusion one often falls victim to in one's quest of narrative identity. From time to time, we find ourselves compelled to reconsider and rectify the narratives by which we have fixed the identity of ourselves. In most cases, we cannot help thinking that it is our singularity, our irreplaceable unicity, which is at stake in vital situations, in crisis-stricken moments. It is important to know that this is not the case; it is important to know this, lest we lose sight of the drama of life, which besides, or even before narration, calls for *acting* as well.

THE WILD REGION IN LIFE-HISTORY

1

Experiential Sense in Life-History

In the previous discussion of the relationship between one's own history and one's self-identity, a crucial role has been assigned to the concept of sense. I have made abundant use of terms like *sense bestowal, spontaneous sense formation,* and *retroactive sense fixation.* An unusually broad meaning has been attributed to the word *sense* in all of these expressions. How can this extended use of the word be justified?

In order to find an answer to this question, I wish to study the relationship between (extralinguistic) sense and (linguistic) meaning in phenomenology. I shall endeavor to show that this relationship raises the more general problem of the connection between experience and expression. I shall argue that all lived experience is related to the spontaneous emergence of a dispossessed sense, whereas the conceptual and linguistic expression of this experience is necessarily based on a retroactive fixation of sense.

I. The Sense of Experience

Phenomenology can be viewed as an attempt to grasp reality in its *sense*—or even *as* a sense. It is not merely the meaning of linguistic expressions which is designated here by the word *sense.* The use of this term had been extended beyond the area of language even by Husserl himself. He admitted that, originally, the word *meaning* was only related to the sphere of speech. However, he considered it as "almost inevitable" and, at the same time, as "an important step for knowledge," to enlarge the meaning of this word.[1] Husserl regularly used the term *sense* as an equivalent for this extended concept of meaning and several phenomenologists followed him in this practice.

But how can the broad meaning of the term *sense* be defined? This is a difficult and controversial question. As long as this question is not satisfactorily answered, the extended concept of sense remains, however, unclear. No wonder, then, that this concept is often considered to be suspect—or even treated as a by-product of the decomposition of the metaphysical idea of a "reason in the world." It is, however, incontestable that ordinarily, terms like *meaning* and *sense* are not only applied to linguistic expressions but also to perceptions, actions, series of events, and the arrangements of (certain) things.[2] Therefore, the attempt to clarify the broader sense of these terms and to determine its relationship with the narrower concept of linguistic meaning seems to be justifiable.

What is, then, *sense* in the extended use of the term? Early phenomenology provides here a fruitful suggestion. Heidegger, and even Husserl, is committed to the view that the structure of sense can generally be framed to the formula "something *as* something." Both of them define *sense* by this "as-structure."

The pertinence of this suggestion can be attested to by a simple example. All of a sudden, I catch sight of a sheet of white paper in front of me; I may express this perception by saying, "I can see a sheet of white paper in front of me." Early phenomenology attributes an as-structure to the expressed perception, as well as to its conceptual and linguistic expression. To put it in Husserlian terms, I may even say, "Whenever I catch sight of a sheet of white paper in front of me, I *recognize* the object of my perception *as* paper, and, at the same time, I *recognize* this paper *as* white." It would, however, be misleading to describe this act of recognition, in a Kantian vein, as a result of the application of a concept to the manifold of an intuition. The term *recognition* is designed here, on the contrary, to indicate an inherent feature of perception rather than the outcome of its synthesis with a properly conceptual representation. I may say, as Wittgenstein would probably put it, that I *can see* the object in front of me *as* paper and the paper *as* white. *Seeing as . . .* specifies a structure peculiar to perception. It may be claimed that it is this structure which is designated by Husserl, already in *Logical Investigations,* as "perceptual sense."[3] That this is not an improper correspondence can be shown by a method of variation which is typically of a Husserlian provenance. A sheet of white paper takes different shapes in different situations. Under certain circumstances, it appears as *paper,* under others (for instance, during a course in geometry), maybe, as a *rectangle,* and it may even count simply as *something white,* and so forth. The general aspect remains in all of these situations one and the same; it is nothing but its *sense,* as one may put it, that changes.

This, of course, is not to imply that a perceptual sense is necessarily inconstant. The same method of variation may be applied to our example in a different manner as well. If, for instance, one and the same sheet of paper is considered from different points of view, then its aspect changes perpetually, while its perceptual sense remains unaltered: the perceived object counts, for instance, constantly as *paper*—and not as a *rectangle* or simply as *something white.* The concept of perceptual sense has, consequently, its identical kernel, its invariably determined core.

It must, nevertheless, be added that the as-structure of extralinguistic sense necessarily contains a difference in itself; it may even be described as a *differential structure.* It is by no means accidental that the German expression *Etwas als Etwas* (something as something), quite often used by Heidegger, is customarily translated into French (by Levinas, for example) as *ceci en tant que cela.*[4] Whenever something appears *as* something, it appears, in reality, as something *else:* "this" as "that." However, this difference indicates an alterity which is far from being arbitrary. Although "this" and "that" are different, they belong strictly together. Otherwise "this" could not be determined, or even viewed, *as* "that." To put it in a somewhat paradoxical way, the particle *as* expresses the identity of two different things—or the difference of two things which are, at the same time, identified with each other. How can this differential identification be accounted for?

Nothing seems to be easier than to apply a purely conceptual dialectics of "sameness" and "alterity," or of "identity" and "difference," to the relationship between "this" and "that" in the as-structure of sense. That would, indeed, be a shortcut from an ordinary example to traditional metaphysics. J.-F. Marquet is right in saying that the little word *as, comme, qua, inquantum,* or *ᾗ*—a particle that, in some cases, consists of a single syllable or even of a single letter—contains in itself perhaps the exhaustive formula of philosophy as a whole, inasmuch as it points to the very event of "appropriation" (in the sense of Heidegger's *Ereignis*).[5] This assertion is more than a mere *bon mot.* The event of "appropriation" in this sense is the process of something becoming what it properly *is.* Thus understood, the term evokes one of the most deeply rooted endeavors of traditional philosophy: it reminds us of the various attempts, undertaken by several thinkers from Aristotle to Hegel, to grasp something individual in its proper essence. One could undoubtedly interpret the differential identification underlying the as-structure of sense in this vein. However, one would then be compelled to take the alterity—which is no less a constant feature of this structure than sameness or identity—as a still unremoved obstacle on the path toward a final stage in which a total adequacy between an individual and its proper essence is ultimately established. Thereby, one would come close to a theory of the "speculative proposition" in the sense of Hegel's preface to his *Phenomenology of Spirit*.[6]

Committed to this approach, however, one could—interestingly, and somewhat paradoxically—not even do justice to Hegel. Heidegger is right in saying that Hegel in his *Phenomenology of Spirit*—a work which originally was entitled *Science of the Experience of Consciousness*—"does not conceive experience dialectically; he thinks of dialectic in terms of the nature of experience."[7] It is even more characteristic of the phenomenology of Husserlian origin to lay out the analysis of the as-structure of sense by taking the structure of experience as a point of departure. Husserl placed himself in opposition to the whole tradition of metaphysics precisely because he tried to find a way which would lead him back from judgment, from predicative assertion—and also from all the speculative dialectics of propositions—to something he called "prepredicative experience." These historical remarks motivate a recourse to experience in the analysis of the as-structure of sense. "Experience" in which sense, however? This question requires a closer examination.

1. Sense Formation in Experience

Experience has rarely been reflected upon, so to speak, in its *poignancy*. In a memorable passage of *Truth and Method*, Gadamer shows how a cramped and truncated view of experience emerges and grows more and more prevalent in Western philosophy. In Aristotelianism, experience is considered as nothing more than an access to the generality of concepts, which, in itself, is taken for granted; and in Baconian empiricism, it is regarded as nothing more than an instance that either confirms or refutes scientific hypotheses. In both of these influential traditions, experience is interpreted as a means by which a desired end—the formation of general concepts or the development of experimental science—is to be achieved. This teleological conception of experience is, however, highly questionable. In its ordinary form, experience, one may insist, is the experience one *gains*. Experience, in this sense, however, has so little to do with any preconceived idea of a desired end that it may rather be defined as the generation of a *new insight*. The first thinker to put this view forward was undoubtedly Hegel. Gadamer, inspired by Hegel, but using a rather Husserlian language, adds a further claim by asserting that all experience that deserves this name "baffles some expectation."[8] Gadamer argues that experience manifests itself by upsetting previous calculations, unsettling inveterated opinions, and countering the designs built upon them. Consequently, experience always touches a sore point; it cuts to the quick, it strikes home; it has, in other words, its characteristic *poignancy.* That is why experience, in its original form—as the experience one *gains*—is one's own *lived* experience, which belongs to one's own life-history and is properly expressed in the first-person singular.

To be sure, not all experience is an experience one *gains.* There is such a thing as *common* or *shared* experience as well. The word *experience* does not necessarily designate an event one goes through; it may just as well refer to a disposition one may appropriate by learning from experiences gained by others. In such standing expressions as "experience shows" or "experience proves that . . . " the word *experience* does not point to a process—not even to a hidden one—but it hints at a commonly acquired disposition. It alludes to an accumulated or sedimented experience that may be shared by each of us, even if it has originally been gained by others. This dispositional sense of experience is, however, only its secondary (derived) sense. It clearly presupposes the primary sense of experience, in which it refers to an *event* or a *process.* The link between the two senses is, of course, obvious: nobody can be called "experienced" without gaining—or having already gained—experiences, while preserving an openness for new ones. From our previous discussion, we may, therefore, draw the conclusion that experience in its primary sense is an event rather than a disposition: namely the event of the generation of a new insight that thwarts some previous expectations.

Nevertheless, we must not entirely lose sight of the dispositional sense of experience, either. What else could we rely on in our attempt to analyze experience in its original form than precisely on our commonly shared experience of what an experience we *gain* is? Phenomenology may generally be defined as an *elucidation of experience* (in the primary sense of experience); it should, however, be added that this elucidation is *guided by experience itself* (in the secondary sense of expereince)—and not simply by a sense of how the word *experience* is properly used *in language.*

Indeed, what else may we cite as an instance than commonly shared experience, if we are to decide whether the experience we *gain* ordinarily includes anything more than the negation of some presumptions? Should we perhaps fall back upon the tradition of dialectics and speak of a "negativity" of experience? Gadamer seems to think so. That is why he draws even more upon Hegel than upon Husserl. The introduction to the *Phenomenology of Spirit* explains the idea that experience can only be seen when a new insight emerges, as it were, *behind the back of consciousness.*[9] However, from this Hegel concludes that experience as such is subject to the rule of the "negative." But one is unlikely to share this opinion unless one accepts the standard by which the negativity of experience is measured in the *Phenomenology of Spirit.* As Gadamer says, this standard is "absolute knowledge," which is characterized by Hegel as the final stage of the whole process presented and analyzed in his work. According to Hegel, the identity of consciousness with its object becomes evident at this stage; nothing *other* than consciousness, nothing *alien* to it, is left any more. Therefore, as Gadamer rightly observes, the dialectics of experience leads, in the *Phenomenology of Spirit,* to a stage in which all experience is overcome.[10] Gadamer does not leave any doubt about his own position regarding the idea of absolute knowledge: he rejects it as a notion that does not meet the requirements of contemporary hermeneutical reflection. It remains, however, somewhat mysterious why, in spite of this refusal, he adopts the idea of a "dialectics of experience." Indeed, there is no reason to place experience under the rule of the "negative." Frustration of previous expectations is more than just a negation of presumptive knowledge, even if it does not become immediately clear how the old convictions can be replaced by new ones. There is nothing sophistical in the assertion that attaining a negative conclusion is already a positive achievement in itself. So much is, however, admitted by Hegel himself. The decisive objection to the idea of a "negativity" of experience can rather be based on a statement formulated by Husserl. Wherever some previous expectation is contradicted by experience, the conflict, we may say with Husserl, "presupposes a certain basis of agreement."[11] That is why experience is never solely a refutation but also a partial confirmation of presumptive knowledge.

This observation suggests that the idea of a "dialectics of experience," as well as that of a "rule of the negative," should be abandoned, even if at least some basic elements of Hegel's approach to experience are to be retained. The elements to be preserved should be transposed into a new framework. In search for such a framework, the phenomenological notion of extralinguistic sense lends itself to a reconsideration.

Hegel and Gadamer's idea of an experience that generates a new insight by baffling previous expectations may easily be linked up with Husserl and Heidegger's conception of extralinguistic sense defined in terms of the differential structure "something as something (else)." For what is the emergence of a new insight frustrating presumptive knowledge if not an event or a process that reveals something *as* something *else?* Here the concept of a "differential identification" shows itself in a proper light; it turns out to be free from any speculative touch. This concept is by no means a mere product of dialectical reasoning. To the contrary, it expresses a general feature of experience. Something *as* something *else:* this differential structure is the very structure of what may be termed as "experiential sense."

The generation of a new insight that thwarts previous expectations may be interpreted as an event in which *a new sense emerges.* In experience, something appears unexpectedly as something else; all of a sudden, "this" reveals itself as "that." Thereby, a new as-structure establishes itself. It seems that to say that here a new sense emerges is merely putting the previous sentence in another way.

This is, however, not a sufficient characterization of experience. It must be added that the new sense emerging in experience cannot be reduced to any sense bestowal by consciousness. That is what Hegel brings to light by insisting that experience takes place, at least partly, *behind the back* of consciousness.

To be sure, in the *Phenomenology of Spirit,* the unconscious process involved in experience is described as the emergence of a new *object* for consciousness rather than that of a new sense.[12] However, the least that can be said of this conception is that it is based on a paradoxical formulation of what happens in experience. Moreover, this conception rests on the anticipatory presupposition of a final stage in which the duality of consciousness and object is surmounted. If frustration of previous expectations is a conflict which, as Husserl claimed, "presupposes a certain basis of agreement," then it is seriously misleading to say that the object itself changes in experience. In reality, it is rather one and the same object which may be said to appear in a new light or to take a new shape. This is clear even from the cases in which, for instance, a human figure in front of us turns out to be a waxwork. Here Hegel leaves out of consideration the fact that, in experience, the object is necessarily given in an intuitive way, i.e., independently of its conceptual identification. We may infer from this that an adequate analysis of experience is not to be expected from a merely conceptual dialectics.

Husserlian and Heideggerian phenomenology suggests a way out from this quandary by providing a concept of *sense* that may serve to account for the changes the object undergoes in experience. Making use of this concept of *sense,* one may describe experience as a *process* of *sense formation.* One will, however, have to keep in mind that this process takes place, at least partly, *behind the back of consciousness.*

This definition of experience sheds a new light on the relationship between experience and reality. I will show this by discussing Husserl's approach to this relationship.

2. Experience and Reality

Husserl is firmly convinced that there are no possible sense formations in a reality that is considered as independent of consciousness because to identify something as something is, necessarily, an intentional accomplishment of consciousness. This conviction seems well founded indeed. Should we not otherwise assume that reality consists of objects identifying themselves without consciousness? It is worth mentioning that this—obviously absurd—assumption is considered by Hilary Putnam as an argument against "realism," taken in the usual sense of the word.[13] We may cite Putnam here even if he formulates the assumption that "objects identify themselves" independently of Husserl,[14] and even if he considers it in the context of an analytic theory of reference instead of the framework of an intentional analysis of consciousness.[15] This instance might be taken as one in which the results of two different traditions of thought may be translated into one another. Putnam's argument, although elaborated as a piece of analytic philosophy, has its ideal counterpart in intentional phenomenology. One could easily infer from this argument that the idea of a mind-independent reality rests on a misconception of experience. Indeed, in contrast with Putnam, Husserl did not hesitate to draw this inference. That is why he linked up intentional phenomenology with transcendental idealism.

Although I do not consider this connection as necessary and, in the following discussion, I intend to break the bounds between phenomenology and transcendental idealism, one thing seems to me incontestable: the idea of transcendental idealism contains in itself an important insight which is neither to be rejected nor to be eluded. This insight can be expressed in the following way: one can conceive of the relationship between experience and reality only from the perspective of one's own consciousness; for substantial reasons, one cannot take any—external, let alone divine—stance allowing for a comparison of experience with reality, and for a nonperspectivistic assessment of the degree of their agreement. This insight is a basic element in Kant's "Copernican revolution," bequeathed to phenomenology. Husserl embraces this legacy; he makes Kant's transcendental idealism his own. He says in the *Cartesian Meditations:* "Whatever exists for a man like me and is accepted by him, exists for him and is accepted in his own conscious life [. . .]."[16] He adds: "The attempt to conceive the universe of true being as something lying outside the universe of possible consciousness [. . .] is nonsensical."[17] The naive realism of everyday life is hardly powerful enough to contest this standpoint.

Husserl thought he was more consistent than Kant himself in his defense of transcendental idealism. Husserl unambiguously rejected the Kantian assumption of things in themselves. Husserl realized that the thing in itself was nothing more than an *idea*—more precisely, an "idea in a Kantian sense"—which, although serving as a "regulative principle" in experience, could not be taken as a reality existing independently of consciousness.

It seems to me, however, that Husserl did not take into account a possibility recognized and, to some extent, exploited by the thinkers of German Idealism. Fichte and Schelling built the system of transcendental idealism on the idea of a "history of self-consciousness."[18] Thereby, they opened a path toward a new interpretation of what is "in itself": for them this term meant the unconscious processes to which they assigned the function of pushing consciousness from one stage of its "historical" development to another. As an heir to this thought, Hegel, in his *Phenomenology of Spirit,* expounds his conception of experience. By the expression "in itself" he means that which emerges for consciousness as a result of processes which take place *behind its back.* It is true that the idea of a "history of self-consciousness" gave rise to a whole "mythology" of unconscious mental activities in German Idealism. Husserl rejected this mythology—in agreement with Paul Natorp—as early as in the *Logical Investigations.*[19] However, his completely justified aversion to the assumption of unconscious activities, postulated by Fichte, Schelling, and even by Hegel in an admittedly intricate manner, prevented him from recognizing the new conception of what "in itself" is in German Idealism. Inspired by this conception, one may now oppose a quite sophisticated version of realism to Kant's original formulation of transcendental idealism as well as to Husserl's restatement of this doctrine.

Indeed, one need not accept the absurd assumption of objects identifying themselves in order to claim that all experience is the experience of the *in itself.* It is sufficient for this claim to conceive of experience as of an event that thwarts previous expectations, frustrates conceptual identifications, and calls for modifying conceptual schemes. Thus interpreted, experience makes it evident that sense bestowal by consciousness is from time to time shattered, put into question and urged to renew itself by impulses coming, so to speak, from the outside of conscious life. The experiential sense of reality is determined by such external impulses. Reality is for us something which may refute our expectations. It is not necessary for us to consider experience from an external perspective in order to form the concept of such a reality. On the contrary; it is precisely the experiences we *gain* that give rise to this concept. For, I wish to argue, experience is permeated with a process of sense formation; although it presupposes a certain basis of agreement, it also upsets previous calculations and unsettles inveterated opinions. What is confirmed by experience may be considered as an *element* of reality. The very *notion* of reality has to do with the fact that, in experience, *confirmation* and *refutation* go hand in hand. This duality of confirmation and refutation makes experience capable of constituting a reality which, in turn, may be considered as independent of this experience.

This version of realism by no means implies that one should ever be able to transcend the necessarily limited perspective of one's own consciousness in order to decide whether one's own experience corresponds to reality or not. Nevertheless, one may claim that all experience is an *encounter* and a *contact* with a mind-independent reality, even if one has to add that the lessons resulting from this encounter and contact are interpreted, in each case, from the necessarily limited perspective of one's own consciousness. These considerations provide a basis for considering experience as the domain of a spontaneous sense formation, which does not fall under the rule of any sense bestowal by consciousness.

One of the main aims of phenomenology, from its very beginnings, has been to give back to experience its weight and significance, in both the reflection upon scientific knowledge and in the methodology of philosophical analysis. Husserl clearly saw that this endeavor did not commit him to any kind of empiricism. For empiricism is based on a reductive view of experience. In empiricism, only those events count as experiences which are repeatable in uncountable ways and which show the same features in all of their occurrences. But where do we find such an experience if not under artificial circumstances, or even under experimental conditions? Husserl, especially in his later philosophy, tries to return from this less ambiguous but seriously impoverished interpretation of experience to a more ambiguous one, which is yet fuller and richer; for him experience is to be encountered not so much in science but in everyday life. He even accuses Kant of having forgotten about the "life-world" and—as a consequence—of failing to admit any other experience than the one pertinent to empirical science. However, Gadamer is right when he claims that even Husserl "did not succeed in getting rid of the one-sidedness he criticize[d]."[20] We may add that Husserl was not in a position to cope with the one-sidedness of the traditional view of experience because he was unable to break with the conviction that experience was the product of a sense bestowal by consciousness. That is why he misconceived the relationship between experience and reality. One cannot, however, give back to experience its weight and significance without setting this relationship in its proper light. Therefore, Hegel may be said to be a more reliable advisor on this question than Husserl. Consequently, contemporary phenomenology may no less draw upon Hegel's *Phenomenology of Spirit* than upon Husserl's transcendental phenomenology.

However, the idea of a process that takes place "behind the back of consciousness" undoubtedly requires some clarification. I will consider it more closely from the perspective of intentional phenomenology.

3. Experience and Intentionality

How does Husserl delimit the sphere of application he assigns to the extended concept of meaning? He claims that this sphere may be circumscribed by the notion of "intentional experience." That is why Husserl's idea of phenomenology, as well as his very concept of phenomenon, is determined by what may be called the "intentional notion" of sense. This notion may be characterized by a simple but by no means harmless formula: "the consciousness *of* something *as* something."[21]

Two structures are intertwined in this formula. The *as-structure of sense* is only one of them. Husserl does not content himself with a definition of phenomenon based exclusively on this structure. It is a peculiar feature of his approach to phenomenology that he inserts and embeds this as-structure into the *intentional structure of consciousness* (marked in the above formula by the particle *of*).

Two parallelisms characterize the dimensions in which this approach unfolds. The first, which is treated by Husserl at length in the *Logical Investigations,* is a parallelism between "meaningful reference"—or "empty meaning"—and "fulfilling intuition."[22] In *Ideas I,* this first parallelism is coupled by a second one: there is a parallelism between the *noesis* and the *noema,* too.[23] If the first parallelism proves to be firm and sound, it can be deduced that (extralinguistic, i.e., intuitive, for instance, perceptual, or, better still, experiential) sense and (linguistic or, more generally, conceptual) meaning are characterized by the same "as-structure." If the second parallelism can equally bear scrutiny, it might be concluded that this "as-structure" is part and parcel of the "of-structure" of intentional consciousness.

It is a consequence of the intertwinement of these two structures that, in Husserl's phenomenology, the attempt to grasp reality as a sense is tantamount to an attempt to prove reality's dependence upon consciousness. This twofold undertaking presupposes a radical break with the natural—*too* natural—conviction that all knowledge of reality rests upon an ontological relation and a substantial correspondence between two entities, one immanent, the other transcendent. It is no exaggeration to claim that modern epistemology, in most of its different versions, has been based on this assumption. It is obvious, however, that this assumption is neither justifiable nor refutable, because it requires a spectator who is in a position to *compare* the two "entities": one, being immanent, resides within the spectator, while the other, belonging to transcendent reality, is the external counterpart of this immanence. As noted above, Kant's "Copernican revolution" was based on the insight that we are never in a position to do this. Husserl shows, no less unambiguously, that no experiential way gives access to such a position. As he says in the fifth *Logical Investigation:*

> There are [. . .] not two things present in experience, we do not experience the object and beside it the intentional experience directed upon it, there are not even two things present in the sense of a part and a whole which contains it: only one thing is present, the intentional experience, whose essential descriptive character is the intention in question. [. . .] If this experience is present, then, *eo ipso* and through its own essence (we must insist), the intentional "relation" to an object is achieved, and an object is "intentionally present"; these two phrases mean precisely the same.[24]

Husserl—and phenomenology in general—wishes to overcome the traditional opposition of what is immanent and what is transcendent on the basis of the above insight. Thereby, the spell which modern epistemology, in most of its different versions, had succumbed to, is broken. However, the intentional notion of sense gives rise to difficulties of another kind, which urge Husserl's successors to surpass the confinements of early phenomenology, or even to submit this heritage to a profound transformation. The following discussion will be dedicated to two difficulties of this sort. The first one, which may be considered as a preposterous consequence of the parallelism between the *noesis* and the *noema,* is a difficulty which Husserl's immediate disciples—for example, Eugen Fink or Jan Patočka—had already to face; the second one, resulting from the parallelism supposed between experiential sense and conceptual meaning, has been brought to the fore only quite recently, especially by Maurice Merleau-Ponty and Emmanuel Levinas. The following attempt to resolve these difficulties is designed to contribute to a reformulation of the concept of phenomenon. In this section, I will deal with the difficulty resulting from the parallelism of the *noesis* and the *noema* in order to clarify the notion of an experiential sense that emerges behind the back of consciousness.

It is a well-known fact that Frege used the terms *Sinn* and *Bedeutung* for the difference between the sense (the meaning) and the reference (the *denotatum*) of linguistic expressions. Husserl finds this terminology misleading. In his opinion, the Fregean distinction between *Sinn* and *Be-*

deutung does not correspond to the ordinary use of these German words; it is a far-fetched and contrived device to designate a difference that might be indicated in a less artificial way. He finds it more natural to reserve the terms *Sinn* and *Bedeutung* to give voice to the difference between experiential sense and conceptual meaning. But as far as the content of the Fregean opposition is concerned, Husserl by no means disagrees, even if he prefers to talk, instead of the Fregean *Bedeutung,* about *Gegenstandsbeziehung* (objective reference) and *Beziehung auf ein Objekt* (relation to an object). It is these expressions that for Husserl stand in opposition with experiential sense (Husserlian *Sinn*) and conceptual meaning (Husserlian *Bedeutung*). (Husserl even uses the pair *Inhalt* [content] and *Gegenstand* [object], proposed by Kasimir Twardowski, one of Brentano's Polish followers who was among the founders of the Warsaw-Lemberg school of logic.)[25]

In spite of such terminological divergences, there are, especially in the *Logical Investigations,* several passages which testify to a certain affinity between Husserl and Frege. In the last four decades, various Husserl scholars have felt encouraged to put the two thinkers side by side. As it is often called, a "Fregean approach" to Husserl's phenomenology has been developed by a whole series of philosophers from Dagfinn Føllesdal to Ronald McIntyre and David Woodruff Smith.[26] One of the characteristics of this approach is the endeavor to understand Husserl's concept of meaning and sense starting from Frege's theory.

At first sight, this endeavor seems rather ill founded. To be sure, in the *Logical Investigations,* Husserl interprets meaning and sense—just like Frege—as abstract entities; yet later on he abandons this view. In *Ideas I,* he elaborates a noematic conception of sense and meaning. This conception allows him to interpret the unchanging, permanent, and recognizable content of a whole series of noetic acts as their common "noematic nucleus." Thus, he is no longer compelled to oppose it as a kind of ideal essence to the real intentional experiences of consciousness. Husserl now defines the concept of sense—or meaning in its extended use—as the "noematic object in its modal setting" (*der noematische Gegenstand im Wie*).[27] The gap between this definition and Frege's position can hardly be bridged. John Drummond rightly points out, in his debate with the proponents of the Fregean approach, that Husserlian "sense" or "meaning," interpreted as a "noematic nucleus," is nothing other than *the object itself in its significance for us.*[28]

Upon a closer examination, however, it turns out that the Fregean approach is nonetheless far from being entirely pointless. Husserl's transition to the noematic view of sense and meaning gives rise to a major difficulty. If sense or meaning is nothing else than the object itself in its significance for us, the question arises as to how to distinguish the object from its sense or meaning. Husserl answers this question by separating the object *simpliciter* from the object *in its modal setting.*[29] This difference can easily be clarified, if attention is given to what has been said about the as-structure of sense and meaning. The distinction may be expressed as follows: whereas "the object simpliciter" is something, "the object in its modal setting" is something *as* something. Yet Husserl finds himself here confronted with an insurmountable difficulty because, in his view, this as-structure is necessarily embedded into the intentional structure of consciousness. That is why he is compelled to assign to sense and meaning the character of an immanence of consciousness which cannot be transferred to the object itself. Thus we have, on the one hand, "the object simpliciter," which is purported to be transcendent; and "the object in its modal setting" on the other, which turns out to be immanent. Consequently, we are once again faced with the question of how that which is immanent can correspond to that which is transcendent. Husserl tries to escape from this predicament by applying the Fregean opposition of sense or meaning and reference not only to noetic acts but also to their noematic counterparts. He writes in *Ideas I,* "Every noema has a *'content,'* namely, its 'meaning' [*Sinn*], and is related through it to 'its' *object.*"[30]

The upshot is a strange conception in which the scope of the Fregean opposition is not only transferred from linguistic expressions to intentional experiences but also extended from intentional acts to their noematic correlates. What are Husserl's reasons for proceeding in this way? Obviously, the parallelism between the *noesis* and the *noema.* This parallelism, as Husserl puts it, is "thoroughly verified" if it can be shown that "the noema also refers to an object and possesses a 'content,' 'by means of' which it refers to the object, the object being the same as that of the noesis [. . .]."[31]

A consequence of this procedure is, however, that the relationship between *content* (i.e., *sense* or *meaning*) and *object* is assimilated to the relationship between (intentional) *act* and *object.* It is not difficult to see that this is a misleading analogy, since the already surmounted opposition between that which is immanent and that which is transcendent makes its reappearance.

No wonder, then, that the intentional notion of sense or meaning proves to be equivocal. This notion can, indeed, be considered as a compromise between two conflicting tendencies: on the one hand, the noematic approach of phenomenology makes it possible, and even plausible, to identify sense and meaning with the object itself in its modal setting or, in other words, in its significance for us. On the other hand, the assumption of a rigorous parallelism between the *noesis* and the *noema* makes it equally plausible, and even necessary, to separate sense and meaning from the object of reference, in order to assimilate them to the act of consciousness. The conflict of these two opposing tendencies results in an *ambivalence* characteristic of the intentional notion of sense and meaning: in an irremediable ambiguity, in an invincible fluctuation between immanence and transcendence. This ambivalence is the first difficulty I wish to discuss.

Eugen Fink was among the first to face this problem. In one of his famous studies on phenomenology, he raises the question in all its poignancy: "Is the noema itself 'immanent' or 'transcendent'?"[32] His answer is based on a distinction between a "psychological" and a "transcendental" concept of the *noema*. Fink says,

> The psychological noema refers to an object which, being independent of it, is manifested and verified in it. The transcendental noema [. . .] cannot refer to [. . .] any entity independent of it, it is the entity itself [. . .].[33]

This quotation clarifies the purport of the distinction between the psychological and the transcendental concept of the *noema*. However, it remains to be asked what, in the case of the transcendental *noema*, the expression "reference to an object" could mean. Here, we cannot follow Fink's line of thought, unless we recall that, in *Ideas I*, Husserl does not content himself with the recourse to the Fregean opposition; he equally makes use of a model of Kantian origin: besides conceiving of the object *simpliciter* as an object of reference, he also attempts to grasp it as something that remains identical in a manifold of senses or meanings. Thus, there are two relations between sense (or meaning) and object, which are superimposed on each other here: the first can be characterized by the key word of *reference;* the second by that of *constitution*. Fink separates these two models from each other: he assigns the first to the psychological, the second to the transcendental *noema*. This dissociation of the two models, which are inseparably linked up with each other in Husserl's original conception, does not leave the superimposition of reference and constitution intact. Fink is engaged in a dubious undertaking: moving from the psychological to the transcendental level, he reduces the relation of reference to the relation of constitution. He undoubtedly succeeds in bridging the gap between that which is immanent and that which is transcendent. Yet this feat has its price: Fink is obliged to assume that sense bestowal by consciousness amounts to a constitution of reality endowed with an almost world-creating power.

Jan Patočka takes the opposite direction in his attempt to overcome the "subjectivism" of Husserl's phenomenology. He interprets noematic sense as an *objective* mode in which the object is given (*eine selbst* gegenständliche *Gegebenheitsweise des Gegenstandes*). He says, "It clearly is an objective appearance, when I consider a cube from its different sides and I, nevertheless, have one and the same object in front of me."[34] He aims at presenting a phenomenal sphere which is not immanent to consciousness but has nothing to do with any allegedly world-creating activity of consciousness, either. At the same time, he sets himself the task of deducing the "essential correlation of the *noesis* and the *noema*" from a "split" of this phenomenal sphere. What is that, however, which prompted Husserl to divide the originally unified field of phenomena into two parts? In Husserl's gesture Patočka discovers the wish to differentiate between empty meaning intention and fulfilling intuition. He himself is far from approving of this distinction. He rather wants to find here "the subjectivism of Husserlian phenomenology *in statu nascendi.*"[35] He says, "It is obviously one and the same object which shows itself once in a deficient mode, then in the mode in which it is given as itself."[36]

Patočka calls the description and analysis of the originally unified phenomenal sphere "asubjective phenomenology." But what does the "objectivity" or "asubjectivity" of this phenomenal sphere consist in? These terms remain unclear as long as it is not shown how experience procures an access to a sense that is not immanent to consciousness. Such a sense may rightly be said to emerge *behind the back of consciousness.* But how can experience procure an access to such a dispossessed sense?

It seems to me that the problem arises from an unwarranted presupposition. One is inclined to take for granted that the structure of experience is necessarily determined by a strict correlation of the *noesis* and the *noema.* This view, however, is untenable unless *actual* as well as *inactual* experiences are admitted. Even a simple perception encompasses some details which fall outside of the range of attention, and its structure may be characterized by a contrast of a central figure with a background that remains at least undifferentiated, if not obscure. Moreover, even a simple perception involves, together with some fully developed moments, certain inchoate moments, as well as fading moments. It is because of such attentional modifications, developmental moments and similar phenomena that, as early as *Ideas I,* Husserl finds himself compelled to allow for several kinds of inactual—or even potential—intentional experiences. It may be added that, in this work, experience is considered merely in the framework of a *static* analysis; it is, in other words, deprived of its *genetic* dimension. That is why it is interpreted just as a lived experience (*Erlebnis*) and not as the emergence of a new insight (*Erfahrung*). A static analysis provides but a curtailed image of experience. If, however, the genetic dimension of experience is restored, the idea of a phenomenology of the unconscious inevitably arises.[37] In this case, something "new" will appear which, in Husserl's own terms, may rightly be said to "ha[ve] come into being as alien to consciousness."[38]

How can this kind of a *genesis spontanea,* of "primal generation,"[39] be accounted for? The concept of inactual experiences will obviously not suffice for this purpose. For such a process will necessarily lead to the emergence of some new sense moments which are not to be considered as merely actualized (awakened) but rather as originally produced (aroused). Such *sense-arousals* may be preceded by, or even included into, intentional experiences—they cannot be *deduced* from them. Rather, they are *induced* by a process of spontaneous sense formation which upsets a preestablished correlation between the *noesis* and the *noema.* The freshly aroused sense moments may unfold; they may pave the way for a fully developed intentional experience that restores the noetico-noematic equilibrium. In between, however, we encounter shreds of sense situated on a path running from one intentional experience to another. We may describe these shreds as *interintentional moments of a spontaneous sense formation,* adding that the phenomenon of "interintentionality" gives its precise meaning to the expression "behind the back of consciousness."

II. Experience and Expression

The difficulty Fink and Patočka are grappling with arises, as we have seen, mainly from the assumption of a parallelism between the *noesis* and the *noema.* But the parallelism between conceptual meaning and experiential sense plays an equally important role in the generation of this difficulty. We must not forget that, in Frege, the opposition between sense (or meaning) and reference applies only to linguistic expressions. Husserl could not have transferred this opposition from linguistic expressions to the noematic nucleus of intentional experiences in general if he had not taken for granted that there is a strong parallelism between the meaning of linguistic expressions and the sense of fulfilling experiences.

The following discussion is dedicated to the difficulty which arises from the assumption of this parallel. It is in this context that the Husserlian idea of a categorial intuition will be analyzed in depth. I shall try to show that there are structural differences between experiential sense and meaningful expression, which justify an attempt to distinguish quasi categories of sense from categories of meaning.

1. Experience and Categorial Expression

According to Husserl, the assumption of a parallelism between experiential sense and meaningful expression is, as a matter of fact, included in the very concept of linguistic—or more generally, conceptual—expression. We are told in *Ideas I* that

> "Expression" is a remarkable form, which permits of being adapted to every "meaning"[40] (to the noematic "nucleus"), and raises it to the realm of the "Logos," of the *conceptual,* and therewith of the "*general.*"[41]

Husserl adds that expression is a

> peculiar intentional instrument [. . .] which essentially possesses the outstanding characteristic of reflecting back as from a mirror every other intentionality according to its form and content, of copying whilst coloring it in its own way, and thereby of working into it its own form of "conceptuality."[42]

Without committing himself to this conception, Husserl could hardly transfer the opposition between sense (or meaning) and reference from the narrower sphere of the "logos" (the expression, the conceptual and the general) to the wider region of the noematic nucleus.

Is, however, the assumption of such a parallelism well founded? In order to decide this, we have to consult the sixth *Logical Investigation,* where Husserl considers whether the expression can be regarded as an "image-like counterpart" of perception or, more precisely, of the percept.[43] He admits that the parallelism between conceptual meaning and experiential sense is suggested by the very idea of expression. Nevertheless, he ultimately comes to the conclusion that

> in the case of structured expressions, the notion of a more or less mirror-like mode of expression [is] quite unavailing in describing the relation which obtains between meanings to be expressed, on the one hand, and expressed intuitions, on the other.[44]

It is true that this is not the case in all linguistic expressions. Indeed, the notion of a more or less mirror-like mode of expression applies to proper names. Husserl says,

> The man who knows Cologne itself, and therefore possesses the genuine "proper meaning" of the word "Cologne," has in his contemporary actual experience something exactly corresponding to the future confirming percept.[45]

However, the case of proper names cannot serve as a "prototype"[46] for a general interpretation of the relation between meaning and intuiting because every structured, articulated expression—like, for instance, "white paper"—includes, as Husserl shows, a "surplus of meaning" that remains over and above the content of the corresponding perception.[47] This surplus of meaning results from the fact that every expression different from a proper name contains *categorial forms* such as "is" and "is not," "a," "the," "and," "or," "if," "then," "all," "none," "something," "nothing," the terms of quantity, the determinations of number, and so on.[48] Husserl here seems to reject the assumption of a parallelism between conceptual meaning and perceptual sense.

Everything changes, however, with the question of whether these categorial forms—and the corresponding logical categories such as being and nonbeing, unity, plurality, totality, number, ground, consequence, and so forth[49]—are only emptily meant, or, rather, they are themselves fulfilled in perception and imagination. At first sight, this question seems rather odd. Is there any fulfilling intuition corresponding to categorial forms such as "is," "and," and "or," just as there is one to each material element of meaning like "paper" or "white"? However strange it might seem, Husserl is convinced that all categorial forms are characterized by "an essential homogeneity of the function of fulfillment."[50] This conception is confirmed by the fact that the "is," the "and," the "or," and the other categorial forms obviously are, in a certain sense, perceived, intuited, or experienced. If it is true that I can see this sheet of white paper before me, it must necessarily also be true that I can see that this sheet of paper is white. The statement according to which I can see that this paper is white *and* this table is brown is no less sound. We can even use the particle *or* in such sentences. An assertion like, for instance, "I can see that a crow *or* a raven has just taken flight" is correct. We are driven by these examples to the conclusion that the distinction between empty designation, imaginative representation, and intuitive self-presentation applies just as much to categorial forms as to material elements of meaning. Husserl is encouraged by this observation to draw a distinction between *sensuous* and *categorial perception* (or, more generally, sensuous and categorial intuition).

The term *categorial perception* refers to an intentional act which, *founded* upon a sense perception, is capable of fulfilling not only the material elements of meaning but also its categorial forms. One of the simplest cases of a categorial perception is the perception of a *state of affairs* (e.g., "I can see that this paper is white") which is, according to Husserl, necessarily founded upon the perception of a *sensible object* ("I can see this white paper"). There are also other kinds of categorial perception. The famous *Wesensschau* itself—"intuition of essences" or "ideative abstraction"—belongs to them. In the perception of a state of affairs, the categorial form of being is said to be fulfilled; in the intuition of essences the categorial form of what is general and conceptual is putatively given in the mode of an intuitive self-presentation. The distinction between sensuous and categorial perception permits Husserl to reconsider and reformulate the problem of a parallelism between perceptual sense and conceptual meaning. As he says,

> our parallelism may be re-established, but it is no longer a parallelism between the meaning-intentions of expressions and the mere percepts which correspond to them: it is a parallelism between meaning-intentions and the above mentioned *perceptually founded acts*.[51]

Thus far, the text is unambiguous. Upon closer view, however, it turns out that this seemingly coherent conception is not flawless. The doubt arises whether a clear line of demarcation can be drawn between what is *sensuous* and what is *categorial*.

This can be seen if the difference between the perception of a sensible object (such as this white paper before me) and the perception of a corresponding state of affairs (such as the fact that this paper is white) is thoroughly examined. Husserl writes,

> the *paper* is known as white, or rather as a white thing, whenever we express our percept in the words "white paper." The intention of the word "white" only partially coincides with the color-aspect of the apparent object; a surplus of meaning remains over, a form which finds nothing in the appearance itself to confirm it. White paper is paper which *is* white.[52]

We are told, however, that the same holds true of the noun *paper*. Husserl adds,

> Only the quality-meanings [*Merkmalbedeutungen*] contained in its "concept" terminate in perception. Here also the whole object is known as paper, and here also a supplementary form is known which includes being, though not as its sole form, in itself.[53]

According to this statement, even the "straightforward" perception of a sensible object (like this paper before me) exhibits an *as-structure;* it contains a *categorial form* which includes not only being in itself but—as the somewhat enigmatic phrase "though not its sole form" may be interpreted—also the form of the conceptual and the general characteristic of every common noun like *paper.* Moreover, not even proper names are exceptions to this rule. The perceived object before me is known *as* paper. The same applies to the streets in which I am roaming: they are known *as* Cologne.

That is why Husserl asks himself, "Ought we not also to attribute to sensuous intuition the character of a categorial act, insofar as through it the form of objectivity is constituted?"[54] Husserl seems to answer this question in the affirmative. However, the interpretation of sense perception as a categorial act blurs the line of demarcation between the sensuous and the categorial. To be sure, in a Kantian model, the sensuous and the categorial could be conceived of as inseparable moments of a unified experience which results from their connection or, as Kant often formulates it, from their *synthesis.* However, the model of *foundation,* which Husserl applies to the relation of these two factors, is different from the Kantian schema. It has nothing to do with synthesis. The sensuous could not serve as the basis of the categorial if it could not occur independently of it. It may even be maintained that this model of foundation marks a radical break with Kant's view of sense and understanding. What are Husserl's reasons to depart from the Kantian tradition?

The main reason is, undoubtedly, in the fact that he elaborates a new conception of the *origin of the categories.* Husserl is able to see that *being is not a real predicate* just as clearly as Kant. Husserl says,

> Being is nothing *in* the object, no part of it, no moment tenanting it, no quality or intensity of it, no figure of it or no internal form whatsoever, no constitutive feature of it however conceived. But being is also nothing attaching *to* an object: as it is no real [*reales*] internal feature, so also it is no external feature, and therefore not, in the *real* sense, a "feature" at all.[55]

Husserl adds that the same is true of the other categorial forms. He insists, however, that the categorial forms "relate to the object itself, *in its categorial structure.*"[56] As this cautious formulation indicates, Husserl is opposed to the traditional view of the origin of the categories, which can be traced back to Locke, and which is to be found even in Leibniz and Kant (at least in the Kant of the precritical period). According to this "natural but quite misguided" doctrine (as Husserl puts it), being, as well as all other categories "arise through reflection upon certain mental acts, and so fall in the sphere of 'inner sense,' of 'inner perception.'"[57] Husserl's main contention, on the contrary, is that the categories, far from arising through *reflection* upon certain intentional acts, have their origin in the *fulfillment* of some intentional acts.[58] It is part and parcel of this view to maintain that the categories have nothing to do with these acts, but they relate, as it has just been quoted, to their objective counterparts.

This view of the origin of the categories is the principal reason why Husserl assumes a genuine kind of intuition which, on the one hand, being irreducible to sensuous intuition but, on the other hand, being founded upon it, can accomplish the task of fulfilling empty categorial meaning intentions. This view also explains why Husserl's doctrine of categorial intuition was embraced as one of the most fruitful insights of early phenomenology, especially by thinkers striving for a renewal of traditional philosophy. Emil Lask was profoundly influenced by this doctrine, and Martin Heidegger considered it as one of Husserl's "fundamental discoveries." Nevertheless, Husserl's view on the origin of the categories encounters new difficulties. The assumption of the "essential homogeneity of the function of fulfillment," which serves as a basis to the whole doctrine of categorial intuitions, cannot be expected to account for the difference between the sensuous and the categorial. Husserl took the example of a white sheet in order to show, as we have seen, that categorial forms manifested themselves through a surplus of meaning. This particularly fruitful notion gave rise to a differentiated and sophisticated analysis which was rightly considered by the later Heidegger as a paradigm of phenomenological proximity to the "things themselves." However, Husserl departed soon from this promising initiative. Instead of adhering consequently to the position according to which categorial forms are to be viewed as moments of a surplus of meaning, he ultimately built his doctrine on the more conventional tenet according to which categorial forms are to be conceived of as "objects of higher levels."

Yet, it testifies to the extraordinary richness of the *Logical Investigations* that it contains some considerations which transcend the limits of this predominant conception. These considerations put the parallelism between conceptual meaning and experiential sense into question. They show that we may speak of a perceptual identification of objects which does not necessarily assume the form of a categorial act. Thereby, they not only encourage but even urge us to distinguish the as-structure which is peculiar to experiential sense from the as-structure attributed to conceptual meaning.

The considerations I have in mind are consecrated to the analysis of a process which is described by Husserl as a "continuous perceptual flux" or "series."[59] In the sixth *Logical Investigation,* the categorial perception of a state of affairs is contrasted not only with the momentary sense perception of an object like a sheet of paper, but also with the case in which such a thing is considered, step by step, from all sides. This is the case of continuous perception. One feature of the categorial perception of a state of affairs is obviously shared by every continuous perception: in both cases, several part-percepts are conflated into a whole. What, then, is the difference between them? The difference becomes clear if they are considered from the point of view of the following three moments of complex perceptual acts.

The first moment concerns what is designated, as early as the *Logical Investigations,* as "perceptual sense."[60] Husserl clearly sees that, in the case of continuous perception, the part-percepts are pervaded by the homogeneous unity of one and the same perceptual sense. In this respect, the case of the perception of a state of affairs is entirely dissimilar. Here a categorial act, capable of producing a surplus over a mere sense perception, superimposes on the part-percepts a categorially formed perceptual sense which is not contained in any of them considered separately.

The second moment to be taken into account is the object of perception. In the case of a continuous perceptual series, the aspect we can see changes perpetually. Nevertheless, we find here, as Husserl insists, "that absolutely nothing new is objectively meant in the extended act, but that the same object is continuously meant in it, the very object that the part-percepts, *taken singly,* were already meaning."[61] To the contrary, in the categorial perception of a state of affairs, an object of "higher level" (namely, precisely a "state of affairs") is constituted. Although what I can see before me is nothing else but a sheet of white paper, now this very sight counts as the percept of the state of affairs *that* the sheet of paper before me *is* white.

The third moment is related to the way of in which, in both cases, part-percepts are united into a whole. Husserl emphasizes that "a continuous perceptual flux involves a *fusion* of part-acts in one act, *rather than a peculiar act founded upon such part-acts.*"[62] He provides some further evidence for the distinction between *fusion* and *foundation.* His argument deserves to be quoted at greater length here:

> In the continuous running on of individual percepts we continuously perceive the single, selfsame object. Can we now call this continuous percept, since it is built out of individual percepts, a percept *founded* upon

> them? It is of course founded upon them in the sense in which a whole is founded on its parts, not however in the sense here relevant, according to which a founded act manifests a new act-character, grounded in the act-characters that underlie it and unthinkable apart from these.[63]

This is a clear difference between the two cases, indicating that, in opposition to categorial perception, which is founded upon its part-percepts, a continuous perceptual series is the product of a passive synthesis, called "fusion." Consequently, continuous perception is to be carefully distinguished from categorial perception. Its unity comes into being, just like the unity of a momentary sense perception, "as a *straightforward* unity."[64]

These distinctions may encourage us to take a further step: we may claim that the as-structure characteristic of continuous perception is separated by an unbridgeable gap from the as-structure attributed to categorial perception. For this purpose, we have only to consider a question which has not been clearly formulated by Husserl himself. As we know, in a continuous perceptual flux, the "selfsame" object remains constantly present, while its aspect perpetually changes. What, however, does the "selfsameness" of the object of a continuous perceptual series precisely consist in? This question is neither properly answered, nor even unambiguously raised in the sixth *Logical Investigation*. Husserl clearly sees, though, that this selfsameness is not an identity "made objective";[65] he rightly emphasizes that "identification is performed, but no identity is meant"[66] here. He even adds that the unity of fusion is transformed into objective identity only "when we use the perceptual series to found a novel act"[67] (in other words, the unity of fusion is transformed into objective identity only by a categorial act founded upon a continuous perceptual flux). However, Husserl does not draw the consequences which follow from these observations.

In fact, these observations entitle us to say that the selfsameness of the object of a continuous perceptual series is due to an identification which does not involve, or even presuppose, any categorial form. Admittedly, this conclusion is hardly reconcilable with Husserl's highly perplexing remark I quoted above on the case in which a noun like *paper* is used to express a sense perception. We may agree with the statement according to which "here also the whole object is known *as* paper." It would amount to a relapse into a phenomenologically unacceptable empiricism to deny that not only categorial intuition but also straightforward sense perception exhibits an as-structure. However, it is an unwarranted inference from the presence of this as-structure to say that "here also a supplementary form is known which includes being, though not as its sole form, in itself." This is an unjustified leap in the argument because it still remains to be seen whether the as-structure peculiar to straightforward sense perception is identical with, or, at least analogous to, the as-structure characteristic of categorial perception. The assumption of such an identity, or even analogy, appears seriously questionable if it is shown that the selfsameness of the object is not an identity made objective.

For, then, this selfsameness by no means implies the *conceptual* identification of the object. Consequently, it does not include any state of affairs in itself, not even implicitly or, so to speak, in seed. Nor does it involve the conceptual and the general, which according to Husserl, is characteristic of the expression of perception rather than of perception itself. Therefore, in the case of straightforward sense perception, the selfsameness of the object is obviously an identity which has not yet been conceptually fixed. It is an identity which may be described, to use a term coined by Merleau-Ponty, as a "cohesion without concept."[68]

We are led by these considerations to draw two main conclusions. The first conclusion concerns the difference between the as-structure peculiar to continuous sense perception and the as-structure characteristic of categorial perception. What, in a continuous perceptual flux, remains "selfsame," while its aspect perpetually changes, cannot be regarded as a definitely settled and conceptually fixed object; it is rather an *object in the making*, an object still awaiting its conceptual identification. Therefore, the as-structure peculiar to continuous sense perception is marked by a *mobility* which is entirely lacking from the case of categorial perception. Inversely, it is precisely by a categorial act, which is articulated in the same way as linguistic meaning is articulated, that a fixed and unchanging as-structure emerges.

The second conclusion is related to the difference between the selfsameness peculiar to continuous perception and the identity resulting from conceptual identification. This difference may be claimed to justify an attempt to distinguish *quasi categories of experiential sense* from categories of conceptual meaning. *Experiential identity*, as it is manifested by the examination of a continuous perceptual series, may be said to be one of these quasi categories. It is, however, certainly not the only one. In *Difference and Repetition*, Gilles Deleuze envisages the concept of a difference that does not amount to a mere conceptual difference. Kant's incongruent counterparts, he adds, are examples of such a difference.[69] This allusion to a difference which is intuitively given without being conceptually grasped may encourage us to form the notion of *experiential difference*, as opposed to conceptual difference, in order to account for the alterity peculiar to experiential sense. An experiential difference, we may say, is encountered wherever, all of a sudden, something appears as something else or, in other words, wherever "this" unexpectedly reveals itself as "that."

2. Expression of Experience and Experience of Expression

The difference discovered between the as-structure peculiar to experiential sense, and the as-structure characteristic of conceptual meaning may be best grasped by the contrast between *sense formation* and *sense fixation. Sinnbildung* and *Sinnstiftung* are terms which belong to the vocabulary of the later Husserl. However, it is only with Merleau-Ponty and Marc Richir that the above contrast is elevated to the rank of a conceptual opposition of general significance, especially when Richir introduces the corresponding French terms *sens se faisant* and *institution symbolique* in order to accentuate it. Simultaneously, he extends the relevance of the distinction between sense formation and sense fixation from the domain of experience to the domain of language and thought, heavily relying upon Merleau-Ponty; in fact the very idea of a *sens se faisant,* of a sense in the making, as one could put it in English, goes back to Merleau-Ponty's phenomenology of language.

Indeed, the later Merleau-Ponty may be said to have initiated a transformation of phenomenology by challenging the parallel Husserl had drawn between experience and expression. It is this transformation which will be considered in the present section.

In *The Visible and the Invisible,* Merleau-Ponty claims that philosophy consists in restoring "wild meaning," in reconstructing the "expression of experience by [an] experience," which "in particular clarifies the special domain of language."[70] It is by no means an exaggeration to claim that such a conception of philosophy demands a radical transformation of phenomenology: Merleau-Ponty created something comparable to a "linguistic turn," especially by calling attention to the diversity between experience and expression.

To legitimate this new conception of philosophy, Merleau-Ponty takes his point of departure from Husserl's *Cartesian Meditations:* "The beginning is the pure and, so to speak, still dumb experience, which is still to be made to utter its own sense clearly [*reine Aussprache ihres eigenen Sinnes*]."[71] It is not without significance that Merleau-Ponty translates "*reine Aussprache ihres eigenen Sinnes*" as "*expression pure de son propre sens.*"[72] The translation is not incorrect, yet it still may be a source of misunderstanding because it suggests agreement where there is, in fact, disagreement: the two thinkers mean something different by the term *expression of the sense of experience.* Husserl, as it was mentioned above, had from the start, suggested a structural correspondence between the experiential sense, and the meaning of the utterance of this experience: for him the utterance, the actual linguistic expression has the ability of "adapting" to the sense considered to be ready-made in itself; moreover, the utterance is capable of raising the sense onto the level of *conceptual generality*. It is easy, then, to see why Husserl draws the conclusion that "The stratum of expression [. . .] is not productive."[73] By contrast, for Merleau-Ponty the utterance (the linguistic expression) has not only productive, but also creative power. He says as early as in the *Phenomenology of Perception:* "Expression is everywhere creative [. . .]."[74] Somewhat later, referring this time to Proust, he describes what he calls the "miracle of speech" as follows: "Speaking or writing is certainly *translating* an experience; an experience, however, which only becomes a text by the very speech which it inspires."[75] The speech that is mentioned here belongs to what Merleau-Ponty calls "operative language"—as opposed to the "ideal system" studied by the linguist.[76] Merleau-Ponty remarks that it is "the error of the semantic philosophies to close up language as if it spoke only of itself," adding that "language lives only from silence."[77] This is undoubtedly a fairly metaphorical formulation. Still, it clearly indicates the specificity of "operative language." This language is inseparable from the experience to be expressed. It is common language considered *in statu nascendi,* taken "in the living or nascent state, with all its references, those behind it, which connect it to the mute things it interpellates, and those it sends before itself and which make up the world of things said [. . .]."[78] While grappling with experience, this language does not content itself with sedimented or instituted meanings. On the contrary, it is constantly in search for a sense which has not yet been, so to speak, domesticated or palliated, and which may, therefore, rightly be characterized as "wild." It is only a language unswervingly groping for an appropriate expression of experience which deserves to be described as a "conquering, active, creative language."[79]

To be sure, the considerations summarized in the posthumous work *The Visible and the Invisible* have a rather tentative character. Therefore, it is hardly surprising that some ambiguous passages may also be found, which at first sight seem to suggest a certain structural correspondence between experience and expression. Taking inspiration from Lacan, Merleau-Ponty endorses, for instance, the assumption that "the vision, the thought itself, are [. . .] 'structured as a language,' are *articulation* before the letter."[80] This assumption undoubtedly encourages the denial of all structural differences between perception, thought, and language. However, it would be a misunderstanding to take such passages as evidence to a view which is obviously inconsistent with the most fundamental insights formulated in the text. *L'originaire éclate:* the original—or the originating—"bursts," it "breaks up into splinters," Merleau-Ponty says, and he adds, "philosophy must accompany this breaking up, this noncoincidence, this differentiation."[81] This partly polemical, partly programmatic statement is addressed, as a matter of fact, to Bergson but its critical thrust does not leave Husserl untouched, either. Indeed, its point is a refusal of all philosophical quests of origin. Thus, it marks a break with the attempt of early phenomenology to reduce language and thought to mute experience and to point out a parallel between the sense to be expressed, and the meaning of conceptual expression. Merleau-Ponty is very far from supposing such a parallel. Emphasizing noncoincidence and differentiation, he undertakes to examine the "deflection"—*écart*—of conceptual expression from experience. Instead of assuming any mirrorlike reflection between them, he tries to describe the process of their dissociation. But here dissociation does not amount to separation. In line with Husserl, Merleau-Ponty considers language and conceptual thought *with regard to* experience. For Merleau-Ponty, however, the expression *with regard to* assumes the meaning of *in contrast with.* But even contrast is different from separation. That is why Merleau-Ponty may be said to transform, but not to abandon, phenomenology. He makes once more "use of the diacritical" in order to account for the structural differences between experience and expression.

This is clear from what he says about the "miracle of speech." Drawing upon Proust, he expressly refuses to attribute to mute experience a ready-made sense articulated in itself as linguistic meaning. On the contrary, he insists that it is the creative power of operative speech which transforms mute experience into a text. Thus, he does distinguish linguistic meaning from experiential sense—he even opposes them. But at the same time he maintains that it is mute experience itself which "inspires" (*suscite*) operative speech. Consequently, the opposition is not obliterated, yet it is characterized by a *diacritical difference* which includes, in itself, inseparability, cohesion, and a belonging together, just as well as a divergence or an opposition.

It is a consequence of this "use of the diacritical" that the phenomenology of language envisaged by Merleau-Ponty exceeds the traditional boundaries. The new enterprise is not centered upon the "ideal system" of language (which is studied, as we have seen, by the linguist); on the contrary, it is entirely dedicated to the analysis of the contrast between mute experience and operative speech. Its basic question concerns, in other words, the *diacritical difference* of *wild sense* and *sedimented meaning.* This is, however, as Merleau-Ponty rightly claims, not a "regional problem" but "an absolutely universal theme, the theme of philosophy itself."[82]

This sharp distinction between the philosophical approach to language and scientific linguistics should not make us forget that the "use of the diacritical" owes a great deal to the impact of Saussure. Merleau-Ponty was one of the first thinkers to study the *Course in General Linguistics*—later the Bible of French structuralism—seriously. As early as in *The Prose of the World,* written in 1951, he credits Saussure with the "immense merit of having taken an initiative which [. . .] makes a new conception of reason possible."[83]

Perhaps Merleau-Ponty learned only one thing from Saussure, but it is of decisive importance: the insight that *there is no meaning without "diacritical" differences.*[84] It follows from this tenet that an isolated utterance, not inserted into the context of a linguistic system, cannot be considered to be meaningful.[85] It is on this conclusion that Merleau-Ponty bases his criticism of Husserl's intentional theory of meaning. Without a whole system of differential relations, he argues, no intentional act can transform a series of sounds into a meaningful expression. It may further be inferred that no intentional content can be regarded as a readily available meaning before it is expressed in public language. The creative power of the utterance (of the linguistic expression) manifests itself in the fact that no full-fledged idea may emerge without it.

However, Merleau-Ponty soon departs from Saussure. He is not concerned with the structural analysis of the system of language (*langue*); he rather sets himself the task of describing language in its actual operations. This task is clearly indicated by the terms he uses: "operative language" and "speaking speech" (*langage opérant, parole parlante*).

How is this goal to be achieved? Here Merleau-Ponty's general approach to diacritical systems provides a valuable clue. Speaking of the diacritical systems of perception and of intersubjectivity, he adopts, as it has been pointed out, an internal perspective. The main question he tries to answer gives rise to an inquiry into how the subject finds himself caught up (almost enmeshed) in, or captured by, or even further—as Merleau-Ponty himself prefers putting it—"being set on," a universal diacritical system.

An external stance is clearly disqualified by the very purpose of the inquiry. It is the very experience of the subject's *inclusion* in a diacritical system which is to be analyzed here. This experience, however, is hardly available from an external stance. On the contrary, it finds its proper expression in the first-person singular. No neutral observer has a direct access to it. And this insight may easily be applied to operative speech as well. A concrete situation of speech presupposes a speaker and a hearer. As opposed to a structural study of the linguistic system, a phenomenological approach to language cannot adopt the *third-person perspective* of the neutral observer. It has to adhere to a *first-person perspective,* in which effective experience originates. It cannot abstract from the differences between the positions taken by the interlocutors, either. If linguistic productivity or, even more generally, expressive creativity is at stake, as it is the case with Merleau-Ponty, the perspective of the speaker may readily be preferred to that of the hearer. It is indeed the speaker who has to pave his way through a whole world of instituted, ready-made, sedimented meanings. The description of the experiential route through this world may, therefore, be regarded as an eminent task of a phenomenology of language.

So far, two approaches to language have been distinguished from each other: a "phenomenological" and a "scientific" one, while two perspectives have also been contrasted: a "first-person" and a "third-person" perspective. It may be claimed that the two opposing pairs correspond to each other: while the scientific approach adopts a third-person perspective, the phenomenological approach, aiming at the analysis of lived experience, remains committed to the first-person perspective. If this is plausible, and if Merleau-Ponty is right in saying that language, considered as operative speech, is not merely a "regional problem" but an "absolutely universal theme, the theme of philosophy itself," then philosophy may be characterized as an attempt at returning from the scientific elaboration of experience to its phenomenological description. This view of philosophy takes shape in Merleau-Ponty's (already quoted) assertion that the whole of philosophy consists in restoring a "wild" sense. It may be emphasized that, in this view, philosophy does not aim at *reducing* the scientific elaboration of experience to its phenomenological dimension—nor, for that matter, at *deducing* the former from the latter. For Merleau-Ponty, the rejection of all philosophical quests of origin involves the replacement of the traditional model of *derivation* by a diacritical model of *contrast.* The endeavor of philosophy consists, according to this model, in making evident the "deflection"—*écart*—of the scientific elaboration of experience from its phenomenological tenor.

Why is the first-person perspective indispensable for a phenomenological approach to language? The reason, upon a closer analysis, might easily be seen in the fact that the adoption of a first-person perspective is inseparably linked up with the possibility of self-awareness (in the sense of the Cartesian *cogito*), so it may save the speaking subject from getting lost in the impersonal relations of the linguistic system. This is, however, not Merleau-Ponty's view. To be sure, Merleau-Ponty's earlier great work, the *Phenomenology of Perception,* is undoubtedly loaded with a massive amount of Cartesianism, primarily in the assumption of a *tacit cogito.* According to this assumption, the silent presence of oneself to oneself is the very basis of one's existence.[86] However, the emergence of the phenomenology of language marks the beginning of a process in which Merleau-Ponty more and more unambiguously distances himself from this stance. He says in *The Prose of the World* that the "*I*" of the "*I think,*" in one's alleged autonomy and unassailability, cannot possibly speak because one who speaks "enters into a system of relations which, while presupposing him, at the same time renders him open and vulnerable."[87] Merleau-Ponty ultimately draws the following conclusion amidst his polemics with himself in one of the working notes of *The Visible and the Invisible:* "What I call the tacit cogito is impossible."[88] The bluntness of this acknowledgment has a lot to do with the results of his phenomenological approach to language.

The indispensability of the first-person perspective for this approach may, however, be understood in another way as well. It might be claimed that the proper significance of this perspective rests upon the primacy attributed by phenomenology to the *living present* of the subject. The term *living present* is, again, of Husserlian origin. In Husserlian phenomenology, conscious life is considered as being eminently a life in the present. The past and the future are, consequently, interpreted as derived modes of the conscious being. Not surprisingly, Derrida here detects some unmistakable traces of what he calls "the metaphysics of the presence."[89] Indeed, just as the notion of a tacit cogito, the term *living present* also expresses the conviction that the presence of oneself to oneself is the very basis of one's conscious being. However, this time, the idea of self-presence takes a temporally determined form. Husserl claims that it is only in the present that the presence of oneself to oneself is fully realized. Furthermore, it can easily be seen that there is no conscious life in the present without perception. Therefore, the doctrine of the living present is closely bound up with the idea of a primacy of perception. This idea is, however, by no means alien to Merleau-Ponty. On the contrary, it is taken as a guideline, with the force of evidence, in his approach to thought and language. Moreover, Merleau-Ponty may be said to base his phenomenology of operative speech on an analogy with the living present of perception. Perception is an immediate encounter and contact with reality. Such an immediacy is certainly not to be found in the case of thought and language. But operative speech collects the disparate elements of the linguistic system and it condenses them into a unique expression in order to meet the requirements arising from the singular experience of reality.[90] In this extended sense, the moment of operative speech is itself the moment of an encounter and a contact with reality. However, even if Merleau-Ponty's view of this moment reminds us of Husserl's conception of the living present, it does not coincide with it. If the edge of the claim that every expression is creative is not to be taken away, the difference should by no means be disregarded. This difference is articulated in a note to *The Prose of the World:* "in the living present"—Merleau-Ponty says—"there is something which has already been expressed, and there is something which still has to be expressed, there is some work still to be done."[91] Hence, the moment of operative speech can by no means be regarded as the moment of total presence. Even if the Derridean objection to a "metaphysics of presence" is justly raised against Husserl's idea of the living present (which is not uncontroversial), it certainly cannot involve Merleau-Ponty's description of the moment of operative speech.

However, as far as this decisive point is concerned, the texts are, unfortunately, not quite straightforward; it seems that it is not *perception* but rather *experience* which Merleau-Ponty takes as a model when analyzing the moment of operative speech. He specifies the phenomenology of language, in opposition to scientific linguistics, as an inquiry into the *experience of expression.* As a matter of fact, he could not possibly characterize it more precisely. However, he still does not seem to be fully aware of the actual weight of such a characterization. This deficiency of awareness is due to a deficiency of distinction: the dissimilarity between perception and experience should be more sharply pointed out by Merleau-Ponty. Although the two terms are far from being synonymous for him, their difference remains without conceptual clarification. No particular emphasis is given to the dynamic aspects of experience, in contrast with the principally static character of perception. That the emergence of a new insight is always *in conflict* with previous expectations is much less accentuated by Merleau-Ponty than, for example, by Hegel or, later on by Gadamer. However, even this lack in Merleau-Ponty does not invalidate the fact that for him the actual content of the phenomenology of language is nothing else than a detailed account of a fundamental experience. This experience is that the struggle for expression engenders an unpredictable sense which does not coincide with the originally intended meaning of the speaker.

Everyone who has ever tried to write a book or a paper is familiar with this experience. It often occurs that an initial idea undergoes a whole series of changes until it takes a—more or less—final shape which does not even resemble its nascent state. In the meantime, freshly conceived thoughts come to the fore, and sometimes they prove to be even more important than the original idea. That is how writing is done: knowledge, wit, practice, taste, imagination, and so on are among the many prerequisites entering the service of an entirely spontaneous process, in which, in turn, a flash of thought is transformed into a more fixed meaning.

Some simpler examples may also be provided. Everybody learning a foreign language is familiar with the experience that sometimes a sentence, which is heard for the first time yet is not immediately understood, assumes a precise sense even if the words which make it up remain unspecified. In such cases, we do not know what the words mean but we do know what the sentence *has to say.* This experience clearly shows that the sense of a sentence is not just the sum total of the verbal meanings of the words constituting it. The peculiar shreds of meaning the words assume in this very sentence could hardly ever be determined if the sense emerging from their particular concatenation as a whole were not obvious. Conversely, if the general sense of an utterance is rightly construed, it may just as well be recast in another linguistic mould. Moreover, the difference between an expression striking home and a less felicitous one may equally clearly be given.

These examples may shed some light on the notion of an experience of expression. They all contrast a sense in the making expressed by language with the ready-made meanings of linguistic expressions. Our examples may also prevent us from an easy misunderstanding: they clearly show that the surplus of a sense in the making over all ready-made meanings is by no means to be considered as arising from the difference between private meaning intentions and public utterances. That this interpretation is untenable is manifested by at least two observations: first, the speaker—or the writer—may be surprised at finding himself or herself led by the expression of his or her meaning intention to a sense which, in its precise shreds, is far from having been intended at all; second, the originally unintended shreds of sense emerging spontaneously from an utterance are no less available for the hearer than for the speaker.

"Wild sense" is a quite appropriate term to characterize the offspring of the creative process which manifests itself in this experience of expression. By this term, Merleau-Ponty hints at a form of generation which is beyond the control of the speaking subject. But what does he mean when he describes a wild sense as an "expression of experience by experience"? This is a mysterious formulation, which remains unclear until it is closely reflected upon.

It becomes, however, evident as soon as the two occurrences of the word *experience* are distinguished in it from each other. The difference of the two occurrences may be construed as follows: it is a *special* kind of experience, namely the experience of expression, which serves as the expression of *experience in general.* We have seen that the experience of expression brings to light a spontaneous formation of sense in language. It has equally been shown that this spontaneous process is not controlled or governed by the original meaning intention of the speaker. What else could, however, induce such an indomitable but, at the same time, entirely intelligible process in language and thought than—*experience?* Not the special experience of expression, of course, but experience in general which may also be described as an experience of *reality*. If that is so, then the experience of expression may, indeed, be said to serve as the expression of experience.

According to this conception, the relationship between experience and expression—or between reality and language—is mediated by what is called in the phenomenology of language the "creativity" or the "fecundity"[92] of expression. The expression of experience by experience is not a mirror-like reflection. The wild sense of experience cannot be retrieved and revealed or, as Merleau-Ponty puts it, "restored" unless language itself gives room to an experience of spontaneous sense formation, or to put it in other words, unless ready-made meanings are enabled by a felicitous turn to produce, or even to "secrete," indirectly—as it were, "laterally"—a new sense.[93] This is what happens in literature. Clear instances are expressions like *Tartuffism* or *Oblomovism.* These expressions testify to a transformation of literary figures into new concepts. A no less typical case is, however, when old concepts are enriched by some new shreds of sense. An example adduced by Merleau-Ponty is the figure of the Public Prosecutor in Stendhal's *La chartreuse de Parme.*[94] Undoubtedly, we have to know what the word *crook* means in order to understand Stendhal. But Rassi, the "snake," is not merely an incarnated crook in the novel; he rather gives us an entirely new idea of what a crook is like. The upshot is that this figure amounts just as well to a new concept of crookery as *Oblomovism* transcends customary sloth and *Tartuffism* surpasses ordinary hypocrisy.

The case of literature indicates that creative expression plays a mediatory role between experience and conceptual thinking. Thereby, it casts some light on the general structure of the operation called "expression." Creative expression—we may say—performs its mediatory function by transmuting a (wild) sense into a (freshly instituted) meaning.[95] This operation may rightly be regarded as creative because the freshly instituted meaning cannot be reduced to the ready-made, acquired, available, sedimented meanings of common language.[96] The productivity of expression is, however, by no means so much as the power of a *creatio ex nihilo*. It is the power of a creation induced and inspired by experience. That is why Merleau-Ponty tries to capture the operation of expression by the contrast of "demand" and "response" (*appel et réponse*). He is the first to make use of this pair of concepts, which is to become of central significance in later phenomenology. He claims that creative expression "infuses a new sense into that which in its turn has already demanded and anticipated this sense"; adding that the transmutation brought about by such an expression is

> not merely a metamorphosis in the sense of fairy tales, miracle or magic, violence or aggression, absolute creation in absolute solitude, but it is also a response to what was demanded from it by the world, the past, the preceding works, it is also consummation, fraternity.[97]

The operation of expression shows the same structure in art and music as in literature and other linguistic forms. It is not even literature but rather painting—especially modern painting—which is credited by Merleau-Ponty with a preeminent and almost paradigmatic role. The prevalent tendency of modern painting to break with the imitation of reality legitimates this preference. In earlier epochs the essence of artistic creation was not rarely said to consist in the imitation—in the faithful representation—of readily given objects. As a matter of fact, this view does not seem to hold true even in the case of classical renaissance painting. This is clear, among other things, from the observation that one of the main "discoveries" of this epoch, the application of geometrical perspective, is a quite artificial procedure, which by no means can be regarded as a means to form a "true picture" of reality. Drawing upon Erwin Panofsky and André Malraux, Merleau-Ponty corroborates this statements by a whole series of arguments in his different writings; relevant passages are to be found in "The Doubt of Cézanne"[98] as well as in *The Prose of the World*[99] and in *The Eye and the Mind.*[100] Still, the appearance of a faithful representation of reality was largely kept up by traditional painting. This illusion is dissipated by Cézanne, Monet, and their followers. Thereby, it is made evident that an expression is never a copy or a passive impression of reality. Merleau-Ponty says, "Modern painting, just as modern thinking in general, imposes on us the absolute obligation to understand what a truth which does not resemble things is like [. . .]."[101]

The parallel drawn by Merleau-Ponty between modern painting and modern thinking deserves to be emphasized. This parallel clearly indicates that, for Merleau-Ponty, the analysis of art—just as well as the analysis of operative language and literary speech—is nothing more than a starting point toward a general theory of creative expression. If he claims that modern painting conveys to us a meaning which "does not refer to any readily given object but it constitutes and inaugurates it," accentuating that it creates, thereby, a mode of communication which dispenses with all "objective evidence" and has no recourse to any kind of a "preestablished nature," and which, as he adds, embodies "a communication before communication" and even a "reason before reason,"[102] then he does not mention a single trait which he does not consider as valid for all other forms of creative expression as well. This is especially true of that thinking which he qualifies as "modern" and which he tries to bring forth by his very attempt to review and to renew, to reconsider and to recast traditional phenomenology. This thinking breaks, indeed, with the presupposition of readily given objects. Far from considering the world as the totality of facts, it rather undertakes to grasp reality *in statu nascendi,* just as it arises from experience. This undertaking has to dispense with all "objective evidence," and it can have no recourse to any kind of a "preestablished nature," either. That is what determines its relationship with the scientific approach to the world, which clearly aims at "objective evidence" and has much to do with a "preestablished nature" as well. Merleau-Ponty by no means renounces to take inspiration from scientific theories—this may be attested by several instances from Saussurian linguistics to Lévi-Straussian ethnology—but he decidedly rejects the traditional function of philosophy in constructing a universal system of objectively valid knowledge. Following to a large extent the later Husserl, he sets himself the task of contrasting the universal but external perspective of "objective" science with the internal perspective of "lived" and, in this sense, "subjective" experience. It is in this experience that he finds the traces of a "reason before reason." This reason inherent to lived experience is nothing else than the wild sense which creative expression tries to restore.

It is not surprising that Merleau-Ponty draws more and more upon Proust in his later writings. His philosophical attempt to break through to a reality in the nascent state may be said to have its literary counterpart in Proust's *Remembrance of Things Past.* Jean-François Marquet shows in an excellent study how Proust comes to think that "man generally lives on a glacial surface of ideas and habits under which he does not surmise anything else [. . .]."[103] He adds that, according to Proust, it is artistic creation alone which "tries to 'defrost' perception and pervade to the injury, the primal impression made by things on us [. . .]."[104] For, in Proust's view, it is this "wound" alone which opens a way to *reality.*

The word *reality* refers here to something which, according to a pregnant formulation of Proust, "bears no relation with possibilities, any more than the stab of a knife in one's body bears to the gradual movement of the clouds overhead [. . .]."[105] As it may be elicited from these words, Proust, and not Lacan, is the first to hold that *the real is the impossible.* But how is this baffling paradox to be understood?

It is, as a matter of fact, far from being unintelligible. It means that the reality of the real predominantly manifests itself by breaking through the "glacial surface" of our habitual expectations, ready-made ideas, and routine practices. A kindred conception of reality has already been set out in the present work. However, our considerations on Merleau-Ponty and Proust lead us up to an extension of our previous discussion of this topic. We may supplement our former train of thought with a new element of utmost importance if we realize that it is the experience of a never entirely surmountable contrast between experience and expression which primarily reveals the reality of the real. Although the wild sense of an experience can, in principle, always be transmuted by a sufficiently creative expression into a freshly instituted meaning, the inevitably ensuing process of conceptual sedimentation never fails to regenerate the tension which has thus been eliminated. It may be inferred from this observation that not just a harmless difference but rather an *irremediable*—because *inappropriable*—*alterity* keeps distinct experience and expression from each other. We may claim that it is the experience of this alterity which gives rise to the very notion of reality.

This experience is alluded to by the metaphors just quoted from Proust. It is indeed something comparable to an "injury," a "wound" inflicted by things upon us, or even to the "stab of a knife" in our bodies. But these metaphors indicate a further difficulty that cannot be eluded if the enigmatic identification of the real with the impossible is to be made clear. They suggest that the experience of the inappropriable alterity between experience and expression cannot be anything more than a breathtaking *shock*. Can the reality of the real be assimilated to such a traumatic event? Here we seem to be confronted with a dilemma: if we take reality to be something else than just the realization of a possibility we are familiar with, then the experience we gain of this reality will not amount to much more than to a dumbfounding and sinister shock; if, however, we reduce the real to the possible, then we shall find ourselves compelled, in spite of our better knowledge, to deny any serious conflict between spontaneously arising experience and conceptually fixed expression.

A reference to Proust's idea of a "primal impression" is, in itself, hardly enough to overcome this difficulty. Yet, we may come upon the right track by considering this idea somewhat closer. The great discovery of Proust lies not just in the insight that a primal impression may be resuscitated by involuntary recollection;[106] more weight is to be attributed to his grandiose attempt to overcome the distance between *im*pression and *ex*pression. It may be maintained that *Remembrance of Things Past* as a whole is designed to accomplish this task. Here, however, we must content ourselves with some illustration. We may take a well-known example, which has already been mentioned.

The little phrase of Vinteuil's sonata has a multifarious role in the unfolding of Swann's passion. The primal impression made by this phrase on Swann has not yet much to do with love. Proust emphasizes that, initially, it seemed rather "to be bringing into Swann's life the possibility of a sort of rejuvenation."[107] It promised to liberate him from "the moral barrenness from which he was suffering."[108] As it is added in the text:

> He had so long since ceased to direct his course towards any ideal goal, and had confined himself to the pursuit of ephemeral satisfactions, that he had come to believe, though without ever formally stating his belief even to himself, that he would remain all his life in that condition, which death alone could alter. More than this, since his mind no longer entertained any lofty ideas, he had ceased to believe in (although he could not have expressly denied) their reality.[109]

After hearing the little phrase of Vinteuil's sonata, Swann, on the contrary,

> found in himself [. . .] the presence of one of those invisible realities in which he had ceased to believe, but to which [. . .] he was conscious once again of a desire, almost, indeed, of the power to consecrate his life. [110]

However, it is not much later when Odette, referring to the little phrase by Vinteuil, says to Swann, "Our little bit; that is all we need."[111] We are indeed witnesses to the slow but steady process in which this little bit becomes "the national anthem of their love."[112] It is only at the end of the whole cycle of novels, during the great meditation in the library belonging to the palace of the Guermantes, that the narrator—who, by the way, had meanwhile the opportunity to get familiar with another work by Vinteuil, the "septet," as well—reveals the real bearing, or at least the ultimate avatar, of this motif. Proust says,

> And thinking again of the extra-temporal joy which I had been made to feel by the sound of the spoon or the taste of the madelaine, I said to myself: "Was this perhaps that happiness which the little phrase of the sonata promised to Swann and which he, because he was unable to find it in artistic creation, mistakenly assimilated to the pleasures of love, was this the happiness of which long ago I was given a presentiment—as something more supraterrestrial even than the mood evoked by the little phrase of the sonata—by the call, the mysterious, rubescent call of the septet which Swann was never privileged to hear, having died like so

many others before the truth that was made for him had been revealed? A truth that in any case he could not have used, for though the phrase perhaps symbolized a call, it was not capable of creating new powers and making Swann the writer that he was not."[113]

We may rightly ascribe a paradigmatic significance to this example because it indicates the way that leads, in Proust, from impression to expression. The main conclusion that may be drawn from the presentation of this example may be formulated as follows: the gap between impression and expression is bridged by a *sense in the making.* Consequently, it is not so much a primal impression as rather a fluent and multiple sense which serves as a vehicle for the experience of reality. Originally, this sense is inseparably bound up with the primal impression. In the sequel, however, it gets increasingly detached from it. Indeed, the little phrase of Vinteuil's sonata becomes more and more saturated by diverse senses during its career. Although Swann sometimes evokes it, with complacence, like "a protective goddess, a confidant of his love,"[114] we know that it is more than that. It is, initially, rather the promise of a rejuvenation and recreation than the symbol of an irresistible passion. It is only later on that these two senses enter into a conflict with each other. Ultimately, the first sense irrevocably yields way to the second. Thus, things take a baleful turn. This event confers a third sense to the analyzed motif: the little phrase of Vinteuil's sonata becomes the emblem of a lost promise. It is difficult to decide whether or not Swann himself is aware of this third sense. He is, however, certainly not aware of the fourth sense: he dies, as we have quoted, before the *truth* that was *made for him* had been revealed. It is only the narrator who realizes that the happiness which the little phrase of Vinteuil's sonata promised to Swann symbolized a *call*—a call for artistic creation. It may be seen here how, in a story told by a great writer, the unfolding shreds of a sense in the making pave the way from a first impression to a final expression: they penetrate not only conscious life but they delve into the very unconscious. It is not necessary to decide if they ever attain to an ultimate stage. Probably no stringent answer can ever be given to the question of whether the truth proclaimed by the narrator coincides with the truth conveyed by the narrated story to the reader. The judgment passed upon Swann's "mistake" may just as well be viewed as bestowing a fifth sense upon the little phrase of Vinteuil's sonata.

Our analysis of this motif has shown an issue from the dilemma we found ourselves confronted with: although the experience of reality never goes without a touch of a sinister shock, this shock should not be called "dumbfounding" (at least not with a view to the literal meaning of this word), because it is the beginning of a spontaneous sense formation which gives not only much to think but also much to say, even if it challenges all instituted expressions. The inappropriable alterity that keeps distinct experience and expression from each other has to be conceived of as a diacritical difference and not as an absolute incompatibility. Therefore, it cannot be correctly interpreted as a sheer inexpressibility. It would be a mistake to deduce this alterity from a lack of sense; on the contrary, the characteristic of experience from which it derives is rather a surplus of sense. If experience challenges all instituted expressions, it is not because it is deprived of sense but because it abounds with a sense which has not yet been instituted. In other words, it is nothing else but the *wild* character of experiential sense which accounts for the alterity under discussion.

Wild sense is Merleau-Ponty's clue to the comprehension of the alterity residing in lived experience and, consequently, in life-history. It remains, however, to be seen if this is a universally applicable clue. Emanuel Levinas is a thinker whose considerations on the alterity of the Other may raise serious doubts here. However, the development of our investigations has not yet reached the stage at which this controversial point can be fruitfully discussed. Let us, therefore, postpone this discussion until later and return now to the problem of the relationship between experience and expression. The next question to be considered concerns the narrative mode of expression.

3. Experience, Action, and Narration

It has been argued that the experience one gains is to be understood as the emergence of a dispossessed sense. Therefore, there is nothing surprising in the observation that experience finds its proper expression in a narrative. A propositional statement is hardly an appropriate form to articulate a spontaneous sense formation because its meaning necessarily settles and fixes an experience that, in itself, is ambiguous and variable. On the contrary, a narrative sequence is capable of adapting itself to a process that gives rise to ever changing sense arousals.

Here the question emerges as to whether a process of spontaneous sense formation necessarily takes the shape of experience before being expressed in a narrative. Is there anything else but experience which can be narrated? It is this question that I shall take up in the following discussion.

An argument may easily be adduced against the idea of a necessary connection between experience and narration: it is mainly with actions, not with experiences, one may contend, that storytelling is concerned. It is this objection which we have to consider first.

a. Action and Narration

Is one to assume a necessary connection between action and storytelling rather than between experience and narration? MacIntyre does not fail to give an affirmative response to this question. We have already seen that he goes so far as to consider action—and even life—as an "enacted narrative."[115]

How does MacIntyre argue for his claim? He takes for his starting point a "conceptual commonplace": the well-known fact that "one and the same segment of human behavior may be correctly characterized in a number of different ways."[116] Some of these characterizations, MacIntyre adds, will express the agent's intentions, others unintended consequences of the agent's action, and of these unintended consequences some may be such that the agent is aware of them while others are not.[117] It is to be noticed, however, that any correct explanation of a given segment of behavior will presuppose some prior answer to the question of how these descriptions of the agent's action are related to each other. One has to know in which description the action is intended and in which it is not. As MacIntyre says, "We cannot [. . .] characterize behavior independently of intentions, and we cannot characterize intentions independently of the settings which make those intentions intelligible both to agents themselves and to others."[118] The settings in question may be institutions or practices, or they may be milieus of some other human kind. But it is central to the notion of setting, as MacIntyre understands it, that a setting has a *narrative history.* These are the premises from which MacIntyre concludes that narrative history is "the basic and essential genre for the characterization of human actions."[119]

I do not intend to challenge this conclusion. I fully agree with the assertion that action becomes "intelligible by finding its place in a narrative."[120] However, I consider it an entirely unjustified leap in the argument when MacIntyre jumps from this statement to the conclusion that action—or even life as a whole—is an "enacted narrative." My contention is that this inference is based on a short circuit: it is overlooked that the connection between action and narration is established by *experience.*

This assertion may be supported by a simple consideration. It is not difficult to see that the narrative intelligibility of an action is due to a determinate relation obtaining between at least two of its possible characterizations (which, at the same time, are logically independent of each other). By no means should a single description of an action, in itself, be considered as a narrative history. It does not even involve the germ of such a history unless it contains some words which imply a different description of the same action. That Oedipus killed a haughty stranger at the crossroads may indeed be regarded as a tale to be told, but only because the expression "haughty stranger" hints at an offense retaliated by the murder. Thus, a situation is alluded to in which manslaughter takes the sense of vengeance. An action becomes intelligible by finding its place in a narrative because a history into which it is inserted assigns to it an implicit or explicit *as-structure* by revealing that the action characterized originally so and so (for instance, as killing a stranger) may be correctly described so and so, as well (for example, as retaliating an offense). It has to be emphasized that this as-structure articulates the relationship between two possible characterizations of one and the same action which are logically independent of each other. No narrative history is suggested by the statement that he who kills a human person commits murder, since here the first description logically entails the second. From this it is only one more step to realize that the as-structure assigned by a narrative history to an action is necessarily established by *experience*.

Here, however, two different cases have to be distinguished. In the first of these cases, it is *common* experience which connects one description of an action with another. Whenever the agent intends to do something by doing something (just as Oedipus intends to retaliate an offense by killing the haughty stranger), the purposeful relation established between the two descriptions of one and the same action rests upon common experience. In the second case, on the contrary, it is the experience the agent *gains* which establishes the relationship between two descriptions of one and the same action. This case is to be seen whenever a narrative history reveals some unintended consequence of an action. Here the agent experiences that the action he intended under one description is in reality an action to be characterized by another description as well. Thus, in Sophocles, Oedipus gains the experience that his act of vengeance is, in fact, patricide.

One may like to claim that a narrative history always expresses an experience of this second kind. Such an experience is manifest in the case of unintended consequences. It is, however, not absent from the case of purposeful action either, even if it remains concealed here. The agent necessarily experiences how common experience applies to his own case. It is, one may infer, this personal experience which is, on the whole, made intelligible by a narrative history. On the contrary, it is not the proper task of storytelling to articulate the common experience underlying purposeful action; this may rather be transformed into empirical generalizations than into narratives.

Therefore, the equation of actions with "enacted narratives" may be seriously contested. Actions, we may say, can only be narrated because they are themselves to be considered as *experiences.* It is not as pieces of purposeful behavior but rather as experienced events of life that they find their places in narratives. Our actions are not only performed by ourselves, they also *happen to us.* They are motivated by experiences we make, and they lead to consequences which, again, take the shape of experiences we go through. Moreover, they include the experience of what it is to do them. Thus, Macbeth experiences what it is to kill a man. In this sense, our actions are not only undertakings we embark upon but also events (adventures) taking place in our lives. The narratives in which they find their places make them intelligible as events happening to us rather than as initiatives taken by ourselves.

Two different dimensions are to be distinguished here: on the one hand, the dimension of experience; on the other hand, the dimension of action. Experience is to be told; action is to be done. Although action may be regarded as an event that is experienced, it is important to see that the dimension of action is irreducible to that of experience. It seems, therefore, to be a misconception to interpret action as an "enacted narrative." It seems that it is not so much as an accomplished deed but rather as an experienced event that action finds its place in a narrative.

b. The Idea of Inchoate Narratives

May we not, however, join Ricoeur, who, although rejecting the idea of "enacted narratives," attributes to action at least a "prenarrative structure"? Should we not, in other words, admit that action—and even life as a whole—is something like a "virtual story," "a story in its beginnings" or "in its germ," which is, so to speak, in search of a narrative?

Ricoeur tries to underpin this view by referring to different authors and different phenomena. First, he commits himself to a narrative interpretation of psychoanalysis. He takes for granted that life rests on untold, or even repressed stories, and he adds that these virtual or inchoate stories call for narratives expressly told. These are narratives for which we may assume responsibility and which we may consider as constitutive of our own self-identity. Drawing upon Roy Schafer, Ricoeur claims that psychoanalytic therapy necessarily aims at transforming fragments of lived experiences, dreams, "primal scenes," and conflict-laden episodes into elaborated narratives which are both more unbearable and less unintelligible than the inchoate ones. This interpretation of psychoanalysis is, however, hardly incontestable. Jacques Lacan would object that such a therapy fails to reach the symbolic subject of the unconscious, and it risks reinforcing the ego in its imaginary constructions. But the entire debate may be said to miss a significant point. For the gist of the original question is not whether unconscious phenomena like repressed fragments of lived experiences, dreams, "primal scenes," and conflict-laden episodes are to be *interpreted* as inchoate stories. The proper question, rather, is whether purposeful behavior and conscious life are, as a matter of fact, *experienced* as consisting of such stories. It is not difficult to see that the latter question is not even touched upon by a narrative—nor, for that matter, by any other—view of psychoanalysis.

Ricoeur adduces, however, a more promising argument for his conception by referring to Wilhelm Schapp's idea of histories we find ourselves caught up, captured, or even enmeshed in. The assumption is that one has no access to another self independently of the stories this self is entangled in. Schapp, a former pupil of Husserl's, relies upon the experiences he gained as a professional public prosecutor. It is always through an indictment that a culprit is encountered by an attorney. The allegations necessarily take the shape of stories. It is in the light of these stories that the accused is first envisaged by the prosecutor. Schapp generalizes these experiences by claiming that the emergence of another person in flesh and blood is only the emergence of his or her stories because another person's visage, face, and entire bodily appearance may be said to tell stories, even if it tries to hide, to conceal, or to cover them up.[121] The histories a person is entangled—*verstrickt*—in are not necessarily narratives expressly told. Moreover, they can never be completely told because every history which is expressly narrated points back to a *Vorgeschichte,* a "prehistory," that remains in the background. It is always from such a background of previous histories remaining untold that an expressly narrated history emerges. It is a person's lived experiences embedded into one another which form this background. When they emerge, the person's self becomes, at least to some extent, transparent. That is why Schapp says that history represents the person: *Die Geschichte steht für den Mann.*[122] If this conception is right, then Ricoeur may, indeed, infer from it that narratives told about one's life are, so to speak, only "continuations" of the histories oneself is involved in and defined by.

However, it may be asked whether the experiences generalized by Schapp are to be severed from the forensic perspective that gave rise to them. The most conspicuous feature of this perspective is its *retrospective* character. A prosecutor is concerned with the past of the culprit; even his personal encounter with him is determined by his investigations. This attitude lends itself to certain modifications and extensions to arrive at some generalizations. But modified and extended as it may be, this hardly seems to be the only attitude which one may adopt toward another person's self. It is one of the merits of Levinas to have pointed out that a visage, a face, or even the curve of a back may not only be the bearer of histories I may inquire into but also the vehicle of demands addressed to me and calling for my response. Consequently, my relationship with the other is not necessarily mediated by the histories he or she is entangled in.

It may be regarded as even more important that one's actions are motivated by the actual demands of the other to a greater extent than by his or her past experiences. It may be added that one's own stories have no greater part in the generation of one's own actions than the stories of the other. It is certainly true that one's deeds are often designed to prolong the line indicated by one's own stories; it is, however, no less true that they often depart from this line. This is not even surprising if we consider that they are never solely determined by the requirement of consistent behavior, but they arise from a more complex endeavor, which is at least partly inspired by the demands of others. Once more, the dimension of action proves to be irreducible to the dimension of experience and narration.

Therefore, it is not an accident if Ricoeur, although setting himself the task of exploring the temporality of action, speaks not so much of the prenarrative structure of action itself than that of experience. Indeed, it is only the experience involved in action which may be interpreted as a virtual or inchoate story awaiting narration, while action itself resides in a dimension that has nothing to do with storytelling.

c. The Split of the Self

Both dimensions have, however, their bearing on what is called a *self.* It is only by one's stories that one's self is to be defined; but it is only by one's actions that one's self is to be proven. The narrative view of selfhood is only one half of the truth; and it is in action that the other half is to be found. But it is even more significant that the self has both these halves. Here one may, indeed, speak of a *split* of the self: the self as it reveals itself in actions remains irreducible to the self as it is grasped in stories.

This split of the self is by no means a pathological phenomenon. On the contrary, it is necessary for normal life. It may, however, incontestably take degenerate forms. How can we know here the normal from the pathological? A passage in one of Freud's last works may show us a way to distinguish between them. The psychoanalytical notion of *Ichspaltung* (split of the ego) is built upon the observation that two psychic attitudes may coexist in a person during a whole life without influencing one another: one of these attitudes corresponds to reality, while the other detaches itself from it under the impact of instinct.[123] It is clear from the text that, according to Freud, the pathological feature of this duality consists in the parallel nature of the two attitudes without transition, without interaction, and without mutual influence. This is, however, a characteristic not to be attributed to the split of the self we have in mind. Here two different attitudes may equally be discerned: the prospective attitude of action has undoubtedly to be sharply distinguished from the retrospective attitude of storytelling. It may even be added that narratives introduce into life a dimension of the imaginary, while actions restore our relationship with reality. Here, however, the two parallel attitudes allow for a transition; they enter into an interaction, and they exert a mutual influence upon one another. It may even be claimed that it is precisely in an *alternation* between the two attitudes that normality consists.

That is why the question arises as to how this alternation is possible. I shall try to answer this question by showing how experience mediates between acting and storytelling.

Let us begin with the observation that the possibility of an alternation between the two attitudes certainly does not exclude the occurrence of conflicts and crises. One may find oneself compelled to engage in a course of action which does not match the stories one would like to be characterized by. One may find a way out of such anomalous situations either by renouncing to fresh initiatives or by rectifying the endorsed stories. We do not need to dwell upon the former alternative at length; it is the price we are sometimes ready to pay for the sake of coherence. As to the latter alternative, we have examined it in depth in our prelude. There we claimed that this issue is provided by a spontaneous sense formation in life-history, which may offer the fundamentals of modified narratives. We will now anchor the idea of spontaneous sense formation in the concept of experience we have been trying to elaborate in the present chapter.

Every lived experience may be said to include a *variable polysemy* which can never be completely exhausted by a narrative, however rich it may be. A story necessarily curtails and impoverishes the experience it is designed to express: by unifying and homogenizing its multifarious shreds of sense, it deprives it of its ever changing ambiguity. However, the discarded shreds of sense do not disappear without leaving at least some traces behind, which may be rediscovered if new challenges find some resonance in them. That is why experience always has some elements in store for a rectified story.

Consequently, it is by the very structure of experience that the transition from a fresh initiative to a renewed narrative is facilitated.

Something similar is true of the movement in the opposite direction. Here the mediating instance is, once again, experience. Stories one is entangled in sometimes pave the way for apparently unprepared actions which are at first sight entirely incompatible with them. This astonishing phenomenon is easily explained if the variable polysemy of experience is taken into account. For the stories held for being characteristic of one's life, as well as of one's self, give an unambiguous and, therefore, necessarily incomplete, or even simplificatory, expression to one's experiences, which often in themselves contain some discarded shreds of sense, secretly intimating, or even prompting, unprecedented actions.

Thus, experience may indeed be said to mediate between storytelling and acting. It is the common ground to which we have recourse in order to find our way from one of these attitudes to the other. It is experience we fix by recounting narratives about ourselves and each other; and it is experience we fall back upon in initiating new actions in response to alien demands. Consequently, it is by experience that the alternation between acting and recounting is made possible. Therefore, if this oscillation, this pendular movement, is hampered, or even trammeled, then it is with experience that something is wrong. Whenever the split of the self we have in mind takes degenerate forms, its pathological turn is caused by a trouble with experience.

But what may go wrong with experience? The answer may be found if attention is paid to the fact that it is not the same side or aspect of experience which is expressed in narratives and which is relied upon in actions. It is mainly with the accepted, expressly endorsed shreds of sense contained in an experience that storytelling is concerned. To the contrary, it is essentially by the discarded shreds of sense involved in an experience that an unprecedented action is suggested and stimulated. Alternation between acting and narrating presupposes a state of a changing equilibrium between accepted and discarded sense moments. Such a delicate balance is, however, easily disturbed. Accepted shreds of sense may often get fixed, immobilized, or may even turn rigid; discarded shreds of sense are frequently put aside, dismissed, or even repressed. Such disturbances have their consequences. The processes of retroactive sense fixation risk being separated from the processes of a spontaneous sense formation. The upshot is that one grows more and more encapsulated in the stories characteristic of one's self, while becoming less and less capable of taking fresh initiatives and opening a new field in life.

We may sum up the considerations presented so far in this section by formulating some theses. First, it may be held that it is solely experience which is grasped by, and expressed in, narratives. However, it must be added, second, that experience can never be exhausted by stories expressly narrated; it always involves some shreds of sense that may be said to wait for being recounted without exhibiting, or even fitting in well with, the explicit structure of narratives. The perception of these inchoate sense moments may encourage us to embrace Ricoeur's idea of a prenarrative structure of experience. But it is with caution that this notion is to be made use of. For nothing prevents discarded, or even repressed, sense arousals from transcending the narratives which are, in each case, designed to capture them. That is precisely why, third, they may be supposed to prepare unprecedented actions which put into question the stories accepted as characteristic of one's life and of one's self. Such a conflict between actions and narratives may, fourthly, be said to lead to a crisis in which an unavoidable split of the self comes to the fore and becomes manifest. It must, fifthly, be emphasized, however, that this split of the self does not inevitably degenerate into a pathological phenomenon because it is normally counterbalanced by a dynamic equilibrium inhering in experience, which, from time to time, rearranges and reorganizes the relationship between acting and recounting. Thus, it is experience that mediates between the two attitudes the self is divided into.

This summary may, however, give rise to a misunderstanding. Considering how experience mediates between action and narration, one easily falls victim to an illusion. One is tempted to conceive of experience not only as a common ground of acting and narrating but also as a field of indifference in which all conflicts between these attitudes are ultimately resolved, so that, in the final analysis, the split of the self seems to be but the result of a transitory disturbance. However, the image of a field of indifference is seriously misleading and even delusory. Although experience mediates between action and narration, mediation by no means amounts here to reconciliation. The split of the self we have in mind can never be surmounted, nor sublated. For, whereas the dimension of one's own narrative history does not transcend the boundaries of one's own self, the dimension of action necessarily surpasses these limits because it arises from the confrontation of the self with the demands of the other, with whom the self, incidentally, enters into a face-to-face relationship. In spite of all mediation between recounting and acting, this difference between the two dimensions remains irreducible. Moreover, it remains so prevalent that it leaves its mark even on the mediatory instance. Indeed, the field of one's own experience is profoundly marked by a difference between what is, in fact, one's *own* and what is, in reality, *alien* to oneself. In other words, the experience one gains never fails to include some hints at the experiences others gain, have gained, or may gain.

d. Radical Alterity in Experience

It is a striking feature of one's own experience that it turns one side to oneself, while reserving other sides to others. This is evidently true of the perception of external things. The castle I can see in front of me has its back side which I cannot see (at least without moving around the edifice), which, however, is immediately visible for others. (If the back side were not visible for others, then, what I can see in front of me, would not be the frontispiece of a castle but, let us say, only a stage scene designed for a play.) In spite of some dissimilarities, due mainly to the differences between spatial objects and temporal processes, the case of the actions we perform, and of the events happening to us, is strictly analogous. According to the testimony of the experience we gain of them, such temporal instances occur, so to speak, at the crossroads of different experiential routes. Each of us traverses only one of these routes. One and the same experience, even if it is shared by others, that is, even if it is rightly considered as part and parcel of what may be called "common experience," takes different shapes, or senses, if regarded from the perspectives of different experiential routes. That is why the experience of actions and events is determined by a perspectivism analogous to that which is characteristic of the perception of external things. Experiences related to one's own states of mind are not exempt of such a perspectivism, either. They are not only marked by it if they are evoked in retrospect, that is, when they are recollected or reproduced in remembrance, but even when they are simply retained during the temporal development of introspective perception. For even such a process bears evidence to an observation which we may formulate—drawing, by the way, upon Husserl—as follows: everything new reacts on the old. In other words, a retroactive effect shows itself not only in recollection but even in retention. The phenomenon of retroactivity imprints a perspectivistic character to all experiences related to one's own states of mind, making it evident that these states of mind result from the reaction of the freshly emerging self upon the old one, the new self inserting them, as it were into the context of an experiential route which is but one among others.

Why is this inner division of one's own experience into what is, in fact, one's own in it and what is, in reality, alien to oneself so important in an inquiry into the relationship between action and narration? It is crucially important because it shows how one's own narrative history is embedded in a more encompassing whole, in which different experiential routes are discernible. Recounting narratives characteristic of one's own life, inserting, at the same time, into these narratives stories told by others about oneself, is obviously designed to serve for *appropriating* one's own experience; and appropriating one's own experience is tantamount to *selecting* one experiential route at the expense of others. This interdependence between *selecting* and *excluding* clearly shows that the narrative appropriation of experience rests on a contrast between what is indeed one's own and what is irretrievably alien in this very experience. While one side of experience is appropriated, another side is irrevocably alienated. From this observation one may draw a conclusion of vital significance: the narrative identity of the self necessarily presupposes a *radical alterity* which it is unable to absorb. This radical alterity may remain concealed in storytelling, a relation with it is necessarily involved in action. That is why an exploration of the tension between acting and recounting, as well as an examination of the split of the self into two corresponding attitudes, reveals a hidden presupposition of the narrative view of personal identity. It is this hidden presupposition which is to be analyzed in the remaining chapters of the present book.

2

The Temporality of Experience in Life-History

Time has the almost magic power to *modify* without *altering:* it confers to every lived experience the character of the past without touching upon its content. Temporal modification seems, therefore, to be an entirely unique kind of change: a transformation which does not presuppose any sublation or negation and does not engender any real difference, either; a transmutation which, consequently, does not exclude recognition, identification, or even the repetition of the same. This kind of modification, as Paul Ricoeur rightly points out, is "a challenge lanced to the logic of the Same and the Other"; this challenge, he adds, is time itself.[1]

Nobody has made more strenuous efforts to account for this peculiar nature of temporal modification than Edmund Husserl. *Modification precedes difference:* this thesis characterizes, according to Ricoeur, his entire approach to time.[2] Husserl holds, in other words, that the difference between the present and the past (as well as that between the present and the future) is engendered, rather than presupposed, by the modification characteristic of the flow of time.

There are, as Ricoeur underscores,[3] some arguments supporting this thesis. How is one to grasp, in fact, the difference between the present and the past? (Since the case of the difference between the present and the future is analogous, we may restrict ourselves to this question.) The answer is obvious: one realizes that something *is not* there—or, at least, *is not* what it was—any longer. Thus, here the realization of a difference includes, or implies, the perception of alterity and negation. However, one does not come to realize something's *being not there* or something's *being not so and so any longer* unless one *fixes*—more or less arbitrarily—an instant in time transforming it, thereby, into a limit or a breaking point. One makes use here, as we may say, of a rather artificial procedure: one simply *abstracts* from the underlying continuity of time. This is, at least, Husserl's firm conviction. If this conviction is well founded, then it can indeed be maintained that the perception of difference, alterity, and negativity in time necessarily presupposes a continuous temporal modification.

Ricoeur adds that this Husserlian view of time may be corroborated by a linguistic or grammatical argument.[4] One can put the verb *to be* into the past tense (or, for that matter, into the future tense) *without denying* it. Consequently, temporal modification proves to be a *positive* modification which, in itself, has nothing to do with difference, alterity, and negativity. Therefore, one may claim that, in a certain sense, the *is not . . . any longer* necessarily presupposes the *was* . . . .[5]

This is an apparently coherent view of temporal modification. Yet, it is far from being unquestionable. It may be objected that this view of temporal modification is modeled upon the *pattern of perception.* No inquiry has an access to time as such; in its proper essence, no investigation is able to grasp time as it is, in itself. Time can only be studied as an unseparable moment of a more complex whole. For Husserl, at least in the course of his earlier considerations on time, this whole is the perception of temporally unfolding objects (like a tune, or a melody). This is, however, certainly not the only option to be taken.

Another possibility is to consider time, in a physical perspective, as a moment of the movement in the universe. This approach to time appears as early as Aristotelianism.[6] It is, indeed, as a number—or measure—of movement that Aristotle interprets time in his *Physics.*[7] This initiative has been followed by several philosophers and scientists up to the present. Modern cosmology from Einstein's general theory of relativity to Stephen Hawking's *Short History of Time,* and even further, stands entirely under this sign. However, it is not difficult to discern a diverging, or even opposite, tendency in the history of Western thought as well. In the eleventh book of his *Confessions,* Augustine, who is the first to develop this opposite tendency, presents time as belonging to the mind and its life.[8] Ricoeur claims that these two historical currents, or trends, represent two possible perspectives one may adopt in considering time: a physical or cosmological one, and a psychological one. He adds that these two perspectives are *mutually conditioned,* as well as *mutually concealed* by each other.[9] Phenomenology is often considered as a continuation of Augustine's psychological approach to time. Even Ricoeur seems to share this opinion. It is, indeed, true that Husserl also takes inspiration from the eleventh book of Augustine's *Confessions.* It is, however, no less true that phenomenology is preserved from a one-sided emphasis upon the psychological approach to time by its doctrine of intentionality. As Rudolf Bernet puts it:

> An analysis of time which is carried out in the framework of a phenomenology of intentional consciousness overcomes the duality of a "psychological" and a "physical" analysis of time because an intentional experience perpetually transcends the limits of intimate self-presence (*innerlicher Selbstzugehörigkeit*) by relating itself to something outside of itself of which it is the very awareness.[10]

It is precisely with a view to overcome the duality of the psychological and the physical perspective upon time that Husserl decides to study the perception of temporally unfolding objects. However, as he delves more and more deeply into this subject, he realizes more and more clearly that temporal modification is not to be sufficiently accounted for by a substantially "static" analysis of the intentional structure characterizing perception. In his later writings and working notes, he seems to be wedded to the opinion that it is rather the dynamic, or as he calls it, "genetic" analysis of self-constitution in the history of a whole life which may be expected to procure a proper access to the comprehension of temporal modification.

The earlier Heidegger may be credited with a kindred conception. In his eyes, time, in its original form, is nothing but the very structure of one's selfhood—or, more precisely, of one's "being a self" (*Selbstsein*)—in its anticipated totality. However, it is not simply on intentionality, it is rather on "transcendence"—in a verbal sense of the word—that he bases his phenomenology of existence.[11] He attributes to transcendence an "ecstatic" character: it is, according to him, an inalienable feature of one's very existence to be able to step out of oneself, to dwell on things different from oneself, and to grasp oneself by returning from them to oneself. He has this ecstatic movement in view when he regards the temporal structure of existence. That is why he interprets the past, the future, and even the present as ecstasies, with the further appendix that the ever changing unity of these ecstasies is itself ecstatic in its nature: it has to be constantly retrieved, recuperated, or reorganized. It is this constant reorganization of the temporal unity of life which is called "temporalization" by Heidegger. The distance of this conception from Husserl's idea of an unbreakable continuity of time may be measured against the famous—and already quoted—thesis: *modification precedes difference.* In the text of a lecture delivered at the university of Marburg in 1928 under the title "The Fundamental Problems of Phenomenology," Heidegger says:

> Upon closer consideration, it turns out that even the *not* (negation), or the essence of the *not, nullity,* can only be interpreted on account of the essence of time, and it is only on account of this essence that the possibility of modification, for instance, of that of presence into absence, is to be understood.[12]

It is clear from this passage that the doctrine of ecstatic temporality marks a break with the thesis under discussion. According to Heidegger, it is not modification which precedes difference. It is, indeed, rather the reverse which is true if the possibility of a modification like that of presence into absence is to be understood on account of ecstatic temporality to which the difference or alterity of the ecstatic dimensions future, present, and past necessarily belong, and from which nullity or negativity (*Nichtigkeit*) is to be derived. Of course, it does not follow that, with Heidegger, time ceases to be "a challenge lanced to the logic of the Same and the Other." On the contrary, what Heidegger chiefly aims at is precisely to reconsider the *not,* the *same,* and the *other* in a way different from what is prescribed by this logic. Inspired by Kant's doctrine of the schematism of the pure concepts of understanding, he sets himself the task of interpreting such logical categories "on account of the essence of time" and reassessing their traditionally instituted content from this novel point of view.

Husserl's idea of a continuous modification of time will not be rehabilitated by French phenomenology, either. Thinkers like Merleau-Ponty, Levinas, Derrida, and Ricoeur maintain even more unambiguously than Heidegger that temporal change may be traced back to an original difference which a theory modeled upon the pattern of perception is in principle unable to account for.[13] Drawing more upon Bergson and Nietzsche than upon Husserl, Deleuze comes to similar results.

There are, of course, profound differences among the thinkers mentioned above. Ricoeur's theory of narrative identity remains largely committed to the old idea that time is to be inquired into within the context of self-identity and life-history. The others dissent and try to break new grounds. They lay emphasis upon a difference in the framework of temporality which attests an otherness than self-identity in life-history. One of the guiding ideas of their inquiries may be hinted at by a dictum quoted from Rimbaud by several of them: *Je est un autre.*[14] Under this intellectual climate, Ricoeur himself feels compelled to account for alterity in his defense of narrative identity. The very title of his work *Oneself as Another* testifies to this aspiration. We shall see, however, in the next chapter that he is never as radical as either Merleau-Ponty or Levinas. The same could be claimed for Derrida and Deleuze as well. From the works of the latter thinkers, a whole series of convincing arguments can be elicited which all point to a radical alterity lying at the very core of the temporality of life-history. It remains, however, quite unclear how, in the light of these discoveries, the analysis of temporal modification could be laid out on new foundations.

My suggestion is that the phenomenological considerations on time should be centered upon *experience* rather than upon perception or upon self-identity in life-history. Here the term *experience* should be taken in the strong sense which has been assigned to it in the course of our considerations. Thus understood, it refers to the spontaneous formation of a new sense, which emerges, so to speak, behind the back of consciousness by thwarting all previous expectations. It indicates, consequently, an otherness than self-identity, an irremediable alterity in life-history which sometimes suddenly gives it a radical turn. This eruptivity is bound to leave its trace on the temporal constitution of experience.

It is often rightly claimed that in Husserl's investigations one unexpectedly finds detours and hints which, at first sight, seem to be alien to his main conception. This is one of the most important reasons for which, even in our days, a strange but incontestable fecundity may be attributed to them. It can be shown that Husserl had, indeed, an inkling of the eruptivity which has been just alluded to. This inkling is obvious from the notion "primal impression" which does not fit in well with the general picture he forms of time. It indicates an alterity which is not accounted for by a temporal modification which is supposed to go without any alteration. This has been emphasized by two thinkers independently of each other: by Emmanuel Levinas and Michel Henry. In the first section of the present chapter, I will consider this peculiar notion, as it had been first proposed by Husserl, and as it was then interpreted, and even appropriated, by Levinas and Henry.

After this interpretative essay, I will dedicate the second section of this chapter to a conceptual inquiry. I shall try to elaborate the concept of a radical turn in life-history by the way of a temporal analysis. This task will give me an opportunity to specify what my investigations owe to the profound initiative which Marc Richir has recently taken in order to renew and recast phenomenology.

I. Temporal Modification and Primal Impression

The book Martin Heidegger edited under the title *Edmund Husserl's Lectures on the Phenomenology of the Consciousness of Internal Time*[15]—based on an earlier collection by Edith Stein—contains writings that had originally not been intended for publication. The main bulk of the volume is the text of a university lecture Husserl gave in 1905, yet we find many of Husserl's manuscripts—the output of almost twenty-five years—in it as well; these are mostly notes he put down for himself between 1893 and 1917. No wonder, then, that the ideas thus collected sometimes lack unity, or even coherence. Yet it is by no means accidental that Michel Henry calls this collection the most beautiful text of phenomenology. Perhaps these are the pieces that witness to Husserl's lifelong project most, highlighted by the well-known imperative of "Back to the things!"; moreover, the "thing" under investigation here, in its mysterious inaccessibility, undoubtedly deserves special attention. This thing is nothing else but *time,* or to be more precise, the *experience* of time, or even—in a more general and simpler account—the *consciousness* of time.

In the collection this "consciousness of time" is closely related to something Husserl calls "original sensation" or "primal impression." These alternating terms refer to the initial element in a series of related experiences; such an element might, for example, be the first note of a tune, or the sound of a ringing that catches one's ear. What is, however, the connection between primal impression thus interpreted, and the consciousness of time?

The investigation in these lectures on time strikes us with the realization that the answer to this problem is far from straightforward. Yet the real difficulty is not in Husserl's inability to clarify the connection under question to the full; the real hindrance is the—otherwise highly rewarding—interpretation of these lectures in the past few decades. Ever since Heidegger objected to the metaphysical definition of being as presence, it seemed obvious that Husserl was overemphasizing the significance of primal impression only because he was prone to take the given, present moment as something deserving special attention, and it was also plausible to say, as a sort of explanation, that no more may be expected from a phenomenology which, in its interpretation of time, follows the *pattern of perception.* From here there was an open road to the claim—first made by Derrida, and then repeated several times—that Husserl, in his analysis of time, remained the *prisoner of the metaphysics of presence.* Under these circumstances it seemed obvious that Husserl surmised a strong connection between primal impression and the consciousness of time because—as Rudolf Bernet puts it—he was unable to escape "the spell of the idea of complete presentness given in the *now.*"[16]

Yet there are some French philosophers who consider as a merit of Husserl's to have linked primal impression and the consciousness of time.[17] Such a thinker is Levinas, who keeps returning to this tenet in various ways. In his *Otherwise Than Being or Beyond Essence* he not only emphasizes the fundamental importance of connecting primal impression and the consciousness of time from the point of view of Husserl's approach but he also inquires into where the weight and significance of the present—perhaps not unfoundedly accentuated by Husserl and others—may come from.[18]

The relationship between primal impression and the consciousness of time is also in the center of those investigations which Henry carries out in his essay "Hyletic and Material Phenomenology,"[19] concerning Husserl's lectures on time. This article differs from Levinas's work, both in its theoretical background and in its aims, in considerable ways. Yet a question they both share still connects them, which—provisionally—might be formulated as follows: Can the present be characterized by the quality of *beginning* (initiality)? In Husserl's analysis of time, this quality becomes accessible through the experience of disruption which an original perception or primal impression brings about in the order of time organized by intentionalities.[20]

In line with Levinas's and Henry's groundbreaking studies, I wish to give an interpretation of Husserl's analyses of time which does not consider the significance he attributes to the present as the imprint of a suspicious metaphysics. The question pertaining to the present characterized by the quality of beginning (initiality) will be in the focus of my attention. However, this question will serve as a guideline for investigations which remain within the framework of the possibilities Husserl opened in his interpretation of time. Consequently, Levinas and Henry will primarily feature as the readers of Husserl's lectures.

1. The Consciousness of Time and Primal Impression in Husserl

"Though it be a rehabilitation of the 'sensorial given' of empiricist sensualism, the primal impression finds again in the context of intentionality [. . .] its power to surprise"—Levinas claims,[21] and adds: in Husserl, the sensible qualities—sounds, colors, hardness, softness, and so on—"are not only the sensed: as affective states, they are the sensing."[22]

In Husserlian phenomenology, "sensation" as "primal content" had been among the experiences of consciousness since the *Logical Investigations,* even if it could not be considered as an "act of consciousness" or as an "intentional experience." The notion of sensation still carries the imprints of its empiricist origin. However, even in the *Logical Investigations,* this notion—as a kind of counterbalance—is coupled with an idea coined in a typically intellectualist vein: Husserl says that consciousness receives sensations—or, as he later calls them, the "hyletic data"—in a specific "apprehension" or "interpretation," and it is thus that they are made its content, while this consciousness "animates" them with its objective intentions. This conception, reflecting the influence of both empiricism and intellectualism, leads to the methodological model which is often called the "apprehension–content of apprehension schema." This schema undoubtedly creates a certain mediation between its heterogeneous elements of different origin, even if their opposition cannot be completely bridged.[23]

The lectures on time, however, quite straightforwardly show that Husserl abandons this scheme from 1909. Simultaneously, he more and more sensitively distinguishes between sensation as sensing (*Empfinden*) and sensation (*Empfindung*) in the sense of the content of sensation (*Empfindungsinhalt*).[24] Thus, it will be useful to investigate the role of these notions in the lectures on time in two steps: the first will interpret "sensation" and "impression" as sense content or sense datum, the second as sensing or consciousness of sense content. It is only after these investigations that we may further consider if the above mentioned process of the separation of sensing and sensation might lead to a new connection, precisely between these two, divided elements.

That sensing (*Empfinden*) and sense datum (*Empfindungsdatum*) might coincide gives a certain ambiguity to the Husserlian notion of sensation (*Empfindung*) from the start. This becomes evident as early as when Husserl distinguishes between subjective and objective time. Husserl—similarly to Kant—takes a point of departure from cases where time relations are different "in the object" and "in the phenomenon." Let us take a piece of chalk. Let us close our eyes and then open them again. During this experiment—Husserl says—"[i]n the object there is duration; in the phenomenon alteration."[25] Yet if we start from this consideration, a certain sensation—for example, a ringing which started and still reverberates for some time—will be ambiguous even "purely as a hyletic datum":[26] it can be taken as an "immanent temporal object" which, on the one hand, might be considered as a "duration in the object," and on the other hand, as a "alteration in the phenomenon." Husserl points out this ambiguity himself: "In the immanent hearing of the sound"—he claims—"my apprehension can aim in two directions: in one instance, towards what is sensed in the temporal flow; in the other, towards what is becoming constituted in this flow and yet is immanent."[27]

A fully legitimate parallel might be drawn between pure sense datum (interpreted as something which is "immanent" for our consciousness, yet is constituted in the temporal flow) and the objects of experience which are transcendent for consciousness. As a consequence, however, "immanent time" itself—Husserl explicitly states—proves to be, in the final analysis, a kind of *objective time:* it proves to be "an objective time, a genuine time in which there is duration and the alteration of what endures."[28] Yet, simultaneously, we may detect—as a kind of second stage of immanence—a "flow" (*Fluß*) which is called by Husserl, around 1907, "preempirical or phenomenological time," in contrast with immanent, yet still objective time.[29]

The notion of original sensation or primal impression is also ambiguous from the start. Husserl identifies primal impression as that which "is primally produced [*das Urgezeugte*]"; it is "the 'new,'" "that which has come into being alien to consciousness [*das bewußtsiensfremd Gewordene*]"; it is "that which has been received [*das Empfangene*], as opposed to what has been produced through consciousness's own spontaneity."[30] In the lectures on time such expressions render the "continuous welling-up of ever new primal impressions"[31] as "primal source [*Urquelle*]," "primal generation [*Urzeugung*]" and "primal creation [*Urschöpfung*]." Yet Husserl warns that these are only "metaphors." He says, "It can only be said: Consciousness is nothing without impression."[32] However, it remains to be seen how the lectures on time describe the relationship between the intentionality of consciousness and primal impression.

At one point Husserl talks about the perception of immanent temporal objects as an "objectivation" with two sides:

> One side of objectivation finds its basis purely in the qualitative content of the material of sensation: this yields the temporal material—the tone, for example. [. . .] A second side of objectivation derives from the apprehension of the representants of the temporal positions [*Zeitstellenrepräsentanten*].[33]

Here Husserl applies the "schema of apprehension–content of apprehension" to the perception of time. Simultaneously, however, within the "phase of consciousness that constitutes the pure now,"[34] he does not only distinguish between two apprehensions but two different contents of apprehension as well: the "temporal material" and the "representants of temporal positions." Thus, distinct sense data bear relation to the ringing which can be heard just now on the one hand, and to its temporal position—the present moment, the "now point"—on the other. Husserl underlines the difference between the two contents of apprehension by introducing two notions: in connection with the ringing he talks about "original sensation," and with respect to the temporal position of the ringing he uses the term "original impression of temporal position."[35] Yet when he attempts to circumscribe what we may understand by *now-point,* the hitherto clear picture becomes blurred, as the definition he arrives at is obviously *circular.*[36] The now point—Husserl claims—is nothing else but "the temporal form of the original sensation." But he also adds that the original sensation is that "belonging to the current now-point." We move in a vicious circle. And these notions totally lose their interpretability when Husserl—even emphatically—adds that "the now-point itself must, in strictness, be defined through original sensation."[37] Yet something still seems to be certain: the original impression of temporal position carries the same meaning as the above mentioned temporal form, consequently it is in opposition with original sensation.

If it is in this context that we call special attention to Husserl's famous dictum according to which primal impression "is something absolutely unmodified [*das absolut Unmodifizerte*], the primal source of all further consciousness and being,"[38] then the ambiguity of this very statement becomes evident as well. We simply do not know if "primal impression" is to be understood as something which "has come into being alien to consciousness" (as the temporal material), or whether it should rather be interpreted as the temporal form of the now-moment, having—ultimately—to do with the spontaneity of consciousness.

At another point Husserl talks about the abiding "form" of the *flow* and that "a now becomes constituted by means of an impression" is taken to be as one of the "regularities" characteristic of this form.[39] This is why Husserl may claim that "the content is certainly not something which was introduced into the form from without"; on the contrary, it is "determined by the regularity of form."[40] It is, however, true that this sentence is appended by the following clause: "only in such a way that this regularity does not alone determine the concretum."[41] This locus, reminiscent of Kant, clearly indicates that primal impression as something alien to consciousness, is *always already forced into an order* which can be traced back to the regularities of the spontaneity of consciousness.

It is thus that the original impression of the temporal position (the temporal form of the consciousness of the now, the present) gets separated from primal impression (i.e., the temporal material). This process reaches its climax in the severing of sensing (*Empfinden*) from the content of sensation (*Empfindunsinhalt*).

Through this severing, the notion of sensation gains a new meaning. As sensing, sensation becomes "the internal consciousness of the content of sensation."[42]

The idea of internal consciousness goes back to Brentano.[43] The hypothesis that all intentional acts are accompanied by internal—or inner—consciousness implies, in *Psychology from an Empirical Standpoint,* the danger of the entanglement of several embedded instances of consciousness. Brentano tries to go around this problem in the following way: "We can say"—he claims—"that the sound is the *primary* object of the *act* of hearing, and that the act of hearing itself is the *secondary object*."[44] His distinction between primary and secondary objects makes it possible for him to separate inner consciousness from inner observation or perception.[45] An intentional act is the *secondary* object of the inner consciousness accompanying this act, while the act is the *primary* object of inner observation (perception).

It is precisely in Brentano's footsteps that Husserl proceeds. First he defines inner or internal consciousness as "absolute consciousness of time."[46] Until he considered the constituting consciousness of immanent temporal objects as an experience which itself belongs to immanent time, he had to face Brentano's difficulty: his conception was threatened by the danger of an infinite complication of mental states or, in other words, of an *infinite regress.* It is not hard to see why. If we, for example, claim that a tune as an immanent temporal object is constituted in the experience of tune perception, and then add that the experience of tune perception might, in its own right, be also considered as an immanent temporal object, then we cannot avoid the question where (*in what*) this newer immanent temporal object will be constituted. If here our answer is that the experience of tune perception as immanent temporal object is constituted in the experience of the perception of tune perception, then we have already supposed the existence of a secondary (second-order) perception of the perception of time. And from now on we are bound to go further and further because secondary experiences will raise the same questions as the primary ones did, ad infinitum. However, Husserl believes that he can avoid this danger by talking about the internal consciousness of tune perception instead of the perception of the perception of tune perception, and by separating this—as Brentano does—from all perceptions. Thus, Husserl may claim that the tune as an immanent temporal object is constituted in the experience of tune perception; in turn, the experience of tune perception as an immanent temporal object is not constituted in the perception of tune perception but in the *internal consciousness* of tune perception which *cannot* be considered as perception. It is true, however, that this answer can only be accepted if the internal consciousness of time, in its own right, is no longer considered as an immanent temporal object. It is this that Husserl, as a first step, tries to show. This is exactly why he talks about the "absolute" consciousness of time. Yet this expression has no intention of referring to a kind of metaphysical *absolute;* Husserl uses this name to simply separate the immediately conscious and vivid experience of time from that temporal process or event in the form of which this very experience is grasped in posterior reflection.

Simultaneously, he believes to have found the deepest layer of temporal experience, from which time, in its true character, emerges to get organized for us—this is the layer in which time is "constituted." Thus, in the lectures on time there are finally three "layers of constitution": the objective time of the objects we experience, the time of immanent temporal objects, and finally, the "absolute time-constituting flow of consciousness,"[47] which—as Husserl claims—we may, strictly speaking, call a "flow" only "*in conformity with what is constituted.*"[48]

This step, however, is even followed by a second one. Husserl makes an attempt at a more straightforward explanation of what the difference between internal consciousness and perception might consist of. We may recall that Brentano did not get further than the separation of primary objects from secondary ones. Husserl does not rest satisfied with this rather artificial and forced distinction. He aims at a more precise grasping of the characteristic of the intentionality that is directed, in the case of hearing, not at the sound which is audible right now but at the listening itself. He concludes that we have to distinguish between two separate components of the intentionality of the consciousness of time: on the one hand, there is a certain *transversal* intentionality, which might be conceived of as if it were intersecting the flow of time: it is directed at the sound that can be heard just now, and it constitutes the building block of the experience of tune perception. On the other hand, there is a certain *longitudinal*—or, as it is sometimes translated into English, *horizontal*—intentionality, having an effect—so to speak—alongside the flow of time: this results in the internal consciousness of the hearing of the sound. In Husserl's interpretation, longitudinal intentionality—as "retention"—holds an earlier shape of the experience of tune perception in one's memory, while—as "protention"—it simultaneously gives out a sign of promise with respect to the subsequent shape of that experience, without opposing either of these shapes with each other as objects. Husserl is quite unambiguous on this point: "the retentional phase is conscious of the preceding phase without making it into an object."[49] Obviously, this applies to protention, too. It is a decisive feature of the internal consciousness that it serves as a kind of *wedge* between that which it still keeps in the memory, and that which it gives a promise of; this is why it cannot oppose either of the two with itself as an object. This is what Husserl realizes and this is why he is not forced—as Brentano was—to try to distinguish between the primary and secondary objects of intentional acts.

Yet the significance of the discovery of an intentionality which is not objectifying in its character is still not exhausted. Husserl is now also capable of ultimately unfastening the analysis of time from the model of perception, something he was so far unable to do. Yet this gesture also invalidates the "schema of apprehension–content of apprehension." Primal impression as the consciousness of the now-moment of the sound thus turns out to be bereft of anything soundlike.[50] Consequently, the primal impression that belongs to the now-moment cannot be identified with the sense datum of sound.

Husserl also builds on the discovery of retentional-longitudinal intentionality when he attributes a posterior "self-appearance"—a to-itself-appearance—to the absolute flow of consciousness; this simultaneously assigns a kind of special, "prephenomenal," "preimmanent" temporality to this flow, which is different from the respective times of both transcendent objects of experience and of immanent temporal objects.[51] It has often been claimed that Husserlian consciousness of time is *nothing but time itself taken in the original meaning.* Heidegger is the first one to say this[52] but similar observations may be found later in Levinas,[53] too. This interpretation is undoubtedly correct in itself but it does not dispel the mystery of the absolute flow of consciousness. It is clear that there is no absolute consciousness of time without primal impression; yet what kind of temporality may we attribute to it? Husserl himself asks, "What about the beginning-phase of an experience that is in the process of becoming constituted?"[54] Yet he immediately adds the following: "if it [the beginning phase] were intended *only* by retention, then what confers on it the label 'now' would remain incomprehensible."[55] This is because retentional-longitudinal intentionality remains hopelessly *posterior.* So Husserl comes to the opinion that the beginning phase has an immediate internal consciousness of its own as well; yet he himself underlines that this "primal consciousness" might be "seen"—i.e., accessible for observation and thus actually grasped—only subsequently, *after* it has elapsed, in the retention, and further, in the reflection based on this retention.[56] But does this insight imply more than that the initial phase is but the *invisible boundary* of—in a certain sense even—*visible time,* which has become revealed in the "self-appearance" of the absolute flow of consciousness?

Husserl carefully considers this possibility, yet this interpretation still does not satisfy him. Perhaps, Husserl says, the initial phase of a "just now" emerging experience

> could be distinguished negatively from its modifications as the one phase that does not make us retentionally conscious of any preceding phase; but the beginning-phase is by all means characterised in consciousness in quite positive fashion.[57]

Where does this positive character of the initial phase come from? The answer is dormant in the claim that the "primal datum" present in the initial phase—in the original form of the "now"—is "already intended" by consciousness, yet without taking the shape of an object, "without its being something objective."[58] Thus, primal consciousness—i.e., sensing (*Empfinden*) by now separated from the content of sensation (*Empfindungsgehalt*)—is no more objectifying in its nature than retentional-longitudinal intentionality. This is why Husserl warns against misunderstanding primal consciousness by taking it "to be an apprehending act."[59] But it remains to be seen if a new kind of connection—or even coincidence—between sensing and sense content is not silently developed again.

For Brentano, inner consciousness always carries some affective content—an accompanying feeling or emotion—as well.[60] Husserl, in the *Logical Investigations,* also talks about a—nonact-like, hence nonintentional—variety of consciousness, which takes the shape of feeling sensations and desire sensations (*Gefühls- und Begehrensempfindungen*).[61] Could we not connect this notion with what was said about the nonobjectifying consciousness of the "primal datum" belonging to the beginning phase? Could we not, in other words, interpret the consciousness of primal impression as a vibration of emotions or desires? If we suppose that the answer is in the affirmative, we will, of course, also have to clarify the interplay which necessarily develops between this in itself nonintentional state of consciousness, and those intentions of consciousness which constitute time.

Is it possible that Husserl already implies this interplay with the surprising notion of "impressional regard" (*impressionaler Blick*)? Let me quote him: "the waking consciousness, the waking life, is a living-towards [*Entgegenleben*], a living that goes from the now towards the new now."[62] And later: "the regard from the now towards the new now, this transition [. . .] belongs to the essence of impression."[63] Finally, he emphasizes that this "is true of every 'primary content,' of every sensation" as well.[64] Thus he establishes a new relationship between the internal consciousness interpreted as the sensing in primal impression, and the sensation taken purely as a "hyletic datum."

As promising as this may sound, the available texts do not allow us to give unambiguous answers to the above questions. Thus the meditation over the nonobjectifying nature of the consciousness of the initial impression cannot be considered to be more than the indication of the possibilities of a theory, without providing a reassuring survey of Husserl's actual views. Yet some of the theoretical possibilities are luckily taken up by Levinas and Henry.

2. Time and Primal Impression in the Reading of Levinas and Henry

The connection between the two approaches might be seen in their common goal: both aim at the clarification of the *initial* character of the present. And both thinkers try to take Husserl by his word: if Husserl identified primal impression as a source-*point* (*Quellpunkt*)[65] of the intentional consciousness constituting time, then they interpret primal impression as a *source* point, as a *point where the source wells up*. In Husserl's lectures on time, which characterize the transformation of experience into retention as a "continuous modification" (*stetige Modifikation*), the ever given beginning phase might easily prove to be the sheer "ideal limit" of a continuum and, hence, it might evaporate in a mere abstraction.[66] However, this tendency is in contrast with Husserl's insight concerning the *positive* character of the initial phase referred to above. Although the respective methods of Levinas and Henry are different, they both wish to show up the positive nature of this "impressional consciousness" in such a way that it becomes as *concrete* as possible and has nothing to do with any kind of *ideal limit*.

Even though Levinas and Henry give careful consideration to all the clues they can find in Husserl's lectures on time, they both think themselves to be in opposition with him. Henry advocates a "final break" with intentional phenomenology,[67] and Levinas emphasizes the "non-intentionality of the primal impression," too, remarking that in Husserl intentionality remains "imperial" (*impérieuse*).[68]

Thus, they both disapprove of the "imperial" role of intentionality. This is exactly why they try to distinguish primal impression from the intentionality of consciousness: through the distinction, they wish to clarify those presuppositions which made it possible for Husserl to unite the two separate elements into the single notion of "impressional consciousness." The method of distinction or separation Levinas and Henry follow here is quite unique, since they are far from questioning the fact that the separated elements belong necessarily together; on the contrary: with respect to the initial phase they even suppose the case to be exactly this.

In what follows, I will put the above special mode of separation into focus. I claim that this procedure belongs to what has been called in the present work *diacritical method*. The word *diacritical* goes back—as it is well known—to the corresponding Greek meaning "separate," "sever," or "distinguish." More specifically, the differential connections which make language into a system are often called "diacritical" differences. However, in the present discussion, *diacritical method* will be even more specifically understood. It will, first and foremost, be meant as way of analysis belonging to *textual hermeneutics*, in which the interpreter starts from certain elements which for a text or for a textual tradition are counted as related or even overlapping ideas, whereas, in principle, they are not indistinguishable; even further, the interpreter, in retrospect, makes a distinction between them, yet without questioning their relatedness; and, finally, he tries to account for those conditions under which the overlapping of the separated elements still seemed plausible.

Yet it is also clear that the diacritical method as an interpretation of a text will only be fruitful if it is able to stand the test as a *phenomenological method* as well. The separation applied during the diacritical procedure may only be considered well founded if it is anchored in elements which demand separation, while, in retrospect, it is also made clear why it was originally plausible to think that they are in overlap. Thus the difference which, through the application of the diacritical method, comes to light as early as the first moment, may phenomenologically be *shown,* yet strictly speaking, it cannot at the same time be *shown up* phenomenologically. It can be shown up only retrospectively, since the initial state—similarly to Husserlian "primal consciousness"—resists direct phenomenological representation.

The germs of the diacritical method as a kind of phenomenological analysis can already be found in one of the arguments of Husserl's lectures on time. Husserl, in connection with the—already quoted—observations which accentuate the opposition he detects between the primal impression coming into being as something alien to consciousness and the spontaneity of consciousness, claims the following:

> The peculiarity of this spontaneity of consciousness [. . .] is that it creates nothing "new" but only brings what has been primally generated to growth, to development. Of course, what from an empirical point of view we call becoming or production belongs to objectivity, and this lies somewhere else altogether. Here it is a question of the spontaneity of consciousness; or, to put it more carefully: of a primordial spontaneity of consciousness.[69]

I read this difficult passage in the following way: Husserl talks about primal impression as the one which has come into being as something "alien to consciousness," as a "primal source," "primal generation," "primal creation," on the one hand, and about the spontaneity, about the autonomous operations of consciousness on the other, but in such a way that while he is *distinguishing* the two, he is simultaneously underlining that they *belong* together *necessarily.* Or, it even seems that he takes the coming into being of primal impression as something "alien to consciousness" to be eventually inseparable from the autonomous operations of consciousness, since here "coming into being" does not mean that something springs into existence or originates—as the result of a supposedly natural process—*objectively.* Here "coming into being" is precisely to be understood as a fact which is not merely surmised but is obvious from experience; it means that something, all of a sudden, *is there* in *consciousness*, it springs forward, by itself, *in experience.* It, thus, comes to the fore, or originates in a way which is *alien* to consciousness, yet it is still not *independent* of that consciousness, even if this kind of coming into being cannot be traced back to the interplay between the various intentionalities of consciousness constituting time. This is why for Husserl the coming into being of primal impression—at least in the moment when the new is just making its appearance, so in the ever given initial phase—is not only inseparable from a "primordial spontaneity" of consciousness, but even overlaps with it. Yet the primordial spontaneity with which primal impression springs into existence remains, in the retention, and in the reflection based on this retention, later clearly separable from that spontaneity of consciousness which—as the absolute consciousness, in its appearance to itself, has testified to it—is expressed in the continuous modifications of the initial impression.

I do not claim that Husserl, with this rather complicated argumentation, was completely able to clarify the relationship between primal impression and the intentionality of consciousness. Yet what remained obscure served as a springboard for the interpretations put forward by Levinas and Henry.

Levinas had a lifelong struggle with the understanding of the Husserlian notions of sensation and primal impression, devoting several writings to this matter. In what follows I wish to show that in these essays the outlines of the diacritical method adumbrated above silently emerge, even if their author was not aware of it. Yet this approach requires serious self-restraint and thus will be highly selective: several significant aspects of Levinas's ideas will have to remain ignored. Still, the connection Levinas detects between corporality and temporality in Husserl will at least have to be touched upon.

The essay entitled "Remarks on Phenomenological 'Technique'" reaches back to the parallel Husserl draws between orienting oneself in time and place respectively in order to carve out his passage to the problem of the splitting up of sense into temporal material and the impression of temporal positions. In Levinas's interpretation, primal impression constitutes the coordinational "origin," the common "zero point" of these two systems of orientation; thus it is taken to belong to the "*here* and *now.*"[70] This is why he is able to claim that the sensual element as the modified shape of primal impression "assigns a place to each content."[71] He further notes that Husserl attributes to "the sensual, in spite of its dullness and thickness, some meaning, and a wisdom of its own—a kind of intentionality."[72] "In the senses [*sens*]"—Levinas says—"there is sense [*sens*]."[73]

Thus understood, Levinas finds a strong connection between primal impression and intentionality, or—in this way—even between sense (sense organ) and sense (meaning). Still, however strongly he may rely here on Husserl's considerations, he undoubtedly makes such a discovery which could hardly be attributed to the old master. Levinas goes a step further and paves the way to the dismantling of a construct Husserl, investigating the connection of sensation and the intentionality of consciousness, erected from such—metaphysically loaded—ideas as the "form" or the "content" of the flow of time. This step is taken in the essay "Intentionality and Sensation."

What happens in this piece might even be called the *déconstruction avant la lettre.* Levinas—well before Derrida—wishes to turn a conflicting pair of metaphysical origin into its opposite and, at the same time, to push onto a new plain of interpretation. Yet here deconstruction is introduced by the application of the diacritical method. As it was quoted above, Levinas accentuates the inseparability of the sensed and the sensing in Husserl, but instead of taking it as a mere coincidence, he interprets it as a "kind of intentionality, which, by the same token" can be taken as "a minimal distance between the sensing and the sensed."[74]

Levinas, when referring to this minimal temporal distance, to this shift in phases, to the infinitesimal detachedness of the primal impression from the "pin-point" of experienced present, and when also emphasizing the disclosedness and growing awareness of this primal impression, "always appearing late with respect to itself,"[75] separates within the initial moment two elements of the sensing and the sensed, yet without questioning their belonging together. This enables him to radically sever the intentionality emerging in the moment of primal impression from all objectifying intentions. For Levinas, this intentionality is a flow in which consciousness and happening coincide,[76] with the further appendix that the "original sense (meaning)" of intentionality lies in the minimal temporal distance between the sensing and the sensed.[77]

This way, he gives an even more uncompromising picture about the unceasing, inerasable posteriority of retentional-longitudinal intentionality than Husserl. Levinas's conception deprives the time-constituting flow of consciousness, always already late with respect to itself, from the idea that it is capable of catching up with itself—a belief Husserl was prone to have cherished. For Levinas, primal impression is what it is more and more through the *difference* it has from itself, yet without thereby totally losing its self-identity. Thus it is possible that although primal impression is kept—in spite of its modifications—in retentive memory, this retention, even from the very initial phase, always means a constant *differing* (*deferring, differance*) at the same time. Consequently, something irredeemably falls out of the flow of time: something irrevocably slips away—there is no means to overhaul it. Levinas writes: "Consciousness is aging and the search for lost time."[78]

As in Husserl, the time constituting flow is given the specificity of "fundamental iteration," the capability that it "constantly returns to itself."[79] In Husserl, this feature is based on the fact that retention comprises not only the corresponding primal impression but also—in a constantly modifying shape—all the earlier retentions of this retention. It would make little sense to talk about continuous modifications in connection with Levinas, for whom primal impression itself comprises a minimal temporal distance, yet he, too, attributes an iterative structure to what we may call *differential distance formation,* detected in the primal impression. This iterative structure can explain why for Levinas the time constituting flow might have a constant form.[80]

According to Levinas, however, this form cannot be traced back to a regularity which the "spontaneity of consciousness" would enforce upon the content of the time flow. For Levinas, as we have seen, sensuality has sense and meaning already in itself, so according to his way of thinking, the differential and iterative distance formation characterizing the flow, and also being the most original intentional achievement, can take its starting point directly from original sensation, i.e., from primal impression itself. Primal impression, however, is "without the difference between material and form"—as Levinas himself notes.[81]

This way, the process that was characterized as *deconstruction before the letter* has reached its goal: the construction erected from the notional opposites of form and material has been dismantled. This is a great achievement in itself, since the possibility is now open to reconsider the relationship between primal impression and the intentionality of consciousness without the disturbing weight of a cumbersome metaphysical tradition. Yet this is only the first step in our application of the diacritical method: so far we cannot boast of more than the discovery that such notional pairs as material and form, or for that matter, sensation and intentionality, totally overlap in the initial phase of primal impression. There is still a second step to be taken: the thus overlapping elements should now be separated anew—but in a new manner. Primal impression is still to be taken out from the narrow order of the intentionalities of consciousness, from the order into which it always already had to fit in Husserl's theory as the "content" of the abiding "form" of "the flow"; as the "material" coming into being as alien to consciousness. Consequently, it has to be shown that the original opposition between primal impression and the intentionality of consciousness turns—so to speak—into its *opposite,* and gets onto a new plain of interpretation, once it has been liberated from the constraints of the metaphysics the opposing notions of "form" and "material" imposed on it. This second step is taken in Levinas's later magnum opus, *Otherwise Than Being or Beyond Essence.*

Here the goal of the investigation is really nothing else than to separate the intentionality of consciousness from primary impression in the initial phase of original sensation. Levinas starts from the claim that the beginning phase of an experience according to Husserl can be characterized as something "unmodified"; this is how primal impression gets distinguished from its own modifications. But does not primary impression so—Levinas asks the decisive question—"precede every protention, and thus precede its own *possibility*"?[82] This gives a clue with respect to what the *initiality* of the ever given initial phase might consist of. The "real" which "precedes and surprises the possible"—this is "the very definition of the *present*" according to Levinas.[83] To make this somewhat clearer we might add that the initial phase can be taken to be a real beginning only as a present which was never pregiven as future in any kind of expectation.

The "real" (*le réel*): it is by no means accidental that this word is put between quotation marks. The "real" is not talked about in the sense of an *ordinary realism.* Primal impression proves to be "primal source," "primal generation," or "primal creation" insofar as it gains significance and prevails *in opposition to* the "spontaneity" of the intentionality of consciousness constituting time. This "in opposition" does not only express a kind of contrast but a belonging together as well. What is real for us is real in consciousness. Husserl is right: the idea of a reality independent of consciousness is the product of a mere abstraction, or even of our forgetting about ourselves. Yet he is still not right: consciousness reveals a reality which prevails *in opposition to* the interplay of the intentions of consciousness, thwarting all expectations, countering all designs, "preceding and surprising the possible"; in consciousness—to put it in another way—such a reality gets organized which *declares its independence from consciousness in this very consciousness itself.* It is this that Levinas discovers when he distinguishes between the two elements of primal impression and the intentionality of consciousness already within the initial phase itself, yet without questioning their belonging together.

This way, we get a full picture of the diacritical method. It is only as difference or as *différance* within identity that the separation of primal impression and the intentionality of consciousness is capable of making the "notion of origin and of creation" directly "intelligible," Levinas claims.[84]

Yet why could Husserl not see the opposition between primal impression and the intentionality of consciousness? Levinas's answer to this question is that in Husserl the particular consciousness of the ever given phase of the present is immediately swept away by the interplay of intentionalities constituting time, and this way "we see the non-intentionality of the primal impression fitted back into the normal order"—unobserved.[85] In Levinas's treatment, the imperial nature of intentionality makes its appearance as something which is incessantly trying to hinder the creative power of primal impression aimed at a new beginning.

However, Husserl's analysis of time raised a question which is hard to answer if we only take Levinas as a point of reference. Is it possible that the *initial* nature of the present has an element which makes the Husserlian phenomenon of "living toward" (*Entgegenleben*) more explicable than the "impressional regard" (*impressionaler Blick*), with which Husserl himself was trying to interpret it? In Henry's expounding of Husserl's analyses of time, it is precisely this question which is put into new light; this is the strongest point of his interpretation.

That it is among the characteristics of life that it goes from the now toward the new now is considered by Henry to be the expression of "instinct" (*pulsion*).[86] Husserl—especially in a later phase of his life—would not take this as a misrepresentation. In the thirties he himself keeps referring to a kind of "universal instinct-intentionality" (*universale Triebintentionalität*) which, as he claims, "drives us on from the present concretely towards the present."[87] There are even thinkers who make the phenomenon of "living toward" central to their interpretation of time. Heidegger, who, in his understanding of time, tries to conceive of the past, the present, and the future as "raptures" (*Entrückungen*), as *ecstasies,* talks about *Drang* (urge) and *Schwung* (swing).[88] Merleau-Ponty anchors the interplay of *ecstasies* in a kind of *poussée,* a sort of "thrust."[89] Yet Henry keeps a distance from these interpretations from the start, since his main goal is to draw a sharp boundary between *pulsion* and all kinds of "ecstatic intentionalities."

In this, we may find traces of a kind of phenomenological dualism, which, instead of the Cartesian dualism of *consciousness* and *world,* is founded on the opposition between *life* and *world.* At a certain point, the late Husserl characterizes phenomenology as an experiment which is aimed at making "the world the phenomenon of life."[90] Henry hurls at this suggestion with a radicalism which could hardly be overdone. In opposition to Levinas, he builds his argumentation on the supposition that the relationship between the sensing and the sensed is not of an intentional nature, and therefore it does not contain "raptures," ecstatic distances. This enables him to oppose two modes of appearance: the self-manifestation of life in emotions on the one hand, which, in his interpretation, lacks all kinds of intentionalities, and the disclosure of the world on the other, which is always expressed in intentional ideas. Simultaneously, he distinguishes between two forms of the coming into being of that given which discloses before us (*donation*): the "self-revelation" of life and the "ecstatic manifestation" of the world. The two kinds of opposition are finally secured as the contrast between "immanence" and "transcendence."

This dualism explains why Henry, in his account on Husserl's lectures on time, is often simply taking a stand instead of giving a genuine interpretation. Yet we would not be fair with Henry if we did not notice that his arguments do not merely wish to explicate, to defend, or to take up the cause of the dualism of life and world, but their role includes the putting of this dualism *to the test* as well. The two above mentioned forms of the coming into being of the given, unfolding before us, meet in the present of the primal impression. Hence, this is the position which is to be explored, if one not only wishes to claim but also to prove that ecstatic intentionality is erected on the self-manifestation of life expressed in sensations and primal impressions.

Henry relies on a kind of diacritical method in his argumentation, too. He tries to disassemble the notion of "impressional regard" (*impressionaler Blick*), which he takes to be inherently equivocal, ambiguous, and, thus, ultimately, impossible. Yet the ultimate aim of taking the notion apart is also to show up its elements, in an original moment, in a unity. In this enterprise, the *initial* nature of the present will be the focus of his attention, too.

The idea Henry tries to work out in detail might be summarized as follows: the present, in its original sense is nothing else but *vie au présent,* (life in the present). Yet "life in the present" understood here is not something which would unfold as an earlier phase of the flow of experience in the various forms of posterior "re-memberings," i.e., in retention or in reflection. This life is *present* in the sense of the linguistic *present tense* as well. Henry takes—or even rips—out the element of the immediate *living through* from the flow of experience. Husserl is also aware of the possibility to distinguish between experience (*Erlebnis*) and experiencing in the sense of living through (*Erleben*), as well as subscribing to the view that the element of this experiencing or living through coincides with the sensing of the sensed. Yet—as it has been shown—he interprets the sensing of the sensed as the internal consciousness of experience and as an "absolute" consciousness of time.[91] Henry goes precisely further than Husserl in differentiating between the content of experience and the experiencing or living through. He even assigns a role to the "life in the present" which is similar to that of Descartes's *cogito.* One is tempted—for the sake of the analogy—to dare to talk about *vivo* (*I live*) here. A hyperbolic argument in the Cartesian vein further shows where this conception differs from the Husserlian enterprise which also keeps up with Descartes to a certain point: "life in the present"—i.e., *I live*—together with its instinct-laden contents of sensation, remains totally untouched, while we imagine that our life when we are awake turns into a dream life, or into a life where an evil spirit of supreme power and cunning is constantly deceiving us.[92] The certainty which might be assigned to the *vivo*—in contrast with the *cogito*—is but the certainty of life, not the certainty of the representation of the world.

This idea puts a strong, yet by no means broad *notion of reality* at Henry's disposal. This reality is nothing else but "life in the present," the living through of the moment. The evidential nature of the *vivo* lends some plausibility to the claim "that not a morsel of this reality does find its way into retention."[93] If this is true, Henry has won the argument against Husserl: to unmask the Husserlian "homogenous, real and concrete" flow of consciousness as a mere illusion is just one further step away.[94]

Henry attributes great importance to the fact that retentional intentionality can be characterized by a dual motion: on the one hand, it keeps distancing itself from the primal impressions whose modified shapes it retains; on the other hand, it is constantly streaming back to the newly emerging primal impressions only to drift them along into the past. This constant streaming back to the present is characterized by Henry as the single source of the reality content in the consciousness of time.[95]

Henry relies on this streaming back also when he tries to separate the primal impression given in the moment of the at all times prevailing present from the intentionality of consciousness; he achieves this by giving, in the form of an opposition, the following corresponding shapes to the above notions: primal impression becomes instinct-laden sensation while intentionality of consciousness appears as the "ecstatic glimpse at the now." It seems, of course, legitimate to ask, if, in the guise of the above opposition, it is not the Husserlian pair of "temporal material" *versus* "impression of temporal position" which makes its reappearance. Yet it is plausible to argue that under this interpretation we would deprive the notional pair of "instinct-laden sense" in opposition with "ecstatic glimpse at the now" from its genuine meaning. We may confidentially claim that Henry takes the Husserlian "temporal material"–"impression of temporal position" pair as a *point of departure* but it would be wrong to suggest that he would *rest satisfied with it,* especially because Henry does not attribute an *impressional* quality to the impression of time positions; he assigns an ecstatic nature to it, he interprets it as a "glimpse at the now," and thus he takes it as belonging to the "ecstatic form of the flow." But the opposition between the "form" and "content" of the flow of time will not satisfy him, either. What Husserl called "temporal material" and considered to be the "content" of the time flow is, for Henry, something in which the movement of life itself might be grasped. We may get an insight into the opposite of this movement if we now exclusively concentrate on the process in which retentional intentionality is constantly streaming back to the always renewing primal impression. In a "material phenomenology"—as Henry himself calls his enterprise—the task at this point will be to disentangle, from the "ecstatic form," the "content" of the Husserlian time flow, in which Husserl did not see more than *hyle* belonging to *morphe;* and, further, to recognize such a *power* in it which makes ecstasy, the rapture—and, thus, even temporality itself—possible at all.[96] In this task we may legitimately see a complete program of a diacritical method.

Yet to put a question mark at the end of this program seems to be legitimate, too, especially if we consider that Henry is also evoking the "eternal present of life,"[97] writing the word *Vie* even with a capital letter. With this gesture, it seems, the cover of "material phenomenology" is ripped up and the metaphysics of the present slowly comes to the fore, even if, in this case, this metaphysics is not carried by an "ecstatic glimpse" but by a sensation which has no hope of clearing up, and which is completely dumb in itself. Expressions such as "life experiences, discloses, reveals" or even "senses itself" are by far less self-evident or self-explanatory than the "*vivo,*" the "*I live*" uttered in the present. In fact, it is *evident* that it is only I who can live my life, and that it is only the life of my *own* which I am able to live.[98] Life cannot live *itself.*

These observations indicate that concerning these problems Henry's material phenomenology cannot be the final word. Thus, attempts of any kind wishing to return to the Husserlian "impressional regard" or to his "universal instinct-intentionality" are—at least in principle—totally legitimate. This, of course, is not to mean that in the form of Husserlian instinct intentionalities—or even in an opposing shape—the problem of "instinct vicissitudes," perhaps taken in a Freudian sense as well, could not be usefully addressed.[99]

Under both interpretations we followed above, the ever given present—by virtue of its quality of being a *beginning,* of being *initial*—proves to be loaded with indications which do not fit into the order of intentionalities of consciousness constituting time. Concerning primal intention, Levinas reads the traces of an otherwise inaccessible origin, while Henry identifies the signs of a hidden, yet vigorously operating instinct. By way of a conclusion, it has to be asked whether—beyond the traces and the signs—there is still an indication concealed in primal impression, simply as a consequence of its coming into being as something *alien to* consciousness, and gaining significance *in opposition to* the spontaneity of this consciousness.

Even if such an indication might be talked about, it cannot be taken as an unambiguous and fully developed relation of meaning. Primal impression does not disclose its origin as being alien to consciousness; it does not refer to something other than itself; it does not become a sign, a picture, or expression of anything; it does not report on any being from which it would be different; it does not bring news about the natural processes it owes its existence. This is exactly why Husserl talks about "primal generation," which "has no seed."[100] Still, primal impression, coming into being as alien to consciousness, clearly gets disentangled from consciousness and thereby, as Levinas said, it "precedes and surprises the possible," it thwarts all expectations, it counters all designs, and thus it alters the picture of reality previously believed to be valid. So even the mere fact of shift and separation indicates the collapse of senses assumed and of meanings conjectured, yet shift and separation also point toward the emergence of a new sense. Thus, the indication discernible from primal impression is not a fully developed meaning, not a fully blown sense; still, it is a commencement which can become a point of origin for senses slowly assuming shape. If the borrowing of a term is allowed from Merleau-Ponty and from Marc Richir, we might say that the becoming of primal impression as something alien to consciousness might be considered as a process which is always already a formation of sense in a germinal shape—or, it is the formation of meaning in "the savage state."[101]

II. The Temporality of a Radical Turn in Life-History

Early phenomenology did not know about any other mode of sense formation than the one ultimately enhancing self-identity. This applies to Husserl, who considers life-history as "self-constitution," just as much as to Heidegger, where destiny interpreted as Dasein's historicality gets defined as "authentic being-one's-self." Taking our hindsight now from the transformation of phenomenology, it may be suggested that the above conceptions could only ensue because in the early period the difference between *sense formation* and *sense fixation* was not yet clear in its full significance.

If this sounds plausible, we have to face a new task, emerging now with clear outlines. Observing the structure of life-history in the first study of this book, an attempt was made at separating the processes of spontaneous sense formation emerging by themselves from narrative sense fixation, recognizing the main source of our self-identity in the latter. It was also pointed out that sense emerging by itself (self-induced sense), in its unavailability for our ownership, takes a course of its own: after it has emerged, creating a new beginning, it is retained and pushed to the fringes again, then once more coming to the fore in a new shape, but still identifiable. Yet this peculiar ability of ungovernable sense to sustain itself—which might as well be interpreted as a special kind of *self-identity*—has not yet properly been distinguished from the *self-identity of our own.* In what follows, this will be our main concern. The difference will be accentuated through *temporal analyses.* We shall be guided by Richir, who, in his *Phenomenological Meditations,* opposes the respective concepts of *ipséité du sens* and *ipséité du soi-même,* too. [102]

1. The Concept of a Radical Turn in Life-History

The emergence of a new sense might be interpreted as an *event* which, within life-history, takes place in the realm of the already mentioned *no-man's-land.* As it was discussed, the narrative fixation of self-identity is based on a "diacritical system" of sense formations grasped and pushed aside; this system, because we can neither possess nor govern it, may never totally be considered as our own, despite the fact that it is, after all, a part of our life-history. We may conclude that our life-history contains elements where it is *alien to itself;* these elements mark out the boundaries of the *no-man's-land* which serves as the scenario of the processes of sense formations emerging by themselves.

Birth, origin, an inherited tradition: these are all facts we are not in a position to alter. Yet these by no means are responsible for initiating what is alien to our self in our life-history, as these fundamental facts precede all the beginnings from which we might claim a lively or vivid reality of experience for our life-history; this implies that these facts are passed down to us in the words of others, i.e., always in more or less ready-made interpretations. There is, however, a common trait in these interpretations: they carry sense fixations which make the above facts appear as the most specific elements pertaining to our self-identity.

Thus, it should rather be claimed that alterity and strangeness in life-history begins to take shape only at points where senses emerging by themselves create in it a *new beginning.* Sense vibrations thwarting our expectations modify the ratio of senses grasped and senses pushed aside, and they shake the sense fixations defining our ever given self-identity. In the flow of our life-history, islands of alterity and strangeness start to cohere. This is not to mean that the basic facts of our life-history *before* all beginnings would totally be bereft of some alien material. Yet this becomes clear retrospectively as well—only *after* sense formations have created a *new* beginning.

a. Senses and Times—in the Plural

The later Husserl comes up with a thesis which might have a larger implication than originally intended. With respect to the intersubjective community of "cosubjects" he says: *The plural precedes the singular.* This interesting insight, it seems, could also be used in a larger context. The qualification *pluralia tantum* (*tantum plurale*) may, for example, be just as readily applied to the events of life-history as to the words of a language. A "single" word in language is no word, and this statement seems to be valid with respect to all diacritical systems held together by the systemic differences of its elements. Once the events of life-history are interpreted as a kind of diacritical system, Husserl's above thesis is applicable to them, too: as a consequence of the changing ratio of senses grasped and senses brushed aside in life-history, every event becomes pregnant with a surplus of meaning and thus in itself becomes a rich resource of a legion of further events.

Yet is Husserl's highly original insight really applicable to the *temporal structure* of life-history? Can we indeed say that sense emerging by itself possesses, in each case, a *time of its own,* and Husserl's warning: *always in the plural,* is pertinent with respect to time as well? If the answer is in the affirmative, then *the* time of a certain life-history in the singular already refers to *times peculiar to each event,* to the *times* events have as their own—it is in these times that senses emerge by themselves.

The above hypothesis is corroborated by the fact that all attempts, even the most impressive ones, trying to argue to the contrary have failed one after the other. Husserl derived the original unity of life time from the "continuous modification of primal impression," while Heidegger tried to grasp the "embracing together" for original temporality in a "fateful destiny in history," in a "fate-like historicality." In the past few decades, however, these interpretations have been seriously contested. It might, therefore, be claimed that it is not only time as a sequence of *nows* which may be considered as the product of sense fixation, but that time "in-itself," always already taken as a unity, might be understood as such a product as well, where sense fixation, for unity's sake, prunes off the ramifying sprouts of the self-emerging senses, or—less metaphorically—where the inception of divergent and deviant senses is heavily checked, or even smothered. How does, then, the wholeness of time in life-history come about? Is it possible that it is produced at the expense of an enforced unification, in which the times peculiar to each event and giving rise to self-emerging senses are sacrificed, are covered up, or buried, or at least forced "underground"?

If we take the risk of giving a positive answer to the above questions, then we enter a brand new, and at the same time immensely large territory of phenomenological investigation. *Sense formation* and *sense fixation* are terms used here in a positively comprehensive sense. Wherever something is taken *as* something (*this* as *that*), i.e., wherever something which is in reality complex, manifold, disparate and even, upon individual consideration, is of a different kind than another, counts, from a certain point of view, as the *same* as the other (*as being identical with* the other), we may witness to the emergence and the fixation of sense, making sense approachable, available, and even graspable. If we assign to the word *sense* such a broad meaning, then it will not only be linguistic and facial expressions, gestures and postures which carry sense but happenings, series of events, and even certain arrangements of objects as well. At the same time, and by exactly the same token, however, it will also be necessary to question or, at least, to problematize, precisely on the basis of the by-themselves emerging sense formations, the seemingly self-evidential nature of the process whereby sense fixation lends *identity*—or perhaps even *self-identity*—to that which is in itself manifold, complex, disparate, or even of a different kind. This is not at all to provide a foundation or a justification for the apparently evidential nature of this process; what should precisely turn out is that such a process, under a one-sided account, is unfounded and unjustifiable. It should be shown that there is a chasm between sense formation and sense fixation, a chasm seemingly covered up by the apparently self-evidential nature of sense fixation. This suspension of sense fixations, which lays the chasm bare, rightfully deserves the name of *epoché*. However, this fundamental phenomenological operation here bears the marks of *criticism,* and even of *subversion.* And if it might still be maintained that the processes of by-themselves emerging sense formations have a time of their own, that they have a time *peculiar* to themselves, then the so-called *phenomenological field*—comprising investigations directed at sense, self-identity, time, and the like—will receive a totally new arrangement. Here the tribute of reorganizing the vast territory of phenomenology and opening new vistas go undeniably to Marc Richir. With an overt reference to the Kantian sublime, he uses the expression *sublime phénoménologique* to describe the scenario the by-themselves emerging sense formations create after the suspension of sense fixations. In his analysis, the vibrations of sense, lacking, in this scenario, any kind of delimitation, enduring shape or unshakable determination, yet at the same time displaying a constant surplus, almost a kind of proliferation, create such a boundless and unending multitude which may rightfully be referred to with a word of a grand tradition: *apeiron.*[103]

A full account of Richir's undertaking cannot be given here—what is rather attempted is finding a way to this newly organized phenomenological field on the basis of the previous questions. If we now put the ambiguous concept of life-history into focus, we will necessarily concentrate on the sense fixations to which we owe our self-identity, disregarding for the time being those sense fixations which lend an objective sameness or identity to the manifold of senses emerging by themselves. This is by no means the only route to the phenomenological field. To be sure, early phenomenology would have favored this approach because—as a continuation of the tradition of transcendental philosophy—it presupposed that ultimately all objective identities are dependent on the self-identity of our own. This supposition, however, is no longer binding for us. If a transformed and renewed phenomenology may still appreciate something in our approach, then it is surely not because we take our point of departure from what is our *own.* There are, indeed, a few suggestions—to be found, admittedly, more in the thought of Levinas than in that of Richir—implying that the road to the *alien* is through what is our *own.* And if this is true, then even a transformed and renewed phenomenology may favor an approach taking its point of departure from the problem of self-identity—even if it is chosen for reasons other than those of early phenomenology.

b. The Concept of a Destinal Event in Life-History

The diacritical method—as it was demonstrated—allows us to peel all those layers of meaning off the notion of destiny which have shown it in an unfavorable, or even dubious, light enabling us to go to its core and to grasp it. This is how we arrived at the concept of *a radical turn in life-history,* which we took as referring to a critical situation, a decisive incidence, a "fateful" or "destinal" event in life-history. This concept can be more precisely circumscribed as follows: the expression of a *radical turn* or *destinal event* in life-history designates a *sense formation* which *starts by itself, takes place without any control,* as if it happened "*underground,*" *creating,* simultaneously, *a new beginning* in life-history.

Should we say that every destinal—or even "fateful"—event is fatal? Not at all. Even the inverse of the above thesis is invalid: a fatal event will only become a destinal event if it is not simply met but it strikes someone down in his or her alleged self-identity.

Thus, it is clear that there is an important connection between destinality and self-identity. Yet the two concepts by no means coincide. The connection is rather ensured by the fact that every destinal event gives rise to a new meaning which is, in the beginning, totally *alien to the self,* and which we try to grasp—with more or less success—and to make, once again, *our own* through fixing our self-identities anew. This connection may serve as an excuse for identifying destiny and self-identity, yet it by no means provides a basis to equate the two. No newly emerging sense, prompting us to correct our stories about ourselves, would be available for us if there were no events when we *find ourselves face-to-face, or even at odds, with ourselves.* If our self were not always already the "self of contradictions"—as the later Husserl liked to say—we would never encounter and counter destinal events. These considerations seem to indicate that the concept of a *destinal event* and the concept of a *split of the self* mutually presuppose each other.

c. The Temporal Structure of Destinal Events

Time can get organized in as many ways as in which senses may emerge. This rather aphoristic statement—even serving as a summary of our previous investigations—is in need of further clarification. It should by no means be contended that this thesis excludes all descriptions with a general validity. What it demands is that in the course of our discussion we keep in mind the correspondences between the various kinds of sense formation and the several ways in which time gets organized, i.e., that we observe a *correlative typology.* Here that mode of time organization will be accounted for which is typical of the sense formation characteristic of a destinal event.

Let us accentuate, once more, the traits this concept comprises. It was stated that by a destinal event we mean a sense formation which *gets started by itself, it takes place "underground," in an uncontrollable, ungovernable way, creating a new beginning in the history of life.* It should be added that sense formation creates a new beginning in life-history by *shaking* (or even shattering, quaking) *the dominant sense fixations which carry our self-identity,* thereby giving rise to *a split in the self,* while simultaneously, it makes a *new sense* available, which in turn will make it possible *to anchor self-identity anew.* The question is what kind of time structure is presupposed by this definition.

Since Merleau-Ponty and Levinas, a peculiar expression has become the vogue in French phenomenology: *a past which has never been present.* The circumscription of the temporal structure of a destinal event will be attempted—with certain modifications—with reference to this expression. It will be claimed that the concept of a destinal event refers to a *present* that *has never been future.*

In what follows, everything will depend on the correct interpretation of the above claim. As a first step it might be recalled that every destinal event thwarts our previous expectations; destinal events create—to use one of Husserl's typical locutions—"a disappointing experience," or—to quote Levinas—they make us face a reality "which precedes and surprises the possible." As a further step, an attempt will be made to derive the temporal structure of the experience of reality from the conflict between two different modes in which time may get organized.

Whenever a new sense becomes, all of a sudden, available for us, we usually discover in ourselves, in retrospect, some presentiments—or inklings—which foreshadowed or foreboded, in various ways, the events to ensue, yet without *anticipating* them in the modes of real expectations. These presentiments may be taken as sense vibrations *pushed aside* by the actual expectations before they may have taken a proper shape. This is why presentiments can only be grasped in their *postvibrations*—or in their *reminiscences.* It is precisely from the point of view of their postvibrations that they might be characterized as presentiments: *pre*sentiments which were never given the chance of becoming *sentiments* in the proper sense of the word.[104]

Here we may track down the traces of a time organized retrospectively, in *retroactive constitution.* This is precisely because the meaning of *pre* in the word *presentiment* can only be grasped by taking our point of departure from the meaning of *post* in the word *postvibrations.* This makes us conclude that the prefix *pre* does not refer to a bygone, actual present which has now become the past but to a *past* which *has never been present.*

The same peculiarity is detectable with respect to the *post* in *postvibration.* This *post* does not refer to a present which, in the moment of the appearance of the new sense, would still belong to the future but rather to that *future* which will *never be present* because when it commences it will not bring something along which is still—or already—imminent or *forth*coming but only something which will retrospectively prove to have preceded even the present moment. For this reason, *this* future will *never become present* without *having become past already.*

The time which gets organized here is one that is *absent* and nothing more; it does not offer anything which would be *present.* No wonder then, that this mode of the organization of time—of temporalization—can never be found independently: it only exits as the inverse of the time spent in the expectations which are thwarted by destinal events.

The time spent in expectations is well known. Instead of a *retrospective* organization, this time rather shows a *progressive* structure: *expectations project into the future what we retain from the past in the present moment.* Yet this mode of the organization of time has the quality of the *temporary* and the *momentary* (in the sense of the "provisional") as well because our expectations are contested, again and again, by our experiences of reality.

The reality which appears in these experiences as something "preceding and surprising the possible" fits into a system of correlations which organizes time retrospectively and in which the presentiments pushed aside become available in their postvibrations. Yet the *progressive* organization of the times of the momentarily dominant expectations is halted by the newly arising sense. The time of the reality which becomes available as a destinal event thus gets unfolded along the lines of the *conflict* between the two contrary modes in which here time is organized: it emerges as the clash between the *retrospective* and the *progressive* temporalization. Consequently, this reality appears as a *present* which *has never been future,* since only after this reality has commenced and has thwarted the previous expectations do the expectations start to take any shape at all—those expectations which are able to harmonize with it. These newly arising expectations, which feed on the presentiments made available in postvibrations, show a progressive organization of time again, yet they do not enter into a conflict with the retrospective organization of time any longer.

2. *Ipseity* as Self-Identity and *Ipseity* as Sense Formation

If the phenomenological field is approached through the investigation of the ambiguous concept of life-history, we may first and foremost catch sight of sense formations emerging by themselves, thwarting, *time* after *time,* our expectations and creating, again and again, a new beginning in the history of life. We might say that the destinal events "make their way" in the phenomenological field, which results in an intricate network of routes. Yet we may also witness to the attempts sense fixations make at the restitution, the recapturing, or even the recreation of self-identity. These attempts have rationale in the fact that destinal events repeatedly bring about a split in the self. The relationship between sense formation and sense fixation is not only one of constant conflicts but of mutual interdependence as well. The new beginnings, created in life-history by the processes of sense formations emerging by themselves, do not only demand a new fixation of self-identity but make it precisely possible by carrying a new sense in themselves. But they are also very much in need of the attempts of sense fixations because the emerging senses, still in their nascent, rudimentary form do not take an exact or definite shape and lack an enduring determination. The inseparability of sense formation and sense fixation is just as important and characteristic of their relationship as their opposition.

Those simply following in the footsteps of *dialectical* thinking could even rest satisfied with the strategies outlined above. The *diacritical* method, however, cannot be content with simply ascertaining the mutual interdependence of the elements in conflict with one another. However challenging and paradoxical this idea may sound, it is still too *orderly* not to obscure the fundamental fact that the newly emerging sense does not, even in the shape of self-identity, get *completely* dissolved, but to a large extent escapes the scope of sense fixation which was to hold it in its grip. But it does not disappear completely, either; it rather shrinks back and closes up itself to make its comeback later, from obscurity. Yet the most significant in this description seems to be that in the meantime it still keeps its identifiableness, i.e., its *identity with itself.* How should we, then, give an account of this special kind of self-sustenance, in the process of our analysis of the temporal structure of sense emerging by itself?

a. The Time of Self-Sustaining and Unfolding Sense

One of the most significant characteristics of newly emerging sense is its lack of a firm determination, i.e., its *undecidedness.* This is the result of the feature which was distinguished as the characteristic "initiality" (nascent, rudimentary nature) detectable in the new sense. This "initiality" refers to a state in which the respective systems of senses grasped and pushed aside are just in the process of transformation. The final outcome of this transformation, in the moment of change, is still undecided.

Once the transformation is accomplished, the dissemination of senses grasped and pushed aside usually take a respective permanent shape for a while. This congealment has to do with our attributing—or lending—a more or less permanent determination to the newly emerging sense, thereby depriving it from its initiality, just as much as of its undecidedness, which go hand in hand. It seems, however, obvious that sense fixations like that cannot be carried out without the pushing aside of certain sense arousals. These pushed aside sense arousals do not cease to exist but remain the latent carriers of the newly grasped sense.

What should we, then, mean by the claim that the sense newly emerging and creating a new beginning in life-history is retained and does not lose its identifiableness? By no means an enduring permanence or a preservation without modification. What should rather be meant here is a self-identity, which—somewhat similarly to the self-identity of our own—is retained amidst changes, or even among tribulations. The Husserlian model of "continuous modification" is hardly capable of grasping this peculiar mode of self-sustainment. Thus, an entirely new model will be tried, which, along the Richirean line of argumentation, will cohere around the idea of the "original deformation" of time.

Richir—like Husserl—does make mention of retentions and protentions. Yet the interpretation Richir gives of the present to which these retentions and protentions refer, and which even give the ingredients of this present, differs radically from that of Husserl's. Richir discards the all too abstract notion of the now-moment of primal impression and rather takes the present to be an *extended phase* which fits into the time belonging to the emergence of sense precisely in the process of emergence. Richir characterizes this phase of the present with a notion reminiscent of the later Merleau-Ponty: he talks about the *chiasmus* of retentions and protentions. This notion is meant to communicate that what we retain from the past in the present moment, and what we expect from, or intend to do in, the future are in a complex way intertwined in the given moment of a just emerging sense formation. From this intertwinement, the Husserlian model of continuous modification cannot grasp too much. It is not enough to say that our expectations are fed on what we retain from the past in the present. Richir, in a highly refined analysis, shows that the word *expectation* conceals the tension which is between the "exigency" (*exigence*) of the past and the "promise" (*promesse*) of the future. In the exigency, retentions and protentions are connected in a way that the latter adjusts to the former, while the promise of the future rests satisfied with the most meager foothold the retained past is able to provide. Thus, in every moment in time, two radically different connections are established between retentions and protentions, which at the same time create a *chiasmus,* either in a crisscross or in an intertwined fashion.

This conception may be considered significant also because in the case of the self-emerging sense formation, there is always a "divergence," an "alterity"—*écart*—between exigency and promise. A sense which further emerges by itself—we may say with Richir—"proceeds both quicker and slower than itself": quicker, to keep its promise, and slower, in order to measure itself to the exigency again and again.[105] Consequently, in the ever changing phase of the present, retentions and protentions keep losing their equilibrium. This *porte-à-faux en mouvement*—as Richir calls it in the French original—makes, at the same time, the notion of the "original distortion" (*distortion originare*) of time explicable as well.[106] The latter French expression may evoke the following images: *the thread of time gets crooked and twisted;* or, somewhat reminiscent of Shakespeare's *Hamlet: the present (time) is out of joint* (act 1, scene 5, line 196), but in English the *warp of time* is also revealing to illustrate Richir's point.

The phase of the present thus proves to be a rupture on the curve of time. Thus, the Husserlian model of "continuous modification" is the last one to be applied to it; Richir's analysis is closer to Heidegger's "ecstatic-horizontal" conception of time. Yet upon a closer examination, there are fundamental differences here, too, which are to unfold in the ensuing account.

What has been so far accounted for may only be taken as the first step in a more comprehensive line of thought. Upon further analysis, a halo of *proto-retentions* and *proto-protentions* will emerge around the kernel composed by retentions and protentions. These expressions refer to the *empty horizons* surrounding the past retained and the future expected or hoped for, which are not products of a mere abstraction but rather gain phenomenological concreteness in the presentiments (premonitions, *prémonitions*) and in the postvibrations (reminiscences, *réminiscences*). These notions have already been touched upon in another context; the premonitions and reminiscences—though somewhat in a different shape than in the above analyses—evoke a *past* in Richir's interpretation which *has never been present,* and point toward a *future,* which *will never be present.* How the interplay of proto-retentions and proto-protentions gets connected with the intertwined retentions and protentions receives a very thorough and complex analysis in the *Phenomenological Meditations,* yet this cannot be pursued here. Our present goals do not require more than the accentuation of the most significant purport of Richir's investigations; he shows how the initial arousals of sense (the *amorces de sens*) pushed aside by some fixations of sense influence the structuring of the time of grasped sense. It becomes obvious that the ever given phase of the present contains the multitude of various kinds of sense formations and a corresponding host of different modes of time structures accompanying them. As opposed to Heidegger, however, who, even in his later work, confirms the idea of "original time," Richir's interpretation of time endorses Merleau-Ponty's tenet: the original is in splinters, it has broken up—*l'originaire éclate.*[107]

It should, nevertheless, be pointed out that in this conception the idea of the *new beginning* remains too much in the background. Therefore, Richir's considerations have to be completed. The references to a past which has never been present and to a future that will never be present have satisfactorily been shown; still, the analysis of the present phase will never be complete unless we simultaneously grasp the present which has never been future, coming to the fore with the force of a destinal event.

This will sound more plausible under the following considerations. The *exigency* of the past projects the future as a direct continuation of what has happened so far. Yet whatever may be planned, reckoned with, expected, or hoped for, it is always clear for us that the future *may thwart* all, or any of these. This does not change the fact that our expectations are fed on what we retain from the past in the present; yet we are not even able to imagine a future which would be incapable of *contradicting* our expectations.[108] If this possibility was not taken into account, the very *promises* the future is pregnant with would also be invalidated. So if the structure of time is really determined by the intertwinement of the exigency of the past and the promise of the future, as it is claimed by Richir, then it is also to be added that into these two threads a third is woven, too: *our conviction that, in any moment, reality may rip up the this way created texture.* This conviction makes room, in every moment, for a *present that has never been future* because it has taken neither the shape of the exigency of the past, nor the form of the promise of the future. It is obvious that in any moment we may be forced to withdraw altogether what we envisaged as the exigency of the past and as the promise of the future; yet we cannot know in advance how this is exactly going to happen. The above conviction is thus not more than an *empty horizon* enveloping the exigency of the past and the promise of the future. Yet when a destinal event does take place, this empty horizon will be rich in premonitions which can be grasped in their reminiscences.

b. The Emergence and Fixation of Self-Identity

Is it possible to claim that every phase of the present is a present which has never been future? In principle, nothing seems to contradict it. Yet it still may sound astounding, especially because we very well know that not every event would prompt us to correct the narratives fixing our self-identity.

It is not to be forgotten, however, that in the correction of previously accepted narratives two factors are in conflict: a sense formation in the making, and a sense fixation which, in the history of life, always counts as the simultaneous fixation of self-identity as well. Whether a given event becomes a destinal event or not will precisely depend on the relationship between these two factors. Even a shipwrecked sense fixation is considerably able to oppose a new, a strange, an alien sense formation. The breakthrough can only be made by a sense formation which contains the necessary amount of *difference* to frustrate all attempts at *appropriation* and *acquisition.* The process must "cross the threshold," as it were, to make its effect.

It seems very likely that the sense emerging by itself keeps its identity with itself even before approaching this "threshold." This ability of self-sustainment, must not, however, be associated with identities pertaining to things or objects, since the sense emerging by itself does not possess a permanent kernel which would remain the same amidst all changes. In its modifications, it might not retain more than the *route* it has taken during its transformations. This route can be accounted for in the form of a coherent, unified narrative. This is exactly why the mode the by-itself emerging sense retains its identifiableness and resembles, in so many ways, how our own self-identity is sustained. Yet the decisive difference should not be neglected, either: it can be grasped in, and understood through, the *original deformation* which dislocates the time of the by-itself emerging sense from the frame of the coherent and unified time of life-history. The coherent time of life-history cannot be separated from the fixation of our self-identity. Thus we must say that the formation of the self-identity of the self-emerging sense can only take the route of its own—there is no way to interpret the coherence of the story telling us about the various stages of this separate route as the imprint of the self-identity of our own. Thus it is obvious that no equal sign is to be put between the self-identity of the by-itself emerging sense and the self-identity of our own.

The question undertaken to be clarified at the beginning of this chapter has thus been answered. However, a further question naturally arises, which now has to be dealt with by way of a worthy conclusion: in what way are the self-identity of the by-itself emerging sense, and the self-identity of our own, *connected?*

Our point of departure may be an idea of Merleau-Ponty's which was mentioned in the previous discussion: it was in connection with this idea that it was possible to claim that diacritical phenomenology cannot rest satisfied with the description of the respective systems of senses grasped and senses pushed aside, but must also clarify *how we find ourselves always already set upon this diacritical system.* If we choose this approach, we may distinguish between *the formation* and *the fixation of our self-identity,* with the additional realization that *the formation of our self-identity finds its primary source in the self-identity of the sense emerging by itself.*

To account for this connection, three concepts will have to be introduced. These concepts are the following: *initiative, undertaking,* and *adventure.* They might be briefly characterized as follows:

1. When, in our life-history, a new sense makes its appearance, we are prompted to alter the dissemination of senses grasped and senses pushed aside. This attempt will here be called *initiative.* That we find ourselves included in a diacritical system of always both grasped and pushed-aside senses becomes clear for us—or at least dawns on us—when we are first prompted to take such an initiative.

2. The initiative gets revealed in a sense formation which simultaneously also means the fixation of self-identity in life-history. Yet the modification of the dissemination of senses grasped and senses pushed aside becomes, at the same time, the starting point of a sense formation emerging by itself. This sense formation does not only become the basis and the frame of the fixation of self-identity but gets connected to it as a part of a unified process as well. This unified process can be named *undertaking.*
3. The fixation of self-identity in a specific sense, as it gets connected with sense formation emerging by itself: this might be understood as the *formation of self-identity.* The formation of self-identity always fits into the framework of undertakings. Each undertaking refers back to an initiative which brought about a modification in the dissemination of senses grasped and senses pushed aside. Though we take such an initiative as a sign of our freedom, we may bring about processes which often break out of the sphere of actions under our control, and become unmanageable. Therefore, each undertaking is an adventure. It is not only the adventure of our self-identity but, at the same time, the adventure of the sense as well: *aventure du sens.*

3. The Question of Wild and Alien Alterity

Destinal events, radical turns in life-history, as it has been demonstrated, have to do with uncontrollable, underground, and by themselves emerging sense formations which resist all attempts at their appropriation or acquisition. Consequently, *alterity,* or even *strangeness,* leaves more and more traces in our life-history.

Could it be claimed that it is precisely these traces of what is alien to the self which pave our way toward the otherness, the alterity of the other? It seems plausible, indeed, that the bridge between self-identity and otherness or alterity is built by the very processes of uncontrollable and unmanageable sense formations, taking place in the *no-man's-land.* Yet the presuppositions behind this suggestion are to be accounted for as well.

It is easy to see that the above supposition is built on the hypothesis that our encounter with the other, taking place at the crossroads of two life-histories, is double-faced, yet can also be understood as an *event which may ultimately receive a unified interpretation.* This is to say that the encounter obviously has a different sense in both respective life-histories. That a *unified* interpretation can still be given of this event is dependent on the question whether the two senses, contrary to all their differences, will fit into the frame of the *self-same* diacritical system of senses grasped and senses pushed aside. Yet this is far from being obvious. It is highly questionable whether the no-man's-land which we find in our life-history can get connected to, and will ever get unified with, the no-man's-land the other discovers in his or her own life-history. This difficulty marks the point in which approaches depart in today's phenomenology.

An answer in the affirmative to the above questions may be read out from the investigations Merleau-Ponty devotes to intercorporality, characterizable as original anonymity. An answer in the negative emerges, however, when the relationship between ourselves and the other is interpreted by Levinas.

It is hard to take a firm and unambiguous stand with respect to these problems. That much, however, seems to be clear: Levinas's position is built on the insight that the encounter with the other in our life-history gives rise to a peculiar kind of sense formation which cannot find room within the framework of the formation of our self-identity: it does not get started upon an initiative of our own, it often demands the suspension of our undertakings, and it results in a split of the self which can no longer be interpreted as a mere adventure of our self-identity. It is precisely here that the exceptional quality of the encounter, including its unique ethical significance, comes to the fore.

3

Self-Identity and the Experience of Alterity

A burden of longeval tradition lies on the notions of the *same* and the *other.* Since Plato's doctrine of the "great kinds," it has been repeatedly attempted to penetrate the obscure region to which these notions belong. Advances on new paths have recently been made toward this region in contemporary French philosophy.[1] Some of these fresh undertakings lend themselves to consideration especially if a proper access to the experience of alterity in life-history is sought for.

We may take as an appropriate starting point for our investigations Paul Ricoeur's interpretation of self-identity in its interdependence with alterity. This interpretation is opposed in *Oneself as Another* to Edmund Husserl's endeavor to understand the other than self as a modified self, as well as to Levinas's attempt to show that the self is nothing without the other than self. It remains to be seen to what extent this double opposition is justifiable.

In order to decide this question, it is necessary to consider, first, Husserl's view of the relationship of what is one's own and what is alien to oneself. This view may, second, be confronted with Maurice Merleau-Ponty's conception of a wild alterity. Third, the radical turn Emmanuel Levinas gives to the notions of the *same* and the *other* has to be dealt with in depth. It should become clear how this radical turn finds its emblematic expression in the Levinasian characterization of the subject's self as "the Other within the Same."

The main goal of these investigations is to show how the experience of a radical alterity is to be integrated into the picture we have been trying to form of the relationship between self-identity and life-history. The importance of a contrast between "proper" and "alien" alterity, as well as the significance of a distinction between "wild" and "alien" alterity for this purpose will emerge in the course of the following considerations.

1. Narrative Identity and Alterity

Ricoeur bases his distinction between the identity in the sense of *idem* and in the sense of *ipse* or, to put it in a simpler way, between the *same* and the *self,* on a special kind of self-understanding. In contrast with Cartesianism, he does not fall back upon an immediately available—and supposedly indubitable—certainty. On the contrary, he holds—using a term borrowed from Martin Heidegger—that no certainty of the self is to be reached without having recourse to *attestation.* Attestation, however, does not cease, as he adds, to be haunted by doubt and tormented by suspicion.[2] That is why, relying this time even more on Nietzsche than on Freud, he radicalizes his earlier expression of a "wounded" *cogito,*[3] evoking now no less than a *cogito brisé,* a "shattered *cogito.*"[4]

Although Ricoeur does not intend to contest the subject's capacity of reflecting upon itself, he can clearly see the difficulties which have been raised by the philosophies of reflection. He takes inspiration from analytic philosophy in order to overcome these difficulties. He enters into a debate with P. F. Strawson, Donald Davidson, and Derek Parfit because, through this confrontation, he expects to be able to give a "*realist* twist" to the comprehension of the self.[5] However, he by no means wants to question the indispensability of reflection. On the contrary, what he aims at in his long debate with analytic philosophy is nothing else than the elaboration of a reliable argument for the indispensability of reflection. This endeavor takes shape in a formula that may remind us of Merleau-Ponty: a "*chiasm* between reflection and analysis" is envisaged.[6] This formula alludes to a far-reaching enterprise which is properly designated as a "phenomenological hermeneutic of the self."[7]

In contrast with analytic philosophy, Ricoeur does not set himself the task of exploring personal identity from an external perspective. Neither does he try to expound a criteriology showing how to decide, in dubious cases, the question of people's personal identity. He commits himself to an internal perspective in his interpretation of self-identity. He relies, therefore, upon a certain kind of self-understanding. But the kind of self-understanding which he finds dependable cannot be taken as a foundation for a philosophy of reflection (in the sense of a respectable but somewhat obsolete tradition of French philosophy, going back to Maine de Biran, and reaching down to Jean Nabert). The assumption of a shattered *cogito* calls for a *hermeneutic* approach.

This approach must be on its guard against everything which might obfuscate the distinction between sameness and self-identity. However, every kind of comparative identification is apt to conjure up this danger. The substantial identity of things is regularly settled by a comparison between the different states of one and the same entity. This is not quite true of self-identity: it is not necessary for me to compare my past I with my present I in order to recognize myself in it. Comparative identification is, therefore, not the proper way to settle the issue of self-identity. That is why a hermeneutic approach to the self has to exclude all kinds of comparison and confrontation from the interpretation of *ipseity*. The exclusion of the perspective of comparative identification, that is, the disqualification of every external point of view, is an unambiguously *phenomenological* ingredient of this hermeneutic inquiry.

However, it seems that this ingredient hardly takes effect in Ricoeur's investigations. The perspective of comparative identification makes from time to time its obtrusive reappearance on the pages of *Oneself as Another*, infringing upon the coherence of the considerations contained in the work. These disturbances can probably be traced back to the "ontological vehemence"[8] by which Ricoeur is driven to seek a foundation of self-identity in being or existence. However, this onotological aspiration comes into conflict with the phenomenological hermeneutic of the self in the last study contained in the work.

The diverse reflections upon the ontological fundamentals of selfhood come to a climax by giving way to the "realist twist" Ricoeur expected as a result of his debate with analytic philosophy. Nothing less is at stake in this breakthrough than the main concept of the whole work, which figures in its very title: *oneself as another*. It is not difficult to determine where, precisely, this breakthrough is achieved. This place is to be found in the train of thought designed to clarify the problem of *body*.

Ricoeur distinguishes between *proper* and *alien* alterity in this train of thought. Drawing upon Didier Franck,[9] he contends that "selfhood implies its own 'proper' otherness, so to speak, for which the flesh is the support."[10] He opposes this kind of alterity to the "otherness of the stranger"[11] or "of the foreign,"[12] meaning by this term the otherness "inherent in the relation of intersubjectivity," that is, "implied by the relation of the self to the *foreign*, in the precise sense of the other (than) self."[13]

This distinction is based on a well-known idea of Husserl's. The phenomenology of intersubjectivity developed by Husserl is centered around the tenet that my own living body (*Leib*), the flesh I inhabit, is, at the same time, itself a (physical) body among bodies (*Körper*). Ricoeur rightly emphasizes the importance of this insight. How does he, however, interpret this inseparability of flesh and body from each other? He finds that "my flesh appears as a body among bodies only to the extent that I am myself an other among all the others [. . .]."[14] *How am I, however, to become myself an other among all the others?* Ricoeur gives to this key question of his entire undertaking an answer which, in its fascinating modesty, is apt to awaken some astonishment: by the calendar, which identifies my living present with an anonymous instant in the time of the universe; by the geographic map, which correlates the *here* of my living body with an indifferent place in the space of the universe; and by the civil register, which I find my name inscribed in. Ricoeur adds that Husserl necessarily failed to give a concise answer to the same question because, instead of grasping the *self* as *another,* he wanted to grasp the *other* as *another self.*[15]

The apparent plausibility of this argument is due to an almost imperceptible change of perspective which may, indeed, be best described as a "realist twist." Unexpectedly, Ricoeur returns to the stance of a *comparative identification.* How this is to be understood is shown by the following considerations.

I hardly could grasp my living present as an anonymous instant in the time of the universe, I would barely be able to interpret my absolute *here,* which I carry with me, so to speak, from one place to another, as a place in the space of the universe, and I would certainly fail to recognize myself in the name inscribed in the civil register, if I had not the capacity to regard myself from an external point of view. That I may, in fact, change my perspective on myself in such a way is beyond any doubt. This, however, does not alter in the least the fact that the two perspectives I may adopt are to be united in a single view. To be sure, it cannot be denied that the external point of view from which I may regard myself gives room to self-referential reflection and even to self-identification. However, the peculiar features self-referentiality assumes here should not be lost sight of, either. These features may be specified as follows.

1. Calendar, geographic map, and civil register are means in our hands to identify ourselves within the framework of a public order, which encompasses us just as well as everybody else. Thereby, we render our personal identity available for, and controllable by, others. By taking such an external point of view, and applying means of this sort to myself, I resort to a kind of self-referentiality which lines me up with all others. Consequently, I settle the question of my personal identity by

the way of a comparative identification, treating thereby my self-identity as an identity in the sense of a special kind of sameness.

2. Whenever I place myself into a public order which encompasses me just as well as everybody else, I consider myself in the *same* way as an *other* might consider me. It is only by adopting the stance of this other that I may be said to regard myself *as* an other among all the others. This is the utmost limit set to self-referentiality: I consider myself *as* a *stranger.*
3. The other, however, who may regard me in this way is not even *the* other with whom I may happen to enter into a face-to-face relationship but somebody who is *an* other for *this* other, just as well as for myself. *An* other—in this indetermination. It is true, however, that this very indetermination assumes here the character of determination because such *an* other is referred to with whom I precisely do *not* happen to enter into a face-to-face relationship. Therefore, this indeterminate other may be said to be rather *a third party,* who considers me and the other, with whom I happen to enter into a face-to-face relationship, with a glance that encompasses both of us. The result is that self-referentiality is committed here to a *third-person perspective.*

It is a fact of extreme significance that I may adopt such an external view regarding myself. This fact has to be integrated into any serious theory of self-identity. Hence, it is certainly a merit of Ricoeur's to have brought this trait of self-identity to light. Does this, however, allow us to connect the terms *oneself* and *another* by the word *as?* And is this permissible if—as Ricoeur expressively says—*as* here does not mean a *comparison* but is in the sense of an *implication?*[16]

In order to decide this question, let us sum up the argument adduced in *Oneself as Another* for the validity of the formula which figures in the very title of the work. The starting point of the argument is the observation that I can adopt a third-person perspective regarding myself. A third person necessarily considers me—from his or her own point of view—as an other among all the others. From this fact it is only a step to draw the conclusion that I can consider myself *as* an other among all the others. However, this conclusion does not warrant the validity of the formula "oneself as another," unless an *as* in the sense of a comparison is taken for an *as* in the sense of an implication. The title of Ricoeur's book is, in reality, a metaphorical abbreviation of a comparison. It is not an accident that one is tempted to take the *as* in the ominous expression "oneself as another" in the sense of an "as if" or "as though." To be sure, this interpretation does not correspond to the intentions of the author. There is, however, no exaggeration in saying that the metaphorical abbreviation amounts here to a conceptual short circuit. The extraordinary tension discharged in this short circuit results from a highly dubious step in the argument: as soon as my living present is inserted into the time of the universe, the absolute here of my living body is identified with a place in the space of the universe, and the immediate self-reference is supplemented by a proper name inscribed in the civil register, *sameness is surreptitiously substituted for self-identity.* Therefore, the expression "oneself as another" is, in truth, nothing more than the sign of an unresolved paradox which is the outcome of a confusion of two irreconcilable perspectives.

It has been claimed that the exclusion of all kinds of a comparative identification is to be regarded as an unambiguously phenomenological ingredient of Ricoeur's hermeneutic approach. Furthermore, it has been maintained that the realist twist of Ricoeur's ontology reenforces the once already shattered status of a comparative identification within this approach. From these two statements it follows that *phenomenology* and *ontology* enter into a conflict with each other in the last study of *Oneself as Another.* It is only because the close connection between the formula of "oneself as another" with a third-person perspective does not come to be revealed in the text that this conflict remains concealed as well.

The insurmountable difficulties arising from this conflict would clearly manifest themselves if we could examine Ricoeur's double polemic against Husserl and Levinas in detail. However, this would be a too far-reaching enterprise; we have to confine ourselves here to some remarks. The undertaking summarized under the title "oneself as another" is equally challenged by Husserl's attempt to reduce the other than self to a modification of the self and by Levinas's endeavor to show the dependence of the self upon the other than self. Indeed, Husserl and Levinas have one thing in common: both of them insist on the radical alterity of the other. This radical alterity, however, seems to be lost sight of by Ricoeur, who tacitly presupposes a common order encompassing the self and the other. This tacit presupposition lies in the very formula "oneself as an other among all the others" because this formula applies to the stranger, just as well as to the self.

Viewed from the angle of such an order, Husserl's and Levinas's attempts assume a peculiar aspect. Both of these attempts, even if they are diametrically opposed to each other, appear, in this perspective, as far-fetched and contrived devices because they are both based on an equally sharp separation of what is alien to oneself from what is one's own. In this twofold separation, Ricoeur discerns a movement of thought which, in the cases of Husserl and Levinas, takes two opposite directions but which, in both cases, is comparable to Descartes's hyperbolic doubt. To be sure, by hyperbole, Ricoeur does not understand "a figure of style, [or] a literary trope, but the systematic practice of *excess* in philosophical argumentation."[17] What is, however, the measure by which excess is assessed in *Oneself as Another?* The answer is plain and obvious: the measure is a tacitly presupposed order which inserts into a unified whole what is one's own and what is alien to oneself. It is, however, not difficult to see that the very idea of such an order is inseparable from a third-person perspective. We may conclude from this that Ricoeur remains captive of a realist ontology which has been dismissed, from the outset, by both Husserl and Levinas. That is why Ricoeur proves to be unable to appreciate the phenomenological radicality characterizing both Husserl's and Levinas's approaches.

II. Intersubjectivity and Wild Alterity

The proper and the alien: Husserl made repeated attempts during several decades to determine the precise relationship of these concepts but his efforts did not prove to be entirely successful. The first step Husserl takes on the road leading up to what he calls "the phenomenology of intersubjectivity" consists in considering the immediate experience one gains from the other in his or her bodily presence. This approach to alien alterity does not go without awakening some surprise. It would be, as it seems, more natural to take an already existing social order as a point of departure: a pregiven community of language, or even a global historical trend because, in most cases, the self and the other find themselves always already bound together by some or even all of these ties. Yet, it is for profound reasons that Husserl refuses to take this course of inquiry. Indeed, by taking a united whole which encompasses the self and the other as a starting point, one commits oneself to regard his or her relationship with the other from a third-person perspective. However, it is a firm conviction of Husserl's—a conviction which is shared also by Levinas—that the distinctive features of this relationship are not even visible from such a perspective.

Undoubtedly, one is by no means unable, as we have seen, to regard his or her relationship with others from such an external point of view. However, the perspective one thereby adopts is necessarily marked by *posteriority* and *temporariness.* Since this perspective obviously presupposes the stance taken by oneself in his or her immediate relationship with others, it cannot be adopted but subsequently; and it cannot be adopted but only transitorily, because the practical tasks arising from any relationship with others soon require a return to the original attitude one changed momentarily for a third-person perspective. Levinas will add that it is precisely this return of the subject to itself which enables it to liberate itself in its relationship with others "from every system and every totality."[18]

There are indeed, as we can see, some arguments worthy to be considered which support the methodological decision to exclude all third-person perspectives from the phenomenology of intersubjectivity. Does not Husserl, however, come to an impasse when he proceeds from here to a sharp distinction between the *proper* and the *alien*, as Ricoeur seems to hold? This reproach requires a somewhat deeper examination of Husserl's considerations on the relationship between oneself and the other.

1. Husserl's Idea of the Other as Another Self

Husserl's considerations on the relationship between oneself and the other are introduced by a methodological device called "primordial reduction." This term may easily give rise to misunderstandings because it may be confused with the famous "phenomenological reduction," although the two procedures do not coincide with each other. The task of the phenomenological reduction is to reveal the sense formations (as-structures) which serve as the *concrete foundations* necessary for the constitution of the objects experienced, or simply conceived of, and emptily referred to. The primordial reduction is, on the contrary, an *abstractive method* applied with the purpose of eliminating from our knowledge everything not properly experienced but borrowed from alien sources.[19] The ultimate goal of this procedure is to delimit and separate our "transcendental sphere of ownness" from everything which refers to a foreign origin.[20]

Such an operation may undoubtedly be suspected of artificiality. It nevertheless gives a clear, almost palpable, sense to what is called a "self." One's self is, according to Husserl's conception, to be defined as the temporally ordered totality—or the "history"—of one's own experiences. However, in contradistinction with the theory of narrative identity, the stress is laid here not so much on the idea of a life-history but rather on the notion of ownness (ownership), of owned experience. That is why Husserl's conception is distinct from the doctrine of narrative identity. Oneself is, in Husserl's eyes, by no means simply "an other among all the others." On the contrary, one's self, interpreted as the temporally ordered totality of one's own experiences, is unique and unrepeatable. This singularity results from what is one's *own* in experience.

It is true, however, that no experience can be owned, or even appropriated, in its totality. It always contains in itself, as it was already mentioned at the end of the first chapter, some ingredients stemming from foreign sources and referring thereby to—real or possible—experiences of strangers. Therefore, one's own experience may be said to involve, or to imply, an otherness which may rightly be qualified, by a term borrowed from Ricoeur, as a "proper alterity." It is a consequence of this structure of experience that one's selfhood necessarily rests upon a *delimitation* and a *separation* from the alterity oneself is, as it were, permeated by.

This conception of selfhood can, however, hardly be correctly assessed unless it is equally taken into account that, according to Husserl's further claim, the proper alterity lying in experience opens a road to understanding the alien alterity of the other as a "modification" of the self. This claim lies at the very core of the phenomenology of intersubjectivity. The guiding idea of the highly complicated investigations designed to prove this claim may be summarized by four main tenets.

The first of these is that a bodily anchored experience is necessarily characterized by an *orientation in space.* It is, in each case, from "here," not from "there," that I am experiencing the world. Accordingly, it is from "here" that I am experiencing the other—namely, the other whom I happen to encounter—in his or her bodily appearance; and I am experiencing him or her as experiencing the same world as myself—not from "here," however, but from "there."

The second tenet around which the phenomenology of intersubjectivity revolves is that it is by this *positional difference* between a "here" and a "there" in the space of experience that the relationship between myself and the other is determined. That is why, in this approach, the other is grasped as a "cosubject" experiencing the same world which I am experiencing myself and, consequently, that is why he or she is interpreted as another self, an *alter ego.*

Husserl adds to these two tenets, third, that it is my experience itself which assigns to my cosubjects the positions they may take in a common space of bodily anchored orientations. It is not difficult to see that every experience of mine is surrounded by a *horizon* of possible experiences which, although anticipated as correlates of my own "potentialities," may just as well be "actualized" by other subjects.

Relying upon this third tenet, Husserl holds, fourthly, that I am experiencing from "here" the other as a cosubject being "there" by experiencing him or her "*as being myself there.*"[21] According to this fourth tenet, it belongs to my own "potentialities" to experience the world as it is "actually" experienced by the cosubject.

If this proposition is correct, then I can, indeed, consider the other as a "modification" of myself. How can I, however, at the same time account for his or her "alterity"? Only by emphasizing that, being "here," I am actually *not* "there," where presently the other is; by insisting, in other words, on the fact that our positions never coincide, they remain, on the contrary, as distinct as "here" and "there" are.

This tortuous argument leads, however, to an ambiguity. The crucial expression "as being myself there" (*wie wenn ich dort wäre*) undoubtedly suggests, on the one hand, a *potentiality;* it amounts, consequently, to so much as "*when* I am myself there" (*wenn ich dort wäre*). But it undeniably implies, on the other hand, also an *irreality;* it must, therefore, just as well be construed as running like "*as if* I were there" (*als ob ich dort wäre*). The two meanings are not distinguished by Husserl; they are, as a matter of fact, conflated in the expression he prefers to use. Consequently, this expression has justly been designated as a *Kontaminationsformel* by Klaus Held, who was the first to detect an ambiguity in it, which results from a fluctuation of its meaning between potentiality and irreality.[22]

How can a way out be found from this quandary? I will confine myself to considering the two main attempts to cope with the difficulties raised by Husserl's phenomenology of intersubjectivity. The first attempt originates with Merleau-Ponty, the second stems from Levinas (who, in his turn, draws upon Sartre). The remaining parts of the present section will be consecrated to Merleau-Ponty's suggestions; Levinas (and, to some extent, Sartre) will be dealt with in the next section.

2. Merleau-Ponty and the Wild Region

Wild region: this term is the emblem of a wild thinking, a *pensée sauvage,* even if not precisely in the sense of Lévi-Strauss's famous book. It is no accident, however, that Lévi-Strauss has dedicated his book to the memory of Merleau-Ponty. We know that the two thinkers were bound together not only by a personal acquaintance—perhaps even by friendship—but also by a close intellectual relationship. It is in an essay treating Marcel Mauss and Claude Lévi-Strauss that the term *wild region* is first used by Merleau-Ponty.[23] Then, it occurs also in *The Visible and the Invisible.* Here, we read, "the communication from one constituted culture to another occurs through the wild region where they all have originated."[24] Although applied preeminently within the context of what might be called the phenomenology of interculturality, the idea of a wild region clearly indicates a way to overcome the difficulties resulting from Husserl's phenomenology of intersubjectivity as well. It refers, so to speak, to a *no-*

man's-land in which the opposition of the proper and the alien is not so much *sublated* (like in a higher-order synthetic unity) but is rather *suspended.* It would be a mistake to consider this no-man's-land as a totality, a whole, which encompasses the proper and the alien. The idea of a wild region is by no means the product of a holistic dialectics. It rather results from what has been repeatedly cited in the course of the present investigations as the "use of the diacritical." The idea of a wild region is inseparable from the notion of a diacritical system of intersubjectivity. It is, of course, not from a third-person perspective that Merleau-Ponty looks upon this system. Here, as elsewhere, it is the subject's inclusion in, its "being set on," this diacritical system which he inquires into. Therefore, he refuses to approach this system *en survol*—"soaring over it." Just like Husserl and all other phenomenologists, it is the subject's own experience which he is concerned with. But he does not accept Husserl's idea of a primordial sphere of ownness. What is proper, what is one's own in experience, has, according to him, no more than a "diacritical value"—a value it derives from its contrast with, its opposition to, or its deflection from, what is alien. It is within one's own experience that, as Bernhard Waldenfels puts it, a "transcendental strangeness"[25] is exhibited in *The Visible and the Invisible.* But Merleau-Ponty does not content himself with pointing out that one's own experience includes in itself an inappropriable otherness. He develops a diacritical phenomenology of intersubjectivity, which, far from establishing itself in a sphere of ownness, penetrates to a region in which the proper and the alien belong inseparably together. What this undertaking is aiming at is, in other words, nothing other than to prove that one's own experience involves an otherness which is *neither* proper, *nor* alien but is characterized by a "strange encroachment,"[26] "reversibility,"[27] or "intertwining"[28] of what is one's own and what remains foreign.

Instead of the expressions just quoted, Merleau-Ponty sometimes uses even the German word *Ineinander,*[29] which he borrows from the vocabulary of the later Husserl. In some of his later texts, Husserl comes indeed close to anticipating the main idea articulated in Merleau-Ponty's posthumous work.[30] We may refer to this main idea under the name of a *wild alterity,* adding that this term is designed to designate an otherness in one's own experience which is marked by what Husserl called the *Ineinander* of the proper and the alien.

How does Merleau-Ponty elaborate his conception? He insists upon the fact that the *visible* is never exhausted by what has actually been *seen* of it, and he tries to show that "my visible, although it is not superposable on that of the other, nonetheless opens upon it" and that, therefore, "both open upon the same sensible world."[31] He argues, in other words, for an intertwining and reversibility of my visible with that of the other by reason of a strange encroachment which is just as little bound to a condition of superposability as the interconnection of the two images sent by the two eyes separately to the brain, or the overlapping of the field of vision with the field of touching.

Merleau-Ponty draws only the last consequence of these observations when he claims that the immediate experience one gains of the other in his or her bodily appearance presupposes an "intercorporeity"[32] which, far from belonging to any "primordial sphere of ownness," is rather characterized by a "primordial anonymity"[33] and is to be considered, therefore, as an entirely disowned, or dispossessed, "*intermonde,*" an "intermundane space,"[34] a no-man's-land. Merleau-Ponty describes this *intermonde* as a "wild world"[35] which—"behind or beneath the cleavages of our acquired culture"—is inhabited by a "wild Being."[36]

These unusual terms may awaken in us the impression of urging a return to a nature behind or beneath of culture. This interpretation is, however, wrong. Merleau-Ponty knows that such an opposition of nature and culture is "abstract."[37] The "search for the 'wild' view of the world,"[38] as he names his undertaking, cannot limit itself to restoring a nature behind or beneath of culture, it has just as well to "restore the very presence of a culture."[39] That is why Merleau-Ponty sets himself the very task indicated by the title of posthumous work: namely, the task of exhibiting the *intertwining* of the *visible* and the *invisible.*

It is clear from this that the *wild* is by no means the *visible,* as opposed to the *invisible.* An immense distance separates this "wild" view of the world from Husserl's early phenomenology which aimed at founding all thoughts upon corresponding intuitions. That is why Merleau-Ponty may speak just as well of a "wild sense" and even of a "savage mind" as of a "wild world" and of a "wild Being."

We have already been led to explore the notion of a wild sense by our considerations on experience and expression. Now we may add that this notion has a role in the experience gained of the other in his or her bodily appearance as well as in the analysis of operative speech. The other I happen to encounter is experienced by me "not as a 'consciousness' but as an inhabitant of a body, and consequently of the world."[40] But what is here precisely meant by the word *inhabitant?* Merleau-Ponty clarifies the relationship involved in this metaphoric designation by putting it in an analogy with the emerging sense of operative speech or, more generally, of creative expression. He writes,

> [The other] is (like the meaning of a sentence) immanent in this body [. . .] and yet, more than the sum of the signs or significations conveyed

> by them. [. . .] Always in process of an unfinished incarnation [. . .]. Beyond the objective body as the sense of the painting is beyond the canvas.[41]

Here the presence of the other is interpreted as the process of a spontaneous sense formation which surpasses the significations conveyed by bodily gestures to the observer. It is this surplus of sense over all consolidated meanings of a corporeal language which, according to Merleau-Ponty, gives an access to the inhabitant of a foreign body.

How are we, however, to understand the expression "savage mind"? By this Merleau-Ponty seems to mean intersubjectivity itself, insofar as it is based on intercorporeity and constituted by operative language. *Esprit sauvage* is, in this sense, not "a 'human' universe, an objective spirit," envisaged by Hegel and his followers, but rather "a milieu of communication [. . .], the spoken tongue [*la langue*] in the present."[42] *Langue au présent:* operative language—a language which, as we may read in another passage, "is a life, is our life and the life of the things."[43] Savage mind is, in a word, nothing else than an "intersubjective diacritical system."[44]

This fundamental concept gives to the *invisible* a sense which binds it to the *visible* without reduction or distortion. Thus interpreted, the invisible is "not the contradictory of the visible,"[45] it is not "an ideal system, a fragment of the intelligible world,"[46] it is, rather, "the invisible *of* this world."[47]

We find, however, at a closer consideration that the "use of the diacritical" falls short of the mark in the theory of the savage mind. In a working note, Merleau-Ponty assimilates the savage mind to "the mind of praxis."[48] He adds,

> Like all praxis, language supposes a *selbstverständlich,* an instituted, which is *Stiftung* preparing *Endstiftung.*—The problem is to grasp *what,* across the successive and simultaneous community of speaking subjects, *wishes, speaks,* and finally *thinks.*[49]

Here, the "wild" view of the world yields the place to a well-known philosophy of history, which considers the diacritical system of intersubjectivity from a third-person perspective. It takes the standpoint of "the mind of praxis," which assumes here the unmistakable characteristics of a *subject of history.* Merleau-Ponty relies in this passage upon the Husserlian contrast between (*Ur-*) *Stiftung* and *Endstiftung,* "primal" and "final" instituting, a pair of concepts which carries indelible traces of a historical teleology. This conceptual opposition outlines a process of sense formation which inserts that which is "instituted" into the framework of a whole, a historical totality.

No less telling a term is the word *selbstverständlich,* which equally marks a break with the "wild" view of the world. Merleau-Ponty considers here even language from the global, holistic perspective of a philosophy of history.[50] We can easily see this if we examine the question of how that which is *selbstverständlich,* which "goes without saying," is generated in language. By *sedimentation,* we may answer: an *Urstiftung,* a primal instituting, gives rise to a tradition by which it is preserved and maintained at the price of becoming a common practice, a custom hardly even reflected upon, or an inured habitude. In order to take into account also the discovery of a wild sense, we have to add that the generation of what goes without saying never fails to bring to a standstill, and even to choke off, a spontaneous sense formation emerging imperceptibly in the depths of a tradition. Merleau-Ponty now turns to what is sedimented and instituted in order "to grasp *what,* across the successive and simultaneous community of speaking subjects, *wishes, speaks,* and finally *thinks.*" He thereby abandons the "wild" view of the world, which is aimed at revealing the hidden processes of a spontaneous emergence of sense, in order to embrace a holistic view of history which considers the great institutions of sedimented, fixed, ready-made sense as the promoting factors of cultural development.

However, we are confronted here with an intellectual bent of the later Merleau-Ponty which, although making its influence felt in some passages, does not get the upper hand in his thought. The wild region discovered and illuminated by this thought remains untouched by the holistic view indulged in at the moments of a not particularly felicitous rumination over history. This is especially clear from Merleau-Ponty's contributions to the phenomenology of interculturality. We may read, for instance, in the essay on Mauss and Lévi-Strauss that ethnology is not simply a science dealing with so-called primitive societies but it is also a "way of thinking" we are compelled to have recourse to whenever the object of our considerations is characterized by an "alterity" requiring that "we transform ourselves."[51] Thus, we may, as Merleau-Ponty adds, become "the ethnologists of our own society," provided that we are able to "preserve a distance from it" in order to consider "as alien that which is our own" and, conversely, "as our own that which was alien to us."[52] Such a distance from our own society procures us an access to the wild region which is not entirely included into our culture but which gives room to a communication with other cultures.

It has already been pointed out that the wild region is not a nature behind or beneath of culture. What could it be then if not a domain of a spontaneous sense formation which has not yet been brought to a standstill, let alone choked off, by any institution of sedimented meanings? It is thanks to this wild region, we may say with Merleau-Ponty and Richir, that we have a chance to remain, to some extent, foreigners in what is our own and to preserve, thereby, an access to what is different from, and even alien to, what is our own.[53]

III. The Experience of Alien Alterity

Levinas reproaches Husserl for having failed to grasp what is radically *alien* in the alterity of the other. The phenomenology of intersubjectivity, he holds, does not describe the other *as* a modified self, it describes, in reality, a modified self *instead* of the other. What makes the other than self *different* from the self remains incomprehensible in this approach.[54]

It is also clear from this fundamental objection why Levinas does not take much inspiration from Merleau-Ponty's discovery of a wild region in which the proper and the alien are intertwined with each other. Although he does not contest the significance of this discovery, he does not expect from it any adequate answer to *his* question, which concerns precisely the *difference* between the proper and the alien.

Levinas agrees with Sartre in holding that Husserl's failure to elucidate this difference was due to his exclusively, or at least predominantly, epistemological orientation. Both Sartre and Levinas are convinced that no experience based solely on a contemplative interest is apt to reveal the radical alterity of the other. It is, therefore, from a situation of action or, more precisely, from a situation in which action is *at stake,* that they take their points of departure in their considerations on the relationship between oneself and the other.

So much is common to Sartre and Levinas. In the sequel, however, their investigations follow up quite diverging paths. This is not the place for a comparison between the two thinkers.[55] Some differences should, however, be highlighted.

It is a striking feature of the considerations consecrated to the relationship between oneself and the other in *Being and Nothingness* that Sartre heavily relies in them on the conceptual opposition of the *subject* and the *object.* Levinas, on the contrary, refrains from making use of this conceptual contrast in his analysis of the encounter with the other. He considers this opposition as pertaining to a merely epistemological inquiry. Therefore, in the analysis of the relationship between oneself and the other, he tries to replace it by a more appropriate conceptual framework. He discovers such a framework in Plato's "great kinds," these "meta-categories," as Ricoeur calls them. That is how Levinas comes to focus his considerations upon the opposition of the *same* and the *other.*

Another claim of Levinas gives rise to a second fundamental difference between the two thinkers. Sartre considers the relationship between oneself and the other as an indispensable ingredient of one's very conscious being, which, in itself, does not impose any constraint or rule, let alone a determinate course, upon action. In other words, he does not find in this relationship anything which would relegate it to moral philosophy; consequently, he treats it within the context of a phenomenological ontology. By contrast, Levinas contends that the relationship between oneself and the other is basically *ethical* in its nature, and that it is, therefore, necessarily curtailed in any ontological approach, be it phenomenologically founded or not. Moreover, it is, according to Levinas, not only bereft of its ethical dimension but it is also categorically distorted: it is wrapped up in a unifying concept of Being which conceals the underlying *split* between the Same and the Other.

I will examine, in this section, how Levinas endeavors to transcend the limits set to a phenomenology of intersubjectivity, just as well as to an ontological approach to the encounter with the other. I shall be concerned primarily with the question of how an experience of alien alterity is revealed by this endeavor. It is, consequently, from a phenomenological point of view that the enterprise of Levinas will be considered on the following pages.[56]

1. Elementary Relation between Oneself and the Other

Levinas considers, in his first great work *Totality and Infinity,* a whole series of different relationships between oneself and the other. War as a relationship between enemies, commerce as a relationship between producers of works, history as a relationship between the survivors and the dead, are among the many subjects treated in the book. The reflections dedicated to the erotic relationship between lovers are especially memorable. One is not surprised to find special attention paid to the relationship between father and son, as well as to that between brothers in a work which lays unreserved (perhaps too unreserved) emphasis on "the marvel of the family."[57] Furthermore, some remarks are concerned with friendship, which was assigned a central role in ethics by Aristotle, and recurring allusions deal with that community of reason which was envisaged by Kant under the name of a "realm of ends" as an ideal inherent in action. Levinas is, however, convinced that these various kinds of intercourse and communication presuppose an "irreducible and ultimate relation" between oneself and the other,[58] which does not coincide with the epistemologically conceived relation between the subject and the cosubject but shows ethical characteristics. In *Totality and Infinity,* this ethical relation proves to be an *elementary* relationship which is implied by intercourses not only between friends, brothers, or lovers, but even between enemies.

How can we, however, have an access to this elementary relation? Here Levinas has recourse to a methodological device which has been bequeathed to him by Husserl: he decides to suspend every pregiven order which cannot be grasped but from a third-person perspective. This procedure leads him up to a discovery of capital significance: he comes to the insight that a peculiar kind of "inequality"—or "asymmetry"—is to be discerned in the elementary relationship between oneself and the other if this relationship is considered from an internal, rather than an external, point of view.[59] This inequality or asymmetry does not result from any difference between personal characteristics. Levinas unmistakably asserts,

> The alterity of the Other does not depend on any quality that would distinguish him from me, for a distinction of this nature would precisely imply between us that community of genus which already nullifies alterity.[60]

The inequality or asymmetry under discussion is rather a consequence of the fact that I am unable to compare the other with myself without adopting the standpoint of a third party. If I regard the other from my own point of view, I cannot grasp any commensurability between us. If I exclude from my approach to the other the possibility of taking any external stance, I am no longer able to find any genus of which both of us would be coordinated instances. Nor am I able, under these circumstances, to specify any series of which I would be the first and he or she the second member, or conversely. The inequality, or asymmetry, under consideration is, therefore, an inequality, or asymmetry, of incommensurable terms. As Levinas emphasizes, it "does not appear to the third party who would count us"; it precisely signifies, as Levinas adds, "the absence of a third party capable of taking in me and the other"; it is tantamount to the very "impossibility of the exterior point of view" which, as it is categorically stated, "alone could abolish it."[61]

It is this inequality or asymmetry, Levinas claims, which manifests the alien alterity of the other. At the same time, he attributes to this unequal or asymmetrical relationship, as we know, an ethical character. He describes the elementary relationship between oneself and the other as a face-to-face conjuncture in which one is confronted with an *ineluctable appeal* calling for a response. This appeal is ineluctable because, in a face-to-face conjuncture, one finds oneself *constrained* to answer; namely, in such a situation, even no response counts as a response. This constraint imposed upon action by an ineluctable appeal of the other defines, according to Levinas, what may be called an ethic of alterity. It is in this—quite peculiar—sense that the elementary relation between oneself and the other can be characterized as an ethical relation.

The question of whether this is a legitimate sense of ethics and, if the answer is in the affirmative, how this unusual version of ethical inquiry is related to the traditional types of moral philosophy, is to be reserved for the next chapter. In this section, I will confine myself to an examination of how Levinas describes the appeal with the other and the role of a third party in the two major works of his later period, namely, *Totality and Infinity* and *Otherwise Than Being or Beyond Essence.*

2. Two Conceptions of the Appeal of the Other

One thing is common in the two versions: namely, the emphasis put upon language, discourse, and speech. It is, in both expositions, taken for granted that one is never confronted with an ineluctable appeal without being addressed by the other—by means of outspoken words or at least by means of a silent glance. Consequently, in a face-to-face conjuncture a response is not extricated, it is rather demanded. However, in analyzing this linguistic or communicative aspect of the encounter with the other, Levinas finds himself in a somewhat awkward situation. The methodological legacy which he has inherited from Husserl does not allow him to adopt a third-person perspective and to envisage from this standpoint a community of language between oneself and the other. Is, however, any interpellation, be it a silent one, possible without such a community of language? Can even a meaningful glance be addressed to someone who is not involved in such a community?

In *Totality and Infinity,* Levinas hopes to overcome this difficulty by tracing back the origin of language and meaning to the immediate experience of the other in his or her bodily presence. He tries to elicit from this experience precisely what has been left out of consideration by the phenomenology of intersubjectivity. As we know, it was one of Husserl's basic ideas that we grasp the other in his or her bodily appearance *as being ourselves in his or her place.* This conception is based on the assumption that we necessarily bestow upon what is alien a sense which we take from our own experiences. This idea of an "analogous apperception" or "appresentation," as it is called in *Cartesian Meditations,* is not unambiguous. Derrida is certainly right in saying that "Husserl takes pains to respect, in its meaning, the alterity of the Other."[62] But Levinas is no less right in objecting to Husserl that a sense bestowal based upon proper experience is not to be expected to give an access to the alien alterity of the other. He holds, however, that it was only because Husserl did not pay any attention to an important feature of the very experience he set out to analyze that he did not find the way leading up to the comprehension of radical alterity: although he was seriously concerned with the bodily gestures of the other, he interpreted them only as possible confirmations or refutations of a sense oneself bestows upon them. Levinas, on the contrary, comes to the insight that these bodily gestures are—just as well as outspoken linguistic utterances—*expressions of an alien sense* which proves to be irreducible to any sense bestowal based upon one's own experiences. He says, "In expression a being presents itself; the being that manifests itself attends this manifestation and consequently appeals to me."[63] That is why Levinas claims that language is "the incessant surpassing of the *Sinngebung* [of the Husserlian sense bestowal] by the signification."[64] He maintains in *Totality and Infinity* that the essence of language consists in the expression of an alien sense that, recalcitrant as it is to all attempts at appropriation, appeals to oneself by calling for a response. This is what he designates by the term *signification*. At the same time, he extends the meaning of this term beyond language. He is convinced that speech, discourse, linguistic utterance is not the only mode of manifesting a radically foreign sense. He writes, "To signify is not equivalent to presenting oneself as a sign, but to expressing oneself, that is, presenting oneself in person."[65] It follows from this conception that the essence of language does not consist in anything which is specifically linguistic in its nature; it rather consists in a "signification of expression"[66] which is by no means peculiar to outspoken words. Levinas does not fail to draw this consequence:

> The primordial essence of language is to be sought not in the corporeal operation that discloses it to me and to others and, in the recourse to language, builds up a thought, but in the presentation of meaning [*dans la présentation du sens*] . . . . Meaning [*sens*] is the face of the Other, and all recourse to words takes place already within the primordial face to face of language.[67]

Just as Husserl and Merleau-Ponty, Levinas defines language by *expression*. However, contrary to Husserl, by expression he does not mean the manifestation of a sense (or meaning) bestowed upon something by an intentional consciousness but he means by it a sense (or meaning) which remains *inappropriable* for any sense-bestowing subject, and, in opposition to Merleau-Ponty, by an inappropriable sense (or meaning) he does not mean simply a *wild* sense which emerges spontaneously as an expression of experience by the experience of creative expression but he means by it an *alien* sense which is presented by the other as an expression of his or her face—or, for that matter, of his or her entire body in a face-to-face encounter. Levinas says, "In the face the existent par excellence presents itself. And the whole body—a hand or a curve of the shoulder—can express as the face."[68]

It is as a par excellence bodily presentation of alien sense that the face fulfills the function of a new principle, of a veritable philosophical *arche* in *Totality and Infinity.* This function is comparable to the role assigned by the Husserlian "principle of principles" to intuition. Just as intuition gives an immediate presence to every sense bestowed upon something by one's own intentional consciousness, the face gives an immediate presence to every sense manifested by the other. Therefore, *Totality and Infinity* may be seen as a work replacing the principle of classical phenomenology by a new philosophical *arche.* However strongly Levinas stresses in this work that "[t]he I's form no totality," and that, consequently, "there exists no privileged plane where these I's could be grasped in their principle," and however unambiguously he adopts the standpoint according to which this "anarchy" is "essential to multiplicity," he is still constantly striving to show that "a principle breaks through all this trembling and vertigo when the face presents itself [. . .]."[69] It is as such a principle, as a philosophical *arche,* that the face proves to be the source of an ineluctable appeal.

This conception is changed in the second major work. The book *Otherwise Than Being or Beyond Essence* marks a new turn in Levinas's thought. One of the most decisive differences concerns language. A new distinction between the *saying* and the *said* is now put to the fore. Levinas holds that the said has its sense and that the very saying of what is said bears additional sense. Moreover, the sense of the saying is not only a surplus over the sense of the said but it is also different in kind from it. This difference is clear even from the simple cases Levinas considers in *Totality and Infinity:* for instance, from the case in which the other presents himself or herself by stating his or her name,[70] or from the no less significant case in which the other attends his or her self-manifestation "in a movement at each instant recovering and deciphering the very signs [he or she] emits."[71] In both cases the saying as a linguistic gesture amounts to more than the mere content of the speech. In *Totality and Infinity* these examples are adduced as so many evidences testifying to the tenet that the bodily features and gestures of the other give an *immediate presence* to the alien sense expressed in them. The distinction between the saying and the said in *Otherwise Than Being or Beyond Essence* marks a break with this earlier interpretation. Levinas comes to the insight that both the sense of the said and the sense of the saying are characterized by a structure in which something stands for, points toward, or indicates something else. Sometimes this structure is referred to by the term *quid pro quo.* This term designates a substitution which does not lend itself to be described as an immediate presence. Therefore, the assumption that a new principle, a philosophical *arche,* can be discerned in the bodily appearance of the other loses its justification.

It is a consequence of this departure from the general standpoint of *Totality and Infinity* that even the generation of an ineluctable appeal is reconsidered in *Otherwise Than Being or Beyond Essence.* The intricate argument Levinas exposes in this work in a rich poetic language and in a somewhat unctuous tenor[72] may be summarized in sober prose as follows.

The decisive step in the argument consists in specifying the surplus of sense which may be attributed to the saying in opposition to the said. Here we are led to the strange result that the structure of this additional sense is analogous to the structure of the elementary relation between oneself and the other. It is not difficult to see that, in all cases, the sense of saying what we say consists in, or is related to, *proposing* a sense—namely, the sense of the said—to the other. This is what Levinas has in mind when he speaks—using an almost untranslatable idiomatic expression—of a *signifiance baillée à autrui.*[73] In this case the indication included in the structure *quid pro quo*—something (standing) for something—which is taken to be characteristic of all sense, signification, and meaning, does not go from the sign toward the designated but from oneself to the other. That is why Levinas makes use of the formula *qui pro quo*—somebody (standing) for somebody, or even the one (standing) for the other—in order to specify the sense of the saying in contradistinction to the sense of the said.[74]

These considerations shed also some light at the "barbarous turn"[75] *otherwise than being* or *beyond essence* figuring in the very title of the work. Levinas interprets the elementary relationship between oneself and the other not as a relationship between two entities, or two existing beings, but as a nexus constituted by the sense peculiar to the saying. It is solely *sense*—and preeminently the sense of the saying—which "is not measured by being,"[76] which, consequently, indicates an "otherwise than being," a "beyond being" or, as Levinas prefers calling the very process of being (in the verbal sense of this word), beyond "essence." In other words, the relationship between oneself and the other is embedded in the process of the emergence of sense rather than in the process of the unfolding of being.

The idea of a sense formation that transcends being is a novelty characteristic of the later period of Levinas's thinking. In retrospect, Levinas himself mentions as an important difference between *Totality and Infinity* and *Otherwise Than Being or Beyond Essence* that the former work makes abundant use of an "ontological language" which the latter tries to avoid.[77] In the former work the elementary relationship between oneself and the other is interpreted as a bond between the *same* and the *other.* To be sure, these Platonic categories—or metacategories—are profoundly transformed by Levinas. Nevertheless, in *Totality and Infinity* they retain their basically ontological nature. This is true without qualifications of the *same* which, in this work, is designed to express the essence of the I, the ego. The I—Levinas says—is "a being whose essence is exhausted in identity."[78] It is—he adds—"not a being that always remains the same, but is the being whose existing consists in identifying itself, in recovering its identity throughout all that happens to it."[79] In this sense the I, the ego, is the very incarnation of the *same.* At first sight, otherness, alterity, seems to lack such a separate existence. As Levinas emphasizes: "Alterity is possible only starting from *me.*"[80] Yet, in *Totality and Infinity,* an ontological status is assigned to alterity as well as to self-identity. Levinas claims, "Being is produced as multiple and as split into same and other; this is its ultimate structure."[81] Thus, the *same* and the *other* are—at least as moments of the ultimate structure characteristic of a split being—unambiguously ontological in nature. It is true that, in *Totality and Infinity* just as well as in *Otherwise Than Being or Beyond Essence,* Levinas is striving to characterize the elementary relationship between the I and the other as something which "can go beyond being";[82] in both works, he tries to replace traditional metaphysics by ethics as first philosophy. But he himself realizes subsequently that this endeavor did not yet prove to be entirely successful in the earlier work.

Why could, in *Totality and Infinity,* the elementary relationship of oneself and the other not be relieved of the remnants of ontological language? The reason lies in Levinas's inclination to interpret the difference between oneself and the other as an "absolute difference."[83] That is why he credits the other not only with a *radical* but also with an *absolute* alterity,[84] just as well as he attributes to the I, the ego, an *absolute* self-identity.[85]

What does he mean, however, by these terms? He tries to express a particularity of the elementary relationship between the I and the other. He says,

> Absolute difference [. . .] is established only by language. Language accomplishes a relation between terms that breaks up the unity of a genus. The terms, the interlocutors, absolve themselves from the relation, or remain absolute within the relationship.[86]

This is true, in particular, of the other: one may present the other as a theme, but as interlocutor, the other may contest the sense one ascribes to him or her; the other "has quit the theme that encompassed him, and upsurges inevitably behind the said."[87] In other words, the other may *retreat* from the relationship without *retiring* into himself or herself. "Evasion of the other": this is the expression Levinas chooses to designate this paradox.[88]

The other term of the relation, the I, the ego, has equally the power of absolving itself from the relation, even if it is pointed out in *Totality and Infinity* that this power "entails a different sense of absolution for each of the different terms."[89] For the I—for myself—absolution has not the sense of evasion but that of "separation." This is one of the basic notions of the entire work; it is highly differentiated and profusely illustrated in the book. Nevertheless, its very definition is founded on a simple observation (which may nonetheless be rightly called "profound"). Levinas claims,

> Separation is the very act of individuation, the possibility in general for an entity posited in being to be posited not by being defined by its references to a whole, by its place within a system, but starting from itself. The fact of starting from oneself is equivalent to separation.[90]

This characterization of separation as "the fact of starting from oneself" may seem to be far too abstract. Levinas tries, indeed, to supplement it by what he calls "the concreteness of egoism."[91] By "egoism" he does not mean a particular attitude to the other but "the very egoism of life."[92] It is not "in the naked will to be" that this egoism consists but "in a relation with contents that are not my being but more dear than my being: thinking, eating, sleeping, reading, working, warming oneself in the sun."[93] Enjoyment of these contents is a happiness which elevates life beyond a pure and naked existence—and even beyond being as such, since "being is risked for happiness"[94]—but which cannot be preserved for a long time without dwelling and habitation, without home, possession, and labor. In a word, as Levinas claims, "separation or ipseity is produced primordially in the enjoyment of happiness."[95]

Yet, the essence of separation and *ipseity* lies deeper: it consists in the independence which derives from the seemingly abstract "fact of starting from oneself." This fact seems to be abstract only as long as it is not connected with the specificity of the relationship between oneself and the other. This relationship is special, or even unique, precisely because it "is not visible from the outside but proceeds from one unto the other."[96] That it "cannot be included within a network visible to a third party" is due to the fact that it is a relationship "proceeding from myself."[97]

By these considerations we are enabled to understand why, in *Totality and Infinity,* Levinas is mistaken when he conceives the identity of the self and the alterity of the other as *absolute* terms. He is certainly right in pointing out that these notions are not "relative" terms in the sense of arising from, or being founded upon, a relation established from the outside by, let us say, a comparison. Nevertheless, these notions are not to be considered as "absolute" terms, either, because self-identity and alterity may be held to be determined by the positions assigned to oneself and to the other in the face-to-face conjuncture into which they enter with each other. Levinas stresses, indeed, that "the alterity of the other does not result from its identity but constitutes it: the other [*l'Autre*] is the Other (*Autrui*)."[98] He adds that it is only "proceeding from myself and not through a comparison of myself with the other" that I may have an access to this alterity of the Other.[99] A similar statement must apply to the identity of oneself if it is true that separation and *ipseity* derive ultimately from the "fact of starting from oneself," since this expression refers itself to the position taken by oneself in the relationship with the other: it is tantamount to saying "proceeding from oneself unto the other."

Therefore, it is highly misleading to speak here of "absolute" terms. However, it might just as well be misleading to describe the identity of the self and the alterity of the other as "relative"—or even as "relational"—terms, since "absolution" is the main feature they are characterized by. Consequently, in order to avoid misunderstandings, we had better prefer a notion which transcends the alternative of "absolute" and "relative" (or "relational"). *Positional* is such a notion, if it is used to emphasize that self-identity and alterity are determined by the positions assigned to oneself and to the other within the elementary relationship they enter upon with each other.

We may add that the basic novelty brought by the second major work of Levinas consists in a systematic reinterpretation of the difference between oneself and the other. In *Totality and Infinity* this difference was considered as an "absolute" one. In *Otherwise Than Being or Beyond Essence,* it comes to be described as a *positional difference.* This turn is indicated by the new definition of subjectivity as "the other in the same" or, more explicitly, as "the intrigue of the other in the same."[100]

3. Responsibility and Order: The Role of the Third Party

Levinas ascribes an ethical character to the ineluctable appeal of the other insofar as, confronting me with a constraint of response, it imposes upon me an *unlimited responsibility.* But what is meant by this term? Nothing other than a responsibility I am assigned to bear not only for myself but also for the other, not only for my own actions but also for alien deeds—deeds which arise from alien freedom and not from my own. Moreover, it is a responsibility not only for alien deeds but also for alien destiny—and this in spite of the fact that the destiny of the other is not only not amenable to my freedom and power, but it is not amenable to the other's freedom and power, either. *What else is, however, such a notion of responsibility than an enthusiastic exaggeration?* we may be inclined to ask. We may even get the impression that here exaggeration is methodically enhanced. It is indeed added that I am always already burdened with this responsibility, even if I am loath to expressly assume it, and even if I expressly refuse to assume it. Moreover, a further claim is formulated, according to which it is not only for *the* other I happen to encounter with but also for *all* the others I do not even happen to encounter with that I am assigned to bear a responsibility. What is the point of this clearly *hyperbolic* argumentation?

Before committing the error of searching for excuses, we should ask ourselves: what is the measure that we apply when we pass this judgment upon the claims raised by Levinas? The answer is obvious: our measure is the customary notion of legal and moral responsibility, which is based upon two underlying principles. The first of these principles is simple: *I am not responsible but for what I do (or omit)*. No less simple is the second principle: *What I shall do (and what I must not) is defined by my legal duties, institutional obligations, and the moral customs of public life.* These two principles may be said to outline a *moral order.* We may realize that the basis of such an order is nothing else than a *limitation*—and *just division—of responsibility.* We should not, however, forget about an experience that is apt to disturb every order of limited responsibility. I mean the experience that an encounter with the other may require more than just an allegiance to legal duties and institutional obligations, or a compliance with moral customs; it may, as a matter of fact, even call for the contrary of this. It is this elementary experience which is contrasted by Levinas with every moral order. This contrast is alluded to in *Otherwise Than Being or Beyond Essence* by the expression of an "anarchy of the Good."[101]

However, Levinas clearly sees that one cannot avoid limiting the initially unlimited responsibility which arises from an encounter with the other.[102] The reason for this inevitable necessity is not simply the finitude of one's power, time, strength, and capacity. The reason is, paradoxically enough, just as well the ethical fact that one's responsibility, according to Levinas, cannot be restricted to *the* other but it must be extended to *all* others.

It is true that the two kinds of responsibility have to be distinguished here. However accidental the encounter with "the" other may be, a face-to-face conjuncture, and thereby a personal bond, results from it. No such bond is established with those indifferently called as "others." One could, therefore, wonder whether in the latter case the question of responsibility arises at all. To speak of responsibility without taking for granted a factual and personal relationship seems to be a far-fetched and contrived procedure which hardly results in anything else than an empty locution.

Things are, however, by no means as plain as that. The personal bond arising from a face-to-face conjuncture is quite peculiar: it has nothing to do with the personal characteristics of the two parties entering into a face-to-face conjuncture with each other. The elementary relationship between oneself and the other, which is considered by Levinas as the ultimate source of responsibility, does not in the least depend upon sympathies between individuals. From this, however, it follows that everybody who figures among those called indifferently "others" has a claim to be regarded as "the" other as well. The emergence of this accessory claim disturbing the relationship between oneself and the other is described by Levinas as the entry of the third party.

This role of the third party is analyzed in *Totality and Infinity* and in *Otherwise Than Being or Beyond Essence* in two different ways. However, for our purposes it suffices to concentrate upon the elements which are common to both versions. The most significant contention runs as follows: *The entry of the third party results in the emergence of a further appeal which one finds himself or herself confronted with; that is why one cannot avoid limiting the initially unlimited responsibility one is assigned to bear for the other.* From this tenet a consequence of crucial importance may be drawn: *This inevitable necessity of the limitation of responsibility and the ensuing requirement of its just division are the two main sources of every moral order.* However, in *Otherwise Than Being or Beyond Essence* this conclusion is followed by the following statement: *As soon as a moral order gets consolidated, the original infinity and unlimitedness of responsibility fades more and more into oblivion.*

This statement reveals what is at stake in the ethic of alterity which is entirely centered upon the elementary relationship of oneself and the other. Levinas brings to light an experience which, recalcitrant as it may be to every moral order, nonetheless makes evident a primordial sense of the ethical from which the ultimate justification of all particular systems of moral prescriptions derives. It is by no means the illusory belief in a moral order that does not require the limitation and the division of responsibility which nurtures the attempt to highlight this experience. Levinas does not even envisage the possibility of replacing the moral impact of legal duties, institutional obligations, and customary rules by the ethic of the face-to-face conjunction with the other. The incentive he is driven by is different. It is a conviction which may be summarized as follows: *A moral order that submerges into oblivion the anarchic event in which an accidental encounter with the other gives rise to an unlimited responsibility is doomed to losing its ethical sense.*

4. The Anarchy of the Good and the Rule of the Law

According to one of Lacan's famous adages, the one who loves gives something he or she does not possess. This idea, which can be traced back to Plotinus, has its place in the ethics of Levinas as well. Yet this place is curiously described in *Otherwise Than Being or Beyond Essence* as a *non-lieu,* that is, so to speak, as "a place nowhere to be found."[103]

This strange expression is the literal equivalent of the Greek *Utopia.* The over- or extrahistoricity, which, in Levinas's view, characterizes the relationship between oneself and another, may indeed remind us of a Utopia. However, the meaning of the expression *non-lieu* has by no means been exhausted so far; and while it is true that Levinas is among those who stand up for the Utopian aspirations of the prophetic tradition, this, in itself, is not enough to make over- or extrahistoricity intelligible, undoubtedly regarded by Levinas as one of the most fundamental features of the ethical relationship. Rather, it is in the direction of what was said in connection with the "anarchy of the Good" that an explanation can be given—at least this is what I wish to claim, and argue for, in the concluding section of this chapter.

The meaning of the term *anarchy of the Good* has already been contextualized; it may be further clarified if we ask how, in Levinas's view, the ethical is related to the historical and, more particularly, to the political.

It is not in an overtly political sense that Levinas first speaks of the anarchy of the Good. The following quotation from *Otherwise Than Being or Beyond Essence* leaves little doubt about this. Levinas says,

> The notion of anarchy we are introducing here has a meaning prior to the political (or antipolitical) meaning currently attributed to it. It would be self-contradictory to set it up as a principle (in the sense that anarchists understand it). Anarchy cannot be sovereign, like an *arche.* It can only disturb the State—but in a radical way [. . .]. The State then cannot set itself up as a Whole.[104]

In another passage, he adds,

> It is [. . .] not without importance to know if the egalitarian and just State in which man is fulfilled (and which is to be set up, and especially

> to be maintained) proceeds from a war of all against all, or from the irreducible responsibility of the one for all, and if it can do without friendships and faces. It is not without importance to know this in order that war may not become the insaturation of a war in good conscience.[105]

Neither of these texts indicates that Levinas would be hostile to the state: the embracing of the idea of an anarchy of the Good does not imply an antistate attitude. On the contrary: to establish and maintain the "egalitarian" and "just" state is, according to him, an important task of the human being. It is also clear that in this process his ethics receives a significant role. It is this role which is first to be specified.

A remarkable interpretation with respect to this role has been put forward by Simon Critchley. His point of departure is as follows: "For Levinas [. . .], ethics is the disruption of totalizing politics: anti-Semitism, antihumanism, National Socialism."[106] Critchley can clearly see, however, that it is not only totalitarianism with which Levinas's position is incompatible; it is also incompatible with every tendency—be it antidemocratic in spirit or not—which, committed to a holistic perspective, insists on the primacy of politics.[107] Still, Critchley maintains that for Levinas *ethics leads finally back to politics.*[108]

How is this claim to be understood? Levinas is so far away from an uncritical justification of politics by ethics that the following passage from *Otherwise Than Being or Beyond Essence* suggests the precise opposite:

> In an alternating movement, like that which leads from skepticism to the refutation that reduces it to ashes, and from its ashes to its rebirth, philosophy justifies and criticises the laws of being and of the city [. . .].[109]

It should be emphasized more unambiguously than it has been done by Simon Critchley that here Levinas insists not only on the inseparability of justification and criticism but he lays an equal stress on the *alternating movement* between the two as well. According to this alternating movement—similarly to the relationship between skepticism and its refutation—justification never reduces criticism to ashes without raising it anew from its ashes, i.e., justification only "annihilates" criticism in order to "resurrect" it in another shape.

Even further, we may distinguish between three significant stages in the alternative movement:

1. Levinas takes it for granted that, at the moment one becomes aware of oneself, one finds oneself already integrated into a given order of customs and morals, obligations and laws. Apart from exceptionally

infelicitous cases, one is from the outset a member of a family and citizen of a state. However, these ties become loose, or may even get undone, in the ethical situation Levinas characterizes as a face-to-face encounter.

2. In a face-to-face encounter, we are confronted with the appeal of the other. This appeal is not to be eluded because in such a situation, as Bernhard Waldenfels rightly puts it, *no answer is itself an answer.*[110] It is, however, not a moral prescription, not an *ought,* from which this inevitability, or inescapability, results. Here one simply *has* to answer; one *cannot* but answer. What kind of place is, however, to be given to an appeal in ethics, which, as it has just been claimed, has nothing to do with any kind of a moral *ought?* Considering the second major work of Levinas's later period, *Otherwise Than Being or Beyond Essence,* we may surmise that this place is by no means insignificant: here the ineluctable appeal of the other is taken to be the source of a responsibility which is not limited by any law, right, or measure.
3. Still, we find ourselves, according to Levinas, compelled to limit this initially unlimited responsibility as soon as we take into account—while simultaneously trying to answer the appeal of the other—the accessory appeal of the third party as well. The entry of the third party entails a conflict of simultaneous appeals.[111] This conflict opens up, as Waldenfels remarks,

> a dimension of the political, which does not merely arise where institutions deliberately aim at forming a separate region—the region of *politics*—out of that which is political; this dimension can be found everywhere where issues of power are raised and conflicts arise: no question and no answer can be rescued from this influence.[112]

It is here that the need arises for an order only law can ensure. Law is required to provide a measure for settling the conflict of simultaneous appeals in the right way. In this sense, Levinasian ethics may indeed be said to lead back to politics, in the broadest possible sense.

Nevertheless, the realm of the initially unlimited responsibility remains once and for all withdrawn from the rule of law. A brief consideration may establish this remarkable point. I may endeavor to correspond to an alien appeal by deliberately adopting a responsive attitude. It is, however, only in such a degree that I shall be able, thereby, to satisfy this appeal. The compliance of my response with the appeal of the other is susceptible to certain degrees; consequently, the adequacy of the answer

I give remains necessarily an issue of *more or less*. Therefore, I shall hardly ever arrive at a point where my response does not leave me still in debt. It is, however, by no means the *laws of the city* to which I remain indebted. It is uniquely to the *other* that I still owe the complete answer. For, as we have already seen, it is not the force of a morally binding *ought* that I am compelled by; it is neither duty nor law that induces me to expressly develop a responsive attitude. It is, consequently, neither duty nor law by which my responsive stance is measured.

Some of the implications here are of crucial importance indeed. It turns out that a full compliance with law and duty is not incompatible with a preposterous refusal of response. The figure of the "refuser of response," acting in full "respect for the law," is far from being a contrived and far-fetched construction. It takes a quite realistic shape if one evokes the *experimentum crucis*[113] Kant was confronted with by Benjamin Constant.

Once encountered, the protagonist of the essay "Über ein vermeintes Recht, aus Menschenliebe zu lügen" is not likely to be ever forgotten. This man gives shelter in his house to a friend who is persecuted by a murderer. The murderer soon appears in the scene, inquiring about the friend in question. Should the protagonist of the essay deny the persecutor the truth? How could he deny it, once he knows that he is not supposed to lie under any circumstances, not even for the sake of humanity? Therefore, he just tells the murderer the truth: he tells him that his friend has indeed taken shelter in his house, and he leaves the rest to fate.[114]

Is this sincere, even *too* sincere, man not the incarnation of a "refuser of response," acting in full "respect for the law"? The mere fact that such a figure is not inconceivable seems already enough to assume with Levinas that the dimension of an unlimited responsibility indeed exists, a dimension which is *not* measured by law.

These considerations may lead us to a new interpretation of Levinas's *non-lieu*. However obvious the allusion to Utopia is, it should not be forgotten that the French expression is taken from the register of jurisdiction: it refers to the cessation of a judicial procedure by a court of justice. This meaning is entirely pertinent here. Indeed, Levinas uses the term *non-lieu* to refer to the realm of a *responsibility before the other*. In this realm, however, something similar to the cessation of a judicial procedure takes place: whoever enters this realm will be, even if only provisionally, *exempted from the responsibility before the law*.

It is this "place of nowhere" that makes room for the "anarchy of the Good." The word *anarchy* substantiates that here the order of customs and morals, obligations and laws we find ourselves integrated into from the start is transitorily suspended, or so to speak, "bracketed," or "put between parentheses," and thereby, invalidated for a while. This is an *epoche* of an unusual sense and of an extraordinary scope, yet it cannot be maintained in the long run because the relationship between oneself and the other, the source of unlimited responsibility, is always already "troubled" by the accessory appeal of the third party. Here the alternating movement between the realm of unlimited responsibility and the rule of the law arrives once again at a turning point: it is a moral order based on a limitation and, as far as it is possible, on a just division of responsibility that one finds oneself relegated to by the entry of the third party. The upshot of these considerations may be retained in a formula that can only be expressed in all its poignancy in French: *Ce n'est qu'à ce point de jointure que le non-lieu a lieu.* The same point may, however, be made in English as well, even if in a slightly different way. Characterizing the realm of unlimited responsibility as a "place of nowhere," we may indeed say: *It is solely on this place of nowhere that the anarchy of the Good can take place.*

4

Elements for an Ethic of Alterity

The aim of the investigations reserved for the last chapter of this book is to adumbrate a phenomenological approach to ethics, for which I take the Levinasian idea of an "alternating movement" between unlimited responsibility and moral ordering as a point of departure.

This option may be surprising, since Levinas himself decidedly opposes ethics to phenomenology. But even if this is true, it is no less true that his ethical inquiries constantly revolve around a question which resides at the very core of phenomenology. Indeed, they are designed to disclose a region of elementary claims and ties which underlies—to use the Husserlian term—the *Urstiftung,* i.e., the "generation by primal instituting," of justice, law, and moral order. It is at the very basis of such a generation that, in Levinas's approach, the third party enters into the sphere of the elementary relationship between oneself and another.

It seems to me that the specific kind of responsibility encountered in this sphere might be best qualified, as Waldenfels rightly suggests, with the word *wild.*[1] This adjective, borrowed from Merleau-Ponty, of course, is to make it clear that responsibility is not yet confined by any particular or well-articulated duties, and it is not yet conditioned or delimited by the universal law. I will argue that the unlimited responsibility Levinas talks about belongs to a *wild region* which lies at the root of all moral order introduced into personal life-history, or created by society.

From what I say below it will be clear that for the study of how moral order arises from the wild region, the Levinasian idea of alternating movement appears to me to be a more appropriate model than the Husserlian notion of a generation by primal instituting. As a matter of fact, the very talk of primal instituting may be judged as inconvenient because it risks the relegation of this question to the obscure areas of a psychological or historical origin. In addition, *Urstiftung,* in Husserl, is closely connected with *Endstiftung;* consequently, it conjures up a teleological perspective, which, in turn, remains committed to a by no means incontestable philosophy of history. Obviously, none of these ingredients of Husserl's original thinking can find a place in a phenomenology inspired by the diacritical method. The model of *alternance,* suggested by Levinas, rather invites us—as the diacritical method requires—to concentrate on critical situations which reveal the indelible contrast between wild responsibility and moral ordering principles.

This model will guide me in locating the first elements of an ethic based on the idea of alterity. This aim involves an inquiry into the role moral ordering principles may play in life-history, so I shall consider how wild responsibility is related to such intricate matters as law, desire, and guilt.

In the first section of the present chapter, I shall expose a generalized model of alternation, applying it to the relationship of wild responsibility and the universal law. The argument to be developed here may be regarded as a more systematic elaboration of the hints formulated at the end of the previous chapter.

In the second section, I will face some of the possible objections which might be raised against the very idea of wild responsibility on the basis of the theory of narrative identity combined with an ethics of a teleological bent. I shall turn with a special interest to Ricoeur's repeated efforts to integrate duty, law, and even moral autonomy into the history of a desire capable of a—teleologically interpreted—process of sublimation. The conclusion which I draw from the reflections upon Ricoeur's undertaking is, however, that all such efforts are doomed to failure.

The third section will still be dedicated to the problem of desire. Here, I shall be concerned first with Lacan's remarkable venture to bestow a properly ethical weight on desire, and then I will make an attempt at the characterization of the relationship between wild responsibility and desire.

The fourth and last section will engage itself with the highly enigmatic problems posed by guilt and evil. I shall try to show how the idea of wild responsibility may provide a clue to a dismantling of what may be described as "the metaphysics of evil," without contesting the insight that guilt (or, as Levinas calls it, "the self-accusation of remorse") may provoke a radical turn in life-history and may prove to be a destinal event of eminent significance.

1. Moral Law and Wild Responsibility

Kant compares conscience to a court of justice where two "lawyers" oppose each other: one for the defense and one for the prosecution, and decision is made in the form of the judge's verdicts (*Richteraussprüche*).[2] By contrast, Heidegger interprets conscience "as a call of care," further emphasizing that "characterising conscience as a call is not just giving a 'picture,' like the Kantian representation of the conscience as a court of justice."[3]

Between these two conceptions of conscience, there is, surely, something like an abyss. The disagreement goes back to the interpretation of the law: while in Kant's ethics it has an absolutely central position, Heidegger's fundamental ontology refuses to assign any role to it in the analysis of conscience. Rather, in *Being and Time,* Heidegger formulates some deep-seated reservations with respect to duty and law; his objection is that Dasein cannot be measured against anything which would be alien to its being: As he says, "Dasein is altogether incommensurable with anything present-at-hand or generally accepted [. . .] which is not it itself, or which is not *in the way Dasein is*—namely, *existing.*"[4]

It remains to be seen, however, to what extent Heidegger's objection is well founded. It should not be forgotten that the moral law—as Kant makes it clear—assumes the form of a command which addresses the moral agent in the *second-person singular.* Consequently, the command is not merely a *demand* or a *claim* on us but it does carry the element of the *call* as well: it addresses, or even issues summons against, us. It was precisely in order to emphasize that the command has the character of the call or the address that Kant coined the metaphor: "the voice of reason."

It was, undoubtedly, Paul Ricoeur's merit to point out the ethical significance of this metaphor. Yet even he had to admit that "the revealing metaphor of the voice ha[d] been eclipsed by the stifling voice of the court."[5] Thus, it can be claimed that, although Kant discovers that we are addressees with respect to the moral law, he fails to see that this address or call has an ethical significance in itself, irrespective of the fact whether the demand the call carries is justifiable or not. This is why Ricoeur cannot and does not rest satisfied with a mere reference to Kant when, in the closing sections of his *Oneself as Another,* he enters into a debate with the interpretation of conscience in *Being and Time,* where Heidegger wishes to separate conscience from everything that has to do with the ethical. Ricoeur tries to find a weightier counterargument than the one he could formulate on the basis of Kant's system and he finds it in Levinas. This is not much of a surprise, since Levinas is, beyond doubt, the first thinker for whom the call is endowed with ethical significance in itself.

Ricoeur's attempt to draw, on the basis of the considerations we reviewed above, a parallel between Kant's and Levinas's respective ethical orientations, is, however, far from unambiguous, since the ethical character Levinas attributes to the call cannot be understood if one takes a duty- or law-based morality as a point of departure. Here the term *ethics* is used, as we know, rather in the sense of wild responsibility than in the sense of duty or obligation.

If we, therefore, abandon the parallel Ricoeur implies, our problem might be reformulated thus: what kind of a connection holds between wild responsibility as it is interpreted by Levinas and the law which is so central for Kant in moral philosophy? It will be argued that with respect to what we conveniently call sometimes "ethics" and sometimes "morality," two sources come into play: these two sources are *distinct* and *neither can be traced back to the other,* yet they are still strangely *inseparable.* The complex thesis which is thus to be formulated contains two claims: it will be attempted to be shown that although wild responsibility cannot be traced back to the moral law, it still requires this law as a principle which provides its boundary and measure; then, in turn, it will be demonstrated that although the moral law cannot be derived from wild responsibility, either, it still presupposes this kind of responsibility as the ultimate source of its own sense.

1. From Wild Responsibility to the Moral Law

One of the reasons why wild responsibility cannot be traced back to the moral law is that it is based neither on duty, nor on moral obligation. It rather occurs when someone addresses us and thereby directs to us an *appeal,* or when—as we may say with an expression we wish to introduce as a technical term in order to emphasize the meaning of "appeal" which is relevant in the present context—we find a kind of *claim of response* on us. If the curious concept of wild responsibility is properly to be understood, it is the claim of response which calls for further specification.

In the footsteps of the pioneering work of Heidegger and especially Levinas, we may talk about the emergence of something like a *phenomenology of appeal* or a *claim-of-response phenomenology,* both in France and in Germany. In spite of their undeniable differences, the initiatives of B. Waldenfels, J.-L. Marion, and J.-L. Chrétien are all marked by the common effort of detecting a *counterintentionality* at the "kernel" of the appeal–response or claim of response–answer relationship, and this may serve as the starting point of an overall refashioning of phenomenology. In line with our primary concern, it is only one aspect of this relationship which can be treated here: I will emphasize that there is a *compulsion for response* which is different from any kind of duty.

Whenever we are faced with a claim of response, we are, in the most literal sense of the word, *compelled* to answer, to respond to, this claim. This is not duty but inevitability: when somebody has addressed us, we are, as we have already seen, simply *not in a position* to refuse to answer, since in this situation even our denial of an answer counts as a kind of response. This is why Levinas claims that "the ethical situation of responsibility cannot be understood if we take ethics as our starting point."[6]

How could the compulsion that derives from the claim of response be properly specified? When Levinas uses expressions like "persecution," "accusation," "assignation," or "obsession" and "trauma," then he contrasts the compulsion not only with the inevitability of that which "cannot be otherwise" but he also tries to delineate it from "the constraint imposed on a will by a situation."[7] Here we might follow Waldenfels, who describes this compulsion—which is, as we could see, neither "eidetic necessity,"[8] nor what we usually and simply call "the force of the circumstances"—as "factual necessity."[9] The concept of *nécessité de fait*—originally introduced by Sartre to characterize the unique certainty of the *cogito*[10]—will prove to be useful here, too, despite the obvious differences between Sartre and Levinas. It is with this expression that I wish to accentuate what I find to be analogous in the otherwise diverse two conceptions; "factual necessity" proves to be, in both authors, the source of a kind of responsibility which is contingent and does neither tolerate, nor need a proper foundation—consequently, there is no way to justify it.

"Factual necessity" should not be mistaken for the unavoidability of the *factum brutum,* either. Crude and brute facts do compel us to reckon with them, yet they do not lay claim to our response, they do not, in themselves, make us give an answer. True enough, the claim of response is not entirely devoid of violence. Levinas—like Nietzsche—wishes to uncover, in his own way, the origins of ethics outside of the realm of ethics; this might even be taken as the common trait of the two philosophers. Such an enterprise involves, in both authors, the detection of the traces of violence in what we may call the "genealogy of morals."[11] Yet the claim of response, triggered by a call, does by no means originate in violence. The connection between the claim and the response, described by Levinas as our "exposure in response to . . . ," as our "being at the question before any interrogation,"[12] cannot be interpreted as a mere *relation* of *power* or *force* or *dominance*—it is rather to be understood as a *sense-relationship.*

The above formulations need, beyond doubt, further specifications. When we talk about a *sense-relationship,* we should concentrate on the sense of *saying,* rather than that of the *said.* What kind of significance may this differentiation carry in ethics? This question cannot be avoided, especially because of one of Ricoeur's excellent insights; Ricoeur, interpreting Levinas's late masterpiece, *Otherwise Than Being or Beyond Essence,* rightfully points out that Levinas's main aim is to demonstrate that "the order of saying [*régime du Dire*] and the ethics of responsibility coincide."[13]

Yet this coincidence is far from obvious or self-evident. To argue on its behalf, it is, first and foremost, the difference between *the said* and *the saying* which should be made clearer. Simon Critchley has applied various models to interpret this difference: the distinction between performative and constative, introduced by J. L. Austin; the distinction between the event of statement and the content of statement (*énonciation, énoncé*), first used by Benveniste and Lacan; and even the distinction which has its origins in Bühler's works: the differentiation between the "descriptive," as well as "expressive" function of speech as opposed to its "addressing," "summoning," "phatic" function.[14] The application of these models is, beyond doubt, useful and valuable; so it is not because of my disagreement that I take an alternative road to the problem. I wish to place the difference between *the said* and *the saying,* as well as the relationship between the claim of response and the answer, into the framework of a *phenomenology of language.* Three main theses will be enough to demonstrate how the "order of saying" and "the ethics of responsibility" are related.

1. It was Merleau-Ponty's feat to make "operative speech"—rather than the system of language—central to the phenomenology of language. Following this hint, which was fruitfully applied and even expanded by Richir, one may detect a fundamental difference between the sense of what is said and the sense of saying the said. It does not, indeed, require great effort to realize that the sense of saying is in the making all the time, whereas the sense of the said is fixed by the accepted and institutionalized system of meanings which can more or less be considered as constant. We may also highlight this difference by using the original Husserlian terms, the opposition of *sense formation* and *sense fixation,* with the significant proviso, however, contrary to Husserl's conception, that sense formation can by no means be traced back to the gesture of sense giving because the sense of saying, of actual speech, of operative language, falls outside the domain of the speaker from the very start. Whether it is the sense of saying identified as "spontaneously emerging sense" (*sens spontané*), as Merleau-Ponty interprets it, or the "sense shaping itself" (*sens se faisant*), as Richir takes it, it will always remain a dispossessed sense, which evades all forms of sense giving intentional consciousness is ready to impose on it. Thus,

what is to be emphasized is not only that here the term *saying* strictly refers to the actual practice of speaking, but also that it designates operative speech only to the extent it is considered as an event during which the emerging sense is in nobody's possession.

2. It is also easy to notice that the relationship between *compatibility* and *incompatibility* will be peculiar to the respective realms of *saying* and *the said:* compatibility and incompatibility will need a different characterization in the two opposing fields. This observation seems to be valid also with respect to successive events of utterances. A protest or a promise, for example, may equally come as answers to a threat, yet a condolence or a thank you would not be adequate responses here, unless the interlocutor wishes to crack a joke or aims at a sarcastic repartee. The relationship between the claim of response and the answer becomes clearer following these considerations. *It seems justifiable to say that an utterance with a claim of response cannot be followed by an utterance that would not count as (some kind of) an answer.* This applies not only to words actually uttered but to silent facial expressions and speechless gestures as well. It is precisely this *incompatibility*—and not a *conflict of forces*—that gives rise to the particular necessity which demands a call to be answered.
3. Since it is evident that there is no utterance without a claim of response, the following conclusion may be drawn from the two observations above: *incompatibility lends the character of an answer to all the senses emerging in the realm of saying* (when the realm of saying is considered as distinct from the realm of the said). This "responsivity," as Waldenfels calls it, puts the spontaneous sense formation characteristic of operative language in an entirely new light. It makes clear that this sense formation necessarily takes place in an intersubjective space marked by an irreducible asymmetry between oneself and the other. Levinas gives voice to this insight by specifying the sense of saying as being always "for the other" (*pour-l'autre*).[15] Levinas's expression is to convey that the giving of an answer is unavoidable: he accentuates that compulsion or constraint which is not only the indispensable prerequisite of the operation of speech but—at the same time—the source of ethics as well.

This is the content of the relationship between "the order of saying" and the "ethics of responsibility" we started out in quest of following Ricoeur. The relationship is established by the compulsion for response triggered by every call. As early as in *Totality and Infinity,* Levinas hints at this peculiar constraint by calling attention to "the ethical condition or essence of language."[16]

However, it is not easy to subscribe to some related tenets of Levinas developed especially in *Totality and Infinity;* for example, it is hard to read the following claim without reservations: "Meaning is the face of the Other, and all recourse to words takes place within the primordial face to face of language."[17] If the consequences of the recent attempts at working out a phenomenology based on the claim of response are properly drawn, one might easily be convinced that statements like those of Levinas cannot be unproblematically taken, since they tend to restrict the validity of the above discussed claim-of-response and answer relationship to a literal *face-to-face* encounter. It is evident that the applicability of this relationship should be carried beyond this boundary. But how? Is it enough to say, with J. L. Marion, that the claim of response "in its anonymity" cannot be traced back to *the other* any more effectively than to *being,* or to *God,* or, for that matter, to *life?*[18] Or should we, after all, still side with Levinas, and stick to his criterion that saying always has the character of being *for the other?* It is not easy to take a stand here. Yet perhaps the obstacle will automatically be removed if *being for the other* is not restricted to a factual encounter with the other, but it is extended, beyond the bounds of the *face-to-face,* to all cases in which we meet an *inappropriable, dispossessible alterity,* be this actually present in the form of a face, a word, a gesture, a deed, or even that of an event. Nothing seems to hinder this extension, since it is not because of the otherness of the other that all these phenomena bear the stamp of dispossessible alterity but the other way round. It is their inappropriable alterity which lends them an otherness even more characteristic and irrevocable than the other's otherness: this is an otherness which is accessible only if it has an inherently *asymmetrical structure,* i.e., it is irreversible in the given context, and thus the relationship we enter into with it does not allow for any kind of reciprocity. It is this asymmetrical relationship which can be characterized as *being for the other.*

Yet it should not be overlooked, either, that the compulsion to answer, triggered by the alien call which cannot be possessed, is always a "factual necessity" as well, so it forever remains a *contingently emerging unavoidabilty.* It must repeatedly be pointed out that here we are dealing with an unavoidability which comes into play as a result of an accidentally emerging claim of response. We cannot say, however, that the claim of response would necessarily be anchored in the condition of a factual encounter with the other, so it does not, in any way, presuppose what Levinas describes as *the face-to-face.* Yet it is very much to be emphasized that it takes shape as a consequence of an accidental, contingent event.

It is in the above insight that the key to our problem is hidden. It is not surprising that wild responsibility cannot replace the universal law once it has been admitted that it emerges as a result of accidental happenings and that, consequently, it remains unique and irreproducible in all its occurrences. Crossing the other's way by chance, or any other situation in which we encounter dispossessible alterity, can give rise to a responsibility which knows no bounds, since it involves neither any measures, nor any law. Yet this indeed wild responsibility, with a wavering sense and with uncertain limits, cannot stand in itself in the long run: sooner or later it will refer us back to the law once again. Even Levinas hastens, as we have seen, to point out that the initially unlimited responsibility is bound to constrain itself as soon as the *third party* makes his or her appearance. In *Otherwise Than Being or Beyond Essence* he writes, "The third party introduces a contradiction in the saying whose signification before the other until then went in one direction."[19] We may add that if it is true that operative speech always assumes the character of an answer, then its signification or sense—the *being for the other*—is always already in contradiction with itself, from the very first moment. This is so because, as Waldenfels points it out, the sense of operative speech always emerges as a resultant of forces in a field where "such claims of response are present which are, at the same point of time, incompatible with one another."[20] In other words, the third party Levinas mentions has been there all the time. So we have to face the question from the start: how can we give an answer which would give its due, which would deal out justice, to each and every competing claim of response? Law finds its origin in this question. A demand for a universal law, thus, comes from the effort to dissolve the inevitably emerging contradiction in the realm of saying.

Our first task has been completed, since we may conclude that although wild responsibility cannot be traced back to the law, it requires it as a kind of principle which measures out responsibility's limits and boundaries. As our second task, it is to be demonstrated that, contrariwise, the law cannot be directly derived from wild responsibility either, yet it still presupposes it as the ultimate source of its own sense.

2. From the Moral Law to Wild Responsibility

The difference between the respective realms of wild responsibility and the law-created order can never be repealed. It is among the significant features of the region of wild responsibility that there is an inequality, a kind of unbalance between the above mentioned, various claims, which, as we saw, are incompatible in the same moment of time. It is not true that these competing claims would, all the time, be arriving partly from *the other* facing us, and partly from a third party who, with his or her appearance, disturbs the straightforwardness of the *face-to-face*. Yet it seems to be very true that some traces of a conflict, structurally akin to *the other-contra-third-party* relationship, are surfacing on all the claims: there are ones which, gaining dominance, aim at an exclusiveness similar to the intimacy of *the face-to-face* relation, while there are some which, in turn, merely count as simple disturbing factors. The line of division between the dominant, decisive features and the ones which get subordinated is sometimes redrawn and placed elsewhere, yet it never totally disappears. Thus, the unbalance we are able to witness here is of a kind which only involves the respective roles of the various claims and, precisely for this reason, makes its appearance in forever changing actual shapes and forms.

It is the always recurring unbalance which prevents the struggle of the mutually exclusive claims from coming to a halt. The origins of the law-established order lie in our effort to give the competing claims their respective due, to justify all of them at the same time. As it would be impetuous to claim that this effort is bound to failure from the start, it is equally heedless to pretend that there is hope for complete success, since the order the universal law establishes has to apply the same measure even where inequality or unbalance is unavoidable.

Consequently, there is an unbridgeable gap between the law-established order and the region of wild responsibility: the law distinguishes itself from wild responsibility precisely by placing itself above the unavoidable unbalance created by the competing claims. Here, however, we have to make amends to avoid a possible misunderstanding. One may falsely conclude that the above mentioned unbalance is a kind of *deficiency*—or worse, a decisively *negative* feature—of the realm of wild responsibility, which simply obstructs the establishment of order and justice. This is far from the truth: the unbalance in question can be traced back to an expressively *positive* trait of the claim of response, since unbalance originates in the fact that each claim of response is *unique* to the point of *incomparability*. The law, with the aspiration to be universally valid, necessarily places one claim of response on the same level as the other, so it automatically disregards the unique and the nonreproducible: *it creates justice at the expense of injustice.* Formulating his well-known charge in the *Gleichmachung des Ungleichen,* it was Nietzsche who unmasked the injustice at the roots of all justice with the keenest eye.

Yet this relationship between justice and injustice should by no means imply that the justification of the order created by the universal law should be called into question. It is for good reasons that Levinas emphasizes the significance of "contradiction" here: it is in the sense, born and emerging from the saying, from the *diction,* where the opposition, or even antagonism, occurs; the sense is in *contra-diction* with itself whenever it encounters the conflict of competing claims of response, and the desire, the demand for a universal law is born in this very contradiction. Yet the "anarchic reason"[21] Levinas also introduces as opposing the justice established by the universal law is equally important. Thus, it will be the opposition between justice and anarchic reason which will be our guideline to clarify the relationship between the respective regions of wild responsibility and the universal law.

To understand what Levinas means by "anarchic reason," we have to recall the analysis of skepticism and its refutation in a memorable section of *Otherwise Than Being or Beyond Essence.* He shows that the refutation of skepticism can detect a contradiction in all statements, denying the possibility of truth, only at the expense of dissolving the difference between the saying and the said on the same level of order: by putting them on the same plane and by "synchronis[ing] the implicit affirmation contained in saying and the negation which this affirmation states in the said."[22] The aim of Levinas's analysis is, as Robert Bernasconi emphasizes, neither to deny the possibility of truth, nor to make a new attempt at the refutation of skepticism but rather to elaborate a "model" apt to elucidate the significant difference between the saying and the said.[23]

It seems to be possible to draw a parallel between the relationship Levinas detects between skepticism and its refutation and the relation which figures between the region of wild responsibility and the order of the universal law. Levinas hints at this parallel himself; our task is to work out the implications.

It sounds plausible indeed that the contradiction encountered in the region of wild responsibility bears the marks of the dissolving of the difference between the saying and the said. If the unbalance between the competing claims of response is transformed into a contradiction waiting for resolution, the transformation—as Levinas is also quick to point it out—will already in itself presuppose "comparison, coexistence, contemporaneousness, assembling, order [. . .], and thence also a copresence on an equal footing as before a court of justice."[24] In this respect, what we encounter here is a case of disregard for the unique, and the neutralization of the incomparable. The unbalance (inequality) between the competing claims of response can be turned into a contradiction awaiting resolution because we wish to give an answer to the claims of response which can *simultaneously,* and at the same time, *completely* satisfy each and every one of them. This ideal might easily motivate us when we have to decide about practical matters, yet it is by no means a good counselor when it comes to working out a theory, because it would entice us to think that it is possible to reach a stage where the answer is in no way lagging behind the claim of response, i.e., where the former is able to match the latter completely. Such a stage could only be reached if the sense emerging by itself, and arising as an answer immediately and without any further mediation to the claim of response directed toward us within the circle of saying, could get dissolved, without any residue, in the meaning fixed by special and separate considerations, i.e., practically in the institutionalized meaning, which here assumes the shape of an organized, well-articulated answer in the realm of the said. Yet the leveling and the complete equality between the sense emerging by itself and fixed meaning would only be possible if the difference that exists between the saying and the said could be abolished without any residue whatsoever.

Levinas finds it important to warn us repeatedly about this fundamentally significant and unsurpassable difference. This gives weight to his "anarchic reason," yet this is not brought into play to create suspicion around the justification of the universal law outlined above. No one is to deny that the universal law has a well-founded origin in the contradiction of the competing claims of response in the region of the said. What is, rather, to be challenged is that that there would only be a single level: as Levinas explicitly says in connection with the relationship between skepticism and its refutation, he wishes "precisely to contest [. . .] this uniqueness of order and level."[25]

What is the actual relationship between the two orders or levels, to be separated from each other? It is, once again the analysis of the relationship between skepticism and its refutation which indicates the direction of an answer. To say that Levinas wishes to defend skepticism is to misunderstand him. "Skepticism is refutable," Levinas declares, yet he immediately adds that "it returns," "*il est le revenant*": it keeps haunting us like a ghost.[26] For Levinas, this means that there is a constant "alternation" between skepticism and its refutation.[27]

This might, once more, serve as a model in our quest for the clarification of the relationship between the region of wild responsibility and the order established by the universal law. It was attempted to be shown that wild responsibility and law represent *two distinct sources* of what we sometimes call "ethics" and sometimes "morality," and *neither of them can be traced back to, or be derived from, the other.* Yet here the word *distinct* implies *discernibility* and even *dissociability* without implying *separability.* This is a paradoxical relationship indeed, which can only be understood if our point of departure is an alternating movement which *unites* the two sources without *unifying* them; which joins them, without fully integrating them.

It is, indeed, an alternating movement that can be detected in the relationship of wild responsibility and the universal law. We are, always already, within the framework of an order which is imbued not only with customs and traditions but with duty and the law as well. If we feel that we are, time after time, torn out of the order we find ready-made, our feeling can be attributed to influences coming from accidental encounters with the other or—to put it more generally—to the effect the facing of a dispossessible alterity may have on us. In such moments we are weighed down by a boundless, limitless responsibility, which knows neither law, nor measure. This initial responsibility, however, has to limit itself—as we saw—as soon as it is faced by various competing claims of response turning toward it. From that moment on, we again have to rely on the order established by the universal law. Yet the movement will not come to a halt. If the order, created by the universal law, were completely able to subjugate the region of wild responsibility, it would have to pay for it by losing the ultimate sense of its own. This totalitarianism would not be perfection at all; it would rather be the sign of a dangerous distortion, since then all the ties, binding the law to the incomparable uniqueness of the claims of response we have to face, would snap. It is this which makes our reliance on an anarchic reason justifiable.

3. Remarks on Moral Conscience

The above considerations may also show the phenomenon of a *voice of the law* (the Kantian "voice of reason") in a new light. There is a considerable ambiguity around this phenomenon: although the only thing the voice of the law demands from the moral subject is to follow the law of *his or her own* (i.e., to become an *autonomous* subject), it still carries the features of a command which remains transcendent. The moral subject cannot withdraw himself or herself from this command: the moral subject's duty is to *obey*. It does not need much demonstration that *morality*, in the sense Kant gave to the word, as distinguished from *legality*, is constantly wavering between these two extremes. It is precisely this wavering in which the mystery of the Kantian "fact of reason" originates: the moral subject has no other duty than to give law to himself or herself, yet it is the law itself which imposes on the moral object this duty. Perhaps it is for this fundamental duality that in Kant the metaphor of the "voice of reason" is inseparably bound to the metaphor of conscience's "court of justice."

Ricoeur challenges this inseparability by erasing all references to the universal law from the analysis of what he calls the "voice of conscience." It is certainly true that, in opposition to Heidegger, he is looking for an "injunction" at the bottom of conscience, yet it is also true that although the injunction he finally identifies is ethical through and through, it is still a far cry from duty. According to the characterization Ricoeur gives here, it is "a form of commandment that is not yet a law"; it is rather an "injunction to live well."[28] Yet the "voice" of conscience cannot be considered as devoid of all ambiguities, even if it is no longer referred back to the universal law. It is clear that because the voice of conscience is an injunction, it talks to the moral subject in the second person singular, yet the otherness Ricoeur attributes to it does not only differ from the otherness of "our own" in our very bodily constitution but from the "alien" otherness of the other as well. It is for this reason that Ricoeur points to the "need to maintain a certain equivocalness of the status of the Other on the strictly philosophical plane," the need to maintain "this aporia of the Other"—an aporia which requires the acknowledgment that "the philosopher as philosopher . . . does not know" and cannot decide, even in principle, "whether this Other, [as] the source of the injunction, is another person whom I can look in the face or who can stare at me," or whether this Other is identical "with my ancestors," or with "God—living God, absent God—or [with] an empty place."[29]

Whatever we are to think of this rather surprising statement, it is suitable to draw at least one conclusion from it: it is not only the metaphor of the voice of the law, or of the voice of reason, which is surrounded by a stubborn ambiguity but the metaphor of the voice of conscience as well. The investigations devoted to the relationship between wild responsibility and law in this section might offer some explanation for this as well. It seems possible to consider "the voice of the law" and the "voice of conscience" as *two-faced limiting concepts,* which do not so much unite but rather obscure and confuse the two sources of ethics and morality we distinguished: the claim of response and wild responsibility, on the one hand, law and duty, on the other; or, to put it differently, "voice" (the call, the summons), on the one hand, and, on the other, the "injunction," which is not duty but still a "form of command." It may even be claimed that the concept of morality, *as opposed to both legality and wild responsibility,* is among the hopelessly equivocal concepts as well. If this sounds plausible, even the mysterious warning the first sentence of *Totality and Infinity* contains can be taken to heart: "Everyone will readily agree that it is of the highest importance to know whether we are not duped by morality."[30]

II. Moral Autonomy and Narrative Identity

The two concepts in the title of this section seem, at first sight, to exclude each other. The notion of "moral autonomy," considered as a principle of obligation and responsibility, "acknowledges," as Kant emphasizes, "no temporal distinctions."[31] In contrast, the theory of narrative identity is an unambiguously temporal view of the self: narrative is inconceivable without temporal distinctions.

This may be one of the reasons why the proponents of the narrative view of self-identity put up a resistance to any influence by the Kantian tradition of moral inquiry and, as far as ethical considerations are concerned, prefer to rely on the Aristotelian heritage. The most striking example of an unconditional rejection of the Kantian approach to morality is, of course, MacIntyre's *After Virtue.* But even a thinker as mildly tempered and as comprehensive in outlook as Paul Ricoeur has put a mitigated version of this rejection forward.

As has become almost common knowledge, MacIntyre sets out to show that "the project of finding a basis for morality," which he takes to be a characteristic enterprise of the Enlightenment era, "was bound to fail" because of the fatal dissolution and decomposition of the "teleological scheme" of ancient and medieval ethics whose articulated structure consisted of three elements: "untutored human nature, man-as-he-could-be-if-he-realized-his-*telos* and the moral precepts which enable him to pass from one state to the other."[32] The destruction of this scheme was in MacIntyre's view "the joint effect of the secular rejection of both Protestant and Catholic theology and the scientific and philosophical rejection of Aristotelianism."[33] As MacIntyre argues in *After Virtue,* the elimination of every notion of "man as he could be if he realized his *telos*" leaves behind the two remaining elements as "incoherent fragments of a once coherent scheme" which can no longer be reintegrated into a whole.[34] Therefore, according to these analyses, all attempts to justify morality, including Kant's foundation of ethics by means of the notion of moral autonomy, were necessarily condemned to fail.

Ricoeur follows MacIntyre and others in specifying the difference between the Aristotelian and the Kantian traditions of ethical inquiry as an opposition between the *teleological* and the *deontological* approaches to morality.[35] But he does not accept the global rejection of any theory of obligation based on moral autonomy. He modifies MacIntyre's view of the Aristotelian and the Kantian legacies by establishing "a relation involving at once subordination and complementarity" between them.[36] He argues for the *primacy* of teleological ethics over the deontological approach to morality, but he does assign at least a limited validity to the latter. However, what is in his approach of utmost interest is not so much his conception of why there is a *complementarity* between the two traditions but rather his idea of why the Kantian view has to be *subordinated* to the Aristotelian heritage. In order to explain this idea he undertakes to show that *a theory of obligation based on moral autonomy has a necessary recourse to the "inherent ethical aim of life."* Part and parcel of this enterprise, he also tries to demonstrate the even more fundamental thesis that *deontological morality has to be integrated into teleological ethics.*

This "Subordination Thesis," as we may term it, can be regarded, if it proves to be valid, as one of the main tenets of the theory of narrative identity. What Ricoeur adduces in favor of this thesis in his book *Oneself as Another* may be supplemented by some observations that we owe to other proponents of this doctrine. Especially Charles Taylor's account of moral reasoning as "a reasoning in transitions" offers itself for consideration. According to this view, we try to convince each other that one moral position is superior to another by showing that the move from the first to the other is an "error-reducing" one: it dispels, for instance, a confusion, or it resolves a contradiction.[37] But Taylor adds that such efforts can, in principle, be successful only if the "move" in question is a *lived* transition.[38] As he puts it,

> You will only convince me by changing my reading of my moral experience, and in particular my reading of my life story, of the transitions I have lived through—or perhaps refused to live through.[39]

Since from this it already follows that this form of argument "has its source in biographical narrative,"[40] it is not difficult to see that this piece of Charles Taylor's "moral phenomenology"[41] points in the same direction as Ricoeur's Subordination Thesis.

The two philosophers agree on some crucial points indeed. First of all, contrary to MacIntyre, neither of them wants to abandon the notion of moral autonomy, although both of them want to deprive it, in Ricoeur's formulation, of its "self-sufficiency"—a formulation which could be Taylor's as well.[42] Second, they seek to find the proper place of this notion in an account of one's search for self-identity. Furthermore, as engaged exponents of the narrative view of the self, they—here already rejoining MacIntyre as well—define this search as a "narrative quest."[43] Further still, in this quest both of them recognize the expression of a fundamental "craving" which, in Taylor's phrase, is "ineradicable from human life"—a phrase which, this time, could also be Ricoeur's.[44] Finally, they assign to this fundamental craving a teleological structure: a direction toward what is, in each case of human agency, taken to be "the good."

Yet, in spite of all these common traits, it would not do justice to Taylor to claim that he holds the Subordination Thesis. He unquestionably shares with Ricoeur (and others) the opinion that "a cramped and truncated view of morality in a narrow sense" has emerged recently.[45] He even formulates the task "to bring out and examine [. . .] the richer background languages in which we set the basis and point of the moral obligations we acknowledge."[46] Yet, from this point onward he dissents, arguing that the real gamut of ethical questions and considerations encompasses three main areas which do not overlap. Moral obligations, he thinks, belong to a cluster of demands concerned with "the respect for the life, integrity, and well-being, even flourishing, of others."[47] The second area of ethical considerations is, in his view, connected with questions of "what kind of life is worth living," or of "what constitutes a rich, meaningful life."[48] Finally, he distinguishes from these areas the "range of notions concerned with dignity" or, in other words, with the "feeling of self-worth."[49] Beside a set of expressions centered around the metaphor of "area," he adopts another language as well in which he compares the different dimensions of ethical interrogation to "axes" of "moral space." This mode of speech clearly indicates that, what, in his opinion, connects the three directions which moral exploration can take is not a relation of dependence: as axes of moral space, they are obviously *coordinated* with, rather than *subordinated* to, each other. Thus, Ricoeur's thesis that deontological morality is to be integrated into teleological ethics can hardly be ascribed to Taylor.

On the following pages I will examine Ricoeur's position by presenting two cases in which thinkers who certainly do not belong to the Aristotelian tradition of ethical inquiry come to the conclusion that the very conception of moral autonomy calls for a narrative perspective. The first case is, significantly enough, Kant's own. My other example is the unduly forgotten French philosopher Jean Nabert. His case is not less relevant than Kant's. It was while grappling with Nabert's quite original contribution to the foundation of ethics that Ricoeur's attempt at deriving morality from teleology first began to take shape. The genesis of Ricoeur's approach is all the more interesting because the Subordination Thesis is not, as such, attested to by the case studies to be presented. Although Kant's and Nabert's examples can be said to support the proposition that moral autonomy and narrative identity belong together, they, interestingly enough, may also serve as evidence *against* Ricoeur's claim that this link between the two notions requires the subordination of deontology to teleology. As we shall see, the link between moral autonomy and narrative identity, in fact, disallows this subordination.

1. Kant's Inquiries into the Origin of Obligation

It is commonly taken for granted that in Kant's eyes the foundation of ethics is tantamount to a *justification of morality*. MacIntyre is one to be committed to this presupposition, too. It is undoubtedly true that Kant speaks of a "deduction of the supreme principle of morality" in his *Foundations of the Metaphysics of Morals.*[50] It is also true that the argument mentioned under this heading is indeed aimed at the "justification" of "the objective and universal validity" of the principle in question, namely the "moral law," as this is clearly shown by a passage in the *Critique of Practical Reason.*[51] But whereas in the former work Kant purports to have completed this task, in the latter he expressly declares that "the objective reality of the moral law can be proved through no deduction."[52] Of course, he hastens to add in the *Critique of Practical Reason* that "the supreme principle of morality" needs "no justifying reasons," because "it is firmly established of itself" as "an apodictically certain fact, as it were, of pure reason."[53] This change in Kant's position is not insignificant. It shows that the task of the foundation of ethics does not coincide in his approach with the task of the justification of morality.

As a matter of fact, the two tasks are at least distinguishable even in the *Foundations of the Metaphysics of Morals.* Here, Kant tries first to discover what the "ground of a possible categorical imperative, i.e., of a practical law" is.[54] He then asks himself, "on what grounds the moral law obligates us" or, in another translation, "*whence the moral law derives its obligation.*"[55] It is the latter question which is answered by the "deduction of the supreme principle of morality." As a response to the former question, we, on the other hand, find a statement which has nothing to do with the attempt to justify moral precepts. As Kant says, "man and, in general, every rational being *exists* as an end in himself."[56] This statement attributes to rational beings a *prerogative* "over all merely natural beings."[57] This "ground of a possible categorical imperative, i.e., of a practical law" is obviously not sufficient to *justify* "the supreme principle of morality." It is in another way that it "grounds" it. It specifies the "supreme limiting condition on the freedom of the actions of each man"[58] and thereby provides room for a possible moral legislation. The foundation of ethics amounts here to laying bare or disclosing the possibility of morality rather than justifying it.

It is due to special circumstances that these two tasks are still considered as finally coinciding in the *Foundations of the Metaphysics of Morals.*[59] These circumstances do not prevail any longer when Kant sets himself to write the *Critique of Practical Reason.* That is why in this work Kant's foundation of ethics undergoes a profound transformation.

This transformation does not entail any rejection of what has been called the "prerogative" of rational beings.[60] But now *personality* is specified as the veritable supporter of this "prerogative." Thus, a new concept comes to the fore. The emergence of this concept is closely connected with a new concern which is characteristic of the *Critique of Practical Reason.* Kant extends here his theory of obligation. He now tries to grasp duty as "the supreme *life-principle* of all human morality."[61] This alteration requires new investigations with the aim of disclosing the conditions of the possibility of a "course of life" (*Lebenswandel*) "conformable" to the moral law.[62]

Thereby, Kant sets a twofold task for himself. He takes the already mentioned "fact of pure reason" as his starting point. He then inquires into the effects brought about by this "fact" directly in the minds of "finite rational beings" and indirectly in the construction of their courses of life. Here, he puts forward his doctrine of respect as the "incentive of pure practical reason." But this is only one part of the task he has undertaken. The other part is proving that the "empirically determinable existence of man in time"[63] exhibits, on its part, a certain receptivity or susceptibility to these effects. As a result of this new undertaking, Kant's foundation of ethics appears in an entirely new light. It has nothing to do with the justification of moral precepts any longer. It revolves rather around the question of *how the very structure of the "empirically determinable existence of man in time" contains the conditions of possibility of a moral "course of life."*

In order to corroborate and elucidate this assertion I will outline how the *Critique of Practical Reason* sets out to find an answer to the question just formulated. The first step Kant takes in this direction is to investigate what features "the empirically determinable existence of man in time" shows *before* the moral law as a "fact of pure reason" begins to exert its influence on this existence. Kant takes it to be natural that first inclinations prevail and "self-love" rules in the "course of life" of a "finite rational being." But he argues that, even at this stage, "the empirically determinable existence of man in time" keeps open, at least, the *possibility of the development of moral personality.* An important observation gives support to this contention. Kant comes to perceive that man, before setting out to follow a "moral course of life," does not simply *yield* to inclinations, but moved by "self-conceit," he makes self-love "legislative," although this is "wholly incapable of giving universal laws."[64] This phenomenon of a *necessarily spurious legislation of self-love,* as we may describe it, shows, so to say, *in the negative* that the "course of life" of a "finite rational being" always contains a place which, however usurped by self-love, is in fact designed and reserved for moral legislation.

Do not all these changes in Kant's foundation of ethics lead to the insight that the theory of moral autonomy as a principle of obligation and responsibility cannot avoid having recourse to a conception of how a human "course of life" evolves? I think the answer is in the affirmative.

And is this conclusion not a confirmation of Ricoeur's Subordination Thesis? Does not the very formula of "duty as a life-principle" indicate that the deontological departure finds its completion in a teleological view of the "empirically determinable existence of man in time"? However astonishing it may be, the answer is, as far as I can see, in the negative.

It would be, indeed, a little overhasty to endorse the latter suggestions. We should not forget that Kant, as it has been pointed out, sets a *twofold* task for himself in the *Critique of Practical Reason*. The twofold character of this task is an expression of his belief that the principle of autonomy does not cease to act upon "man's existence in time" *from without*, even if it is at the same time not unreasonably regarded as "the supreme *life-principle* of all human morality." This clearly shows that, in Kant's view, the notion of moral autonomy cannot be separated from its "deontological" context.

But even apart from Kant's view, the proposition that this notion does not lend itself to any restatement in the framework of a "teleological scheme" can be supported by a further argument. Before specifying it, let me, however, insert a preliminary remark here in order to prevent misunderstandings. By saying that the notion of moral autonomy does not lend itself to any reformulation in the context of a teleological scheme I do not want to imply that any teleological scheme entails what has been called by Kant "heteronomy." As MacIntyre has rightly claimed, "Aristotle's view is teleological, but it is not consequentialist."[65] Therefore, in contrast to utilitarianism, Aristotle and his followers are not compelled to consider moral action as a means to an end which is not moral in its character. On the contrary, the author of the *Nicomachean Ethics* emphasizes that it is *for their own sake* that the virtuous man chooses the virtues.[66] Thus, it is incontestable that the Aristotelian tradition is in a position to meet one of the most important requirements involved in Kant's notion of moral autonomy. It is for a different reason that this notion still resists being transposed into the framework of a teleological scheme. This reason is that moral autonomy includes, or even presupposes, a *radical change of attitude* which can never be replaced by any imperceptible transitions in a continuous development. To put it in Kantian terms: man can never take the "standpoint" of freedom without a "revolution in his way of thinking." From this it already follows that the character of "ought" and, consequently, a certain sort of constraint or compulsion can never be removed from moral autonomy. It is, therefore, not a mere accident that this notion originates in a deontological approach to morality.

But why not interpret this deontological approach as a necessary *detour* which the teleological unfolding of any human course of life finds itself forced to take? Ricoeur's intention is, in fact, to elaborate such an interpretation. This is an integral part of the legacy bequeathed to him by Jean Nabert.

2. The Genealogy of Obligation in Nabert, Ricoeur, and Freud

The first to delineate such a genealogy of obligation was indeed Nabert, who deserves by far more attention than he receives today. *Déduire le devoir:* this is one of the great tasks Nabert undertakes to complete in his work *Elements for an Ethic.* He attempts to derive duty from what he calls "desire to be."

This attempt is to be analyzed within the broader context of an endeavor which is to show that "the history" of the desire just mentioned is the main concern of what deserves the name "ethic." As Nabert expressly formulates it, "An ethic can only offer itself as the structure of a concrete history which each self begins again and which it does not always complete."[67] This statement clearly marks a break with any deontological conception of morality. Moreover, this conclusion is explicitly drawn in the text. "The ethic," we are told, "does not prescribe; it reflects on a becoming whose beginning, palpably identical for all, it discerns and whose ideal direction it seeks to discover."[68] It is from this perspective that Nabert tries to "deduce and determine" the "significance" of moral imperatives.[69] He describes duty as "a moment or a condition of the unfolding of our desire to be."[70]

It can, however, be claimed that Nabert's "deduction of duty" has a chance to be successful only because "our desire to be" is regarded in it as "a desire deeper than all desires" or as "an aspiration deeper than all aspirations born of nature."[71] This quotation implies a significant dichotomy. In Nabert's view, the realm of desire is indeed divided into two distinct parts. The aspiration which has been identified with "our desire to be" is said to have "nothing in common with the desire for satisfaction related to this or that determined tendency."[72]

Nabert's derivation of duty from "our desire to be" would remain entirely incomprehensible without this dichotomy. The distinction between "natural tendencies" and "desire to be," or "aspiration into existence,"[73] is an indispensable premise of the deduction. In this distinction a further presupposition is involved: it is taken for granted that, left to themselves, natural tendencies "engender a dissatisfaction," in Nabert's own formulation.[74] The exposition of the main idea is built on these assumptions. Yet the deduction of duty has not only the task to draw the conclusion from these premises. Nabert attempts at the same time to *show up* an *event* which makes it clear that these premises are not unjustified. In other words, it is not from an external point of view that he makes a distinction between two kinds of desire; he rather tries to find an event where desire separates itself from desire by—as it were—itself.

It seems equally obvious that if this *event of split*—as the self-initiated separation within desire might be called—does occur, it must simultaneously bring about a situation where *we find ourselves divided* as well, since as Spinoza pointed out, we are desire itself; desire is not an accidental appendage to our real being but rather the other way round: our real being coincides with our very desire. Thus, the event where desire gets separated from desire should also be considered as an event, as a sign in the *split of the self.*

The course of the deduction Nabert undertakes is as follows. The initial step of the argument is to state that "the fundamental desire to be inserts itself invincibly into tendencies and knows itself first of all within them." In the next step, Nabert explains then the emergence of duty by alluding to a "nonempirical act" of self-recognition by which the fundamental desire to be discerns itself from all natural tendencies. As we read: "it reacts to inner dissatisfaction which bothers it by accepting, with the supremacy of a nonempirical act, the authority of a law strong enough to defeat the tendencies." After this crucial assertion nothing is left but to draw the conclusion: "The desire to be withdraws in favor of duty."[75]

Can this argument support Ricoeur's Subordination Thesis? The answer seems to be "Yes," but it is, in fact, "No." It seems to be "Yes," because Nabert takes a stand against the deontological conception of morality. But the answer is "No," because Nabert is far from taking sides with Aristotle's teleological approach. The event of split which we encountered in his theory of desire unmistakably indicates that he does not break all ties with the Kantian tradition. He rather completes by his "deduction of duty" what Kant had begun but left undeveloped. In his account the idea of "duty as a life-principle" expands to an articulated theory. But just as in Kant's *Critique of Practical Reason,* it remains rooted in a "nonempirical act." Furthermore, just as in Kant's view, this "nonempirical act" leads to *a radical change of attitude* in Nabert's conception as well. The dichotomy which demarcates the "aspiration into existence" from "natural tendencies" is only a theoretical expression of this change of attitude. It is only in the sense of "a desire deeper than all desires" that morally legislative reason and its authority are to be reduced to desire.[76] And it is only in the sense of "an aspiration deeper than all aspirations born of nature" that Nabert can say "Duty masks aspiration."[77]

It is Ricoeur himself who tries, first in the early sixties, to reinterpret the lesson which he has drawn from Nabert's "deduction of duty" in a teleological framework. However, in assuming the legacy bequeathed to him by the work *Elements for an Ethic* in this modified form, he finds himself confronted with another heritage: the heritage of Freud. It does not escape him that in the statement "Duty masks aspiration" there lies the possibility of an interpretation unintended by Nabert, but proposed before him by Freud, according to which *duty masks desire and repression of desire.* Thus, in contrast to his later book *Oneself as Another,* in the sixties Ricoeur is led to face a hermeneutical situation which he characterizes as an inevitable "conflict of interpretations."

Are his efforts to cope with this situation successful? Does he glimpse a way "to arbitrate the war between two opposed hermeneutics,"[78] as he describes the task emerging from this situation? In seeking to find an answer to these questions, it is worthwhile to consider here briefly his remarkable essay on Freud.

He approaches the conflict of the two interpretations from the basis of what he calls "*philosophical reflection.*" By this term he refers back, once again, to the heritage taken over from Nabert. In order to understand how the notion of philosophical reflection can be brought into connection with Freud's theory of desire, it will be instructive to draw on an observation of Ricoeur's which concerns, once more, Nabert's conception of morality. In his preface to the second French edition of the work *Elements for an Ethic,* Ricoeur sharply remarks that "Nabert rediscovers a meaning of 'Ethics' which is closer to Spinoza than it is to Kant."[79] We can really appreciate the pertinence of this remark if we take a look at the meaning of the "nonempirical act" which played such an important role in Nabert's "deduction of duty."

As we have said, it is an act by which the "fundamental desire to be" comes to self-recognition. At the very core of the work *Elements for an Ethic,* we find a train of thought which is designed to shed light on this process. Nabert elaborates here his own version of the thesis *Cogito, ergo sum.* He assumes with Descartes that self-awareness includes the affirmation of one's being, but, in opposition to Descartes, and in agreement with Spinoza, he gives a "dynamic interpretation" of the "I am": he discloses in it, so to say, desire at work. In his view, the emergence of a "consciousness of self" is the very process in which the "fundamental desire to be" comes to self-recognition. Moreover, Nabert shares with Spinoza the conviction that "the initiative of affirmation is wrested from me," as the emphatic formulation of the work *Elements for an Ethic* goes.[80] Consequently, we are no longer surprised to learn that the "I am," in Nabert's interpretation, is "far from being the autonomous positioning of a subject."[81] Almost the opposite is true: the "I am" expresses, as we are told,

> nothing less than the absolute affirmation affirming itself through the act of a consciousness which becomes consciousness of self at the very moment it discovers that it is not in virtue of itself.[82]

In his essay on Freud, Ricoeur revives this doctrine of a "primary" or "primal affirmation," as it is called in the work *Elements for an Ethic.* He finds in it the indication of an essential mark of what he himself tried to describe as "mere human freedom" in his book *Le volontaire et l'involontaire* (translated into English as *Freedom and Nature).*[83] He summarizes this highly original interpretation of the thesis *Cogito, ergo sum,* an interpretation proposed first by Nabert and adopted then by himself, too, for reasons dictated by his own investigations, as follows: "I posit myself as already posited in my desire to be."[84] This restatement of Nabert's main idea is to emphasize that "primal affirmation" is not contained in self-consciousness but in a desire which is a *prerequisite* of self-consciousness. If, instead of adopting an external point of view to describe this affirmation, I take the perspective of my awakening self-consciousness itself—similarly to how Proust describes his hero's awakening in his early childhood—I find at the very root of my existence a desire directed at the maintenance and the unfolding (the dénouement) of my being. The moment I arrive at the affirmation, at the conscious undertaking of my being, I have to realize that the desire to be in me has already overtaken me, it has arrived *before* me. This is why Spinoza's *conatus* proves to be more *original,* more *primordial* than Descartes's *cogito.* The desire to be turns out as inseparable from my real being, from the *self* which I, in my awakening, become conscious of. An expression coined by Ricoeur is usefully applicable here: it is indeed a *cogito blessé,* "wounded cogito," which is revealed here. The reason for this wound is *the event of split in desire:* the desire to be, preceding self-consciousness, gets by itself separated from all the other desires tying the self to the particular entities of the world. It is this insight which prompts Nabert to base his ethics on the desire to be.

It is in this Nabertian sense that we may claim that Ricoeur, in the sixties, wishes to give an *ethical* tint to the whole of philosophy. From the idea Ricoeur borrows from his master about the desire which precedes self-consciousness, there is a logical, or even necessary step toward the reevaluation of psychoanalysis.

Ricoeur makes efforts to show that Freud's "metapsychology" can be integrated into philosophical reflection precisely as a description of "the emergence and positing of desire through which I am posited, and find myself already posited."[85] In this view, the main achievement of psychoanalytical theory is the revelation of what is anterior to any consciousness and, in this sense, "the manifestation of the ever prior."[86] That is why Ricoeur tries to capture the contribution of Freud's analysis of desire to a philosophy of reflection by forming the concept of "an archeology of the subject."

It is from this perspective that Ricoeur reconstructs the psychoanalytic account of morality. He points out that this account consists in a genetic explanation of the agency called "superego," and he adds that this explanation is "aimed at bringing authority into the history of desire" or, to put it in different terms, at showing "how the sublime arises within desire."[87] It is not difficult to recognize a certain affinity of these formulations with Nabert's phrase "*déduire le devoir*" or even with Kant's notion of "duty as a *life-principle.*" But what is the result of Freud's attempt?

After having devoted painstaking analyses to the problems of identification, ideal formation, and sublimation, all closely related to the question of how the superego takes shape, Ricoeur comes to a general assessment of the psychoanalytical explanation of morality. He first states that

> Freud maintains two theses with equal force: the superego is acquired from without and, in this sense, not primal; on the other hand, the superego is the expression of the most powerful instincts and the most important libidinal vicissitudes of the id.[88]

With regard to this ambiguity, he speaks then of a "compromise between two requirements: to *internalize* an 'outside' (authority, father figure, any form of master) and to *differentiate* an 'inside' (libido, narcissism, id)."[89] Finally, he draws the following conclusion:

> For my part I doubt that Freud succeeded in reducing the fundamental gap between the externality of authority, to which he is condemned by his refusal of an ethical foundation inherent of the positing of the ego, and the solipsism of desire, which stems from his initial economic hypothesis that every formation of an ideal is ultimately a differentiation of the id.[90]

Ricoeur's way out of this cul-de-sac is to supplement the archaeology of the subject with the *teleology of consciousness.* He reaches back to the Hegelian phenomenology of the spirit to identify the event of split in desire. Hegel's formulations about the "reduplication of self-consciousness"[91] serve as a convenient starting point: Hegel defines self-consciousness here as *desire.* Through an intricate line of argument, it is further demonstrated that this self-consciousness "*finds satisfaction only in another self-consciousness.*"[92] Ricoeur gives a detailed analysis of Hegel's reasoning, pointing out that desire "is revealed as *human* desire" only to the extent it is defined as "desire for the desire of another consciousness."[93] The phenomenon of the *reduplication of desire,* as a result of Ricoeur's investigations, gives an interpretative content to that idea of

Nabert's which claims that we have a desire which is more primordial than any of the others tying us to the particular entities of the world. Self-consciousness, Ricoeur claims, is the result of a process in which "the desire of self disengages itself from the desire of things," yet it does not try to find its way to the self directly (or, as Freud would put it, in a narcissistic way) but—similarly to the Hegelian conception of self-consciousness—"by seeking itself in the other," by turning, so to speak, to the other for mediation.[94]

An event of split in desire: this description precisely seems to fit what is going on here. Ricoeur follows Nabert, yet his joining forces with Hegel's teleological dialectics has a price as well. Ricoeur does show a *self-split in desire,* yet this split for him is a "wound" of self-consciousness which, eventually, gets "healed" in the dialectical teleology of history. The most effective "ointment" is the Hegelian model of *mutual recognition.* Ricoeur is not hesitant to apply this model: he easily identifies "the desire for the desire of the other" with "man's desire to be recognised by man."[95] Following in Hegel's footsteps, he engages himself with a holistic perspective which—directing attention to the "whole," to the "totality"—gives priority to *man's* desire of mutual recognition and thus pushes the difference between the desire *of one's own* and *alien* desire to the background. This finds expression in Ricoeur's claim that it is "the desire of self" which ultimately finds *itself* in "the desire for the desire of the other." *Désir de soi:* this notion could hardly be rescued from the threat of solipsism, had Ricoeur not applied, in Hegel's footsteps, the dialectical model of mutual recognition to the desire to be.

Is this teleology of consciousness in a better position to bring "authority into the history of desire" or to show "how the sublime arises within desire" than the archaeology of the subject? I think this is quite doubtful. However disconcerting it may be, in the essay on Freud no positive attempt is made to derive deontology from teleology. Ricoeur contents himself here with a merely critical analysis of Freud's interpretation. But he does not show how this interpretation, which he is certainly fully justified to call "reductive," could be complemented by a "more comprehensive" interpretation.

The general way of Ricoeur's "arbitrating" the war of these two hermeneutics may give rise to further doubts. In the concluding chapter of the essay on Freud the initial monism of teleology is replaced by a new dualism: inspired by Hegel, Ricoeur develops first a "phenomenology of spirit or mind"; then, inspired not so much by Karl Barth and Rudolf Bultmann but rather by Mircea Eliade and Gerardus van der Leeuw, he proceeds to a "phenomenology of the sacred," while he expressly states that "the phenomenology of the sacred is not a continuation of a phenomenology of spirit [. . .]."[96] It is not the "phenomenology of spirit" but it is the "phenomenology of the sacred" by which, as we are told, "another dependence of the Cogito or self is revealed, a dependence that is first seen not in the symbol of its birth but in the symbol of an eschaton, an ultimate [. . .]."[97] Therefore, the circle of philosophical reflection is not closed by teleology itself but only by an "eschatology" which is carefully distinguished from philosophy.

If archeology and teleology are related, archeology and eschatology are even more closely connected. The latter connection is also marked by a name that figures in both contexts. This name is, astonishingly enough, Spinoza's. We have seen how Ricoeur discovered in Nabert's description of "primal affirmation" a Spinozistic approach to ethics and how he connected this departure with Freudian "archeology." We now may add that he finds in Spinoza's *amor Dei intellectualis* the culmination of what he calls "eschatology." The following of Ricoeur's descriptions characterizes the attitude of faith as distinguished from all religions of "accusation" and "consolation": "I give up my point of view; I love the whole; I make ready to say: 'The intellectual love of the mind toward God is a part of that very love of God whereby God loves himself.'"[98] He believes that by this attitude "a path of non-narcissistic reconciliation" is opened, a path on which, as he puts it, "the giving up of desire is no longer death but love."[99]

These references to Spinoza both in the context of archeology and in the context of eschatology reveal a permanent endeavor of Ricoeur's in the sixties that underlies his essay on Freud as well. He regards his confrontation with psychoanalysis as well as his renewal of Nabert's reflective thinking as an attempt to develop a philosophy which is *ethics* without being a mere philosophy of morality.[100] We may here repeat one of Ricoeur's remarks on Nabert: this meaning of "ethics" is closer to Spinoza than it is to Kant; and we may add: it is closer to Spinoza than it is to Aristotle, too. "Ethics," in this sense, is not a mere deontology; but it is not a mere teleology either.

Ricoeur does not conceal that this enterprise encounters serious difficulties. As he reaches the point of *amor Dei intellectualis* in his essay on Freud—a point that seems to him to be "unsurpassable"—he frankly admits, "It is not a point of repose but of tension, for it is not yet apparent how the 'personality' of God who pardons and the 'impersonality' of *Deus sive natura* could coincide."[101]

This ultimate difficulty invites us to take a retrospective view of the construction accomplished by Ricoeur in his essay on Freud. It is easy to see that the main building blocks, such as deontology and teleology, or archeology and eschatology, remain *maladjusted* in the final structure.

However, the fact that difficulties are here so conspicuous is one more reason for giving our full attention to Ricoeur's study on Freud even today.

In Ricoeur's more recent book *Oneself as Another* these difficulties are not overcome; in fact, they are not even raised. The introduction of the new concept of "narrative identity" to designate that which earlier bore the name of "history of desire" is certainly illuminating and fruitful. The Subordination Thesis is, however, but a faint reminiscence of the former attempt at mobilizing all resources of deontology and teleology, archeology and eschatology in order to reveal and retrieve what one of the papers collected in the volume *The Conflict of Interpretations* calls in French "*l'originaire éthique.*"[102] Therefore, it seems that the great adventure of the sixties, undertaken by Ricoeur in company with Nabert, Freud, Hegel, Kant, and Spinoza, has not yet found its consummation.

III. The Philosophical Discovery of Desire

To look for the sources, the "ancestry," of our present endeavors and fields of interest, we should go back to the late fifties and early sixties. Present day philosophy has largely been shaped by those special key words, those peculiar questions and daring ventures which were all born in those exciting years. This period was witnessing highly significant works, all having a lasting influence on our thinking: Heidegger, Merleau-Ponty, Levinas, and Henry had created a new beginning for phenomenology; philosophical hermeneutics emerged with Gadamer and Ricoeur; Lévi-Strauss, Lacan, Foucault, and Barthes opposed Sartre's and Camus's existentialism with structuralism; speech-act theory, in Austin's and Searle's groundbreaking studies, began to take a central position in analytical philosophy; Habermas and Apel published their first challenging works; Derrida cast his account, on a grand scale, with Husserl, Levinas, and Freud, while Deleuze did the same with Hume, Kant, Nietzsche, Bergson, and Proust. New vistas were opened in philosophical ethics as well, and it is also in this period that French thinkers made an attempt at the reevaluation of the role desire plays in ethics. Thus, the significance of psychoanalysis for philosophy became deeper than it had ever before. The first decisive moves were made by Ricoeur, Lacan, and Levinas, and their insightful observations are still worthy of our considerations.

It is a deeply rooted, age-old philosophical conviction that moral self-consciousness and practical reason are in opposition with desires, inclinations, and propensities. It is this conception the thinkers who aim at a revision of the ethical tradition in the late fifties and early sixties all wish to challenge. It cannot, of course, be denied that desire displays the structure of self-centeredness: it comes from basic necessities which gush forth often without control, it serves self-interests and even works with a passion behind it that does not consider anybody or anything. Thus, the question might be put in the following form: is there a kind of desire which has a positive relevance for ethics? This is the question Ricoeur, following in Nabert's footsteps, was after but this will be Lacan and Levinas's problem as well.

1. Lacan on the Ethical Weight of Desire

No one was expecting more from Ricoeur's book on Freud than Jacques Lacan—and nobody was more disappointed in it when it was published. This is hardly surprising, considering how differently Lacan tried, somewhat even earlier than Ricoeur, to measure out the ethical weight of desire.

In the fall of 1959 and the spring of 1960, Lacan, in the framework of his famous "seminar," gave a series of lectures with the title *The Ethics of Psychoanalysis.* This gave him the opportunity to review the tradition of philosophical ethics. Lacan's series was centered around three major types of ethical theory: Aristotle's teleologically anchored ethics, Kant's deontologically structured moral philosophy, and Bentham's utilitarianism. In line with his major topic, Lacan's "standard to that reconsideration of ethics to which psychoanalysis leads us" was "the relationship between action and the desire that inhabits it."[103]

The specification of the standard indicates in itself Lacan's major objection to traditional theories of ethics. He claims that *no version of philosophical ethics has been able to put desire where it properly belongs.* Utilitarianism only knows about need, but not about desire; in Kant, desire belongs to our natural being and thus it is in constant opposition to reason, i.e., to that toward which we are turned with our real being, while Aristotle relegates a whole legion of desires into the realm of beastly behavior, thereby excluding them from the region of ethics. In contrast with all these, Lacan points out, "the genesis of the moral dimension in Freud's theoretical elaboration is located nowhere else than in desire itself."[104]

Yet, if one wishes to disclose "the genesis of the moral dimension" *via* Freud's theory, he cannot avoid the question whether this genesis is "limited to"—i.e., is in coincidence with—"the genesis of the superego."[105] This is a question of crucial importance, which Ricoeur was perhaps too quick to answer in the affirmative. Lacan is more cautious: first of all, he makes it clear that "this genesis of the superego is not simply a psychogenesis and a sociogenesis," that "it is impossible to articulate it by limiting ourselves to the register of collective needs," and that its "unique scope" can only be appreciated "in terms of the relation to the signifier and to the law of discourse."[106] Then he makes use of the concepts of the *symbolic,* the *imaginary,* and the *real,* none of which can be neglected in the interpretation of the genesis of the superego. These notions are of course in need of further clarification.

Here the discussion cannot go beyond the circumscription of the following notions: the "relation" of desire to the "signifier," "the law of discourse," the "symbolic," the "imaginary," and the "real," on the basis of the lectures in 1959 and 1960. (These lectures have received expert treatment in respective essays by Rudolf Bernet and Hans-Dieter Gondek, and I will heavily rely on them here.) Yet, even from Lacan's remarks quoted above it is clear that his approach to the problem of ethics is not the usual one in psychoanalytical theory. The main difference is that Lacan does not consider the Oedipus complex to be a necessary accompaniment of healthy development and, contrary to Freud, he does not derive the superego from its disintegration.[107] "Lacan discloses the figure of the tyrannical and revengeful father as an 'illusion,' as a fantasy of compulsive neurosis," Bernet observes.[108] Thus, in Lacan's treatment, the "genesis of the moral dimension" will not coincide—at least in the traditional sense—with the "genesis of the superego." This will suffice as a preliminary overview for the more detailed discussions of the above notions.

We may start by pointing out that for Lacan the "law of discourse" *creates a split in the desire.* The "law of discourse," as Bernet puts it, "functions like a categorical imperative: it imposes on the human that he or she should express, or represent, his or her desire in language."[109] This explains why Lacan connects desire with the "signifier" from the very beginning. This connection contains the insight that objects become objects arousing desire only through the mediation of language. Yet, it is not only the discourse of the others which plays a role here but anonymous language games and linguistic associations as well. Desire takes an especially favored footing in equivocal expressions since these, as Bernet points out, "outwit" the vigilance of the repressive instance and make "the satisfaction of suppressed desire possible."[110]

The signifier—as the philosophical tradition drawing on Saussurean linguistics is prone to put it—has its place in a *diacritical system.* As we know, this concept involves the assumption that the signifier gains meaning in its difference from the other signifiers, or more precisely, in the "differential relationship" it has with them. Since desire is necessarily bound to one of the signifiers by the law of discourse, desire will, from the very beginning, engage itself in the diacritical system which ties the signifier in question to the other signifiers. It is to express this relationship that Lacan coined the famous notion of the "chain of signifiers" (*chaîne de signifiants*). The emergence of such a chain "obeys"—as Bernet puts it—"the general laws of language, while it is the precipitation or the distilment of the personal history of the subject as well."[111]

What emerges in the relationship between the desire and the signifier is a *double split in the subject.* As the human being is the subject of a linguistically expressed desire, he or she is at odds with himself or herself because the (symbolic) subject of discourse and desire does not coincide with the (presymbolic) subject of needs. The second split occurs because he or she gets constantly separated from himself or herself as the subject of discourse and desire as well. As the subject of the event of the utterance, i.e., as the maker of the utterance (*sujet de l'énonciation*), he or she never completely recognizes himself or herself in the subject of what is uttered (*sujet de l'énoncé*) to the full. The split of the symbolic subject accompanies all discourse with the force of necessity. We may recall instances when we try to express something significant about ourselves, yet we find that we strive at sincerity in vain: our statements sound phony, because our words construct a narrative which—as a result of our conscious (or even tendentious) selection from among the events of our life—has been created out of ready-made building blocks, widely accepted patterns of speech, or even clichés. This is an unavoidable distortion, which testifies to a split of the self in life-history.

It can be shown that the self-split originating in language is accompanied by an event of split in desire as well. One brings his or her *need* (*besoin*) into language, puts it *into words,* as an appeal, or as a command, or—with a more comprehensive expression—as a *demand* (*demande*). Considering a diacritical system of signifiers, this very fact is already enough to trigger the emergence of additional (or, even a surplus of) meanings which point beyond the actual need. This is the mechanism on which advertisements are built: "Granny's strawberry jam" is no ordinary strawberry jam! A single call word is enough, and a whole chain of signifiers already emerges, lending the aura of childhood's yummy goodies to the ordinary jam. Meaning gets, thereby, *shifted.* The words suggest something more and something different than they actually express. Thus, we need something more and something different for the satisfaction of our needs than it would be dictated by bare necessities. We, of course, do not receive anything "more" when we buy "Granny's jam"—and this immediately shows that advertisements are a worldwide delusion. Yet, it should be quickly added that we allow our arms to be twisted because we would not be human if our need did not go beyond the bare necessities in which it originates. One of the best poetic formulations of this is in Shakespeare's *King Lear,* when Lear tells his two elder daughters, Goneril and Regan:

> O, reason not the need! Our basest beggars
> Are in the poorest thing superfluous,
> Allow not nature more than nature needs,
> Men's life is cheap as beast's.
> (2.2.453–56)[112]

Lacan calls the above semantic shift—adopting Roman Jacobson's term—*metonymy.* As Lacan claims, the nature of *desire* (*désir*) can be traced properly down along the lines of the above considerations. The process we designate by the term *the shift of meaning* is not solely carried by the general reference relations of the linguistic signifiers but it is also supported by the desire, which "is formed as something supported by this metonymy," i.e., by the desire which comes into being in the *gap* that opens up between the actual meaning and the additional sense.[113] This desire is idiosyncratic with respect to the individual; it varies from speaker to speaker, it is inalienably unique. This desire—triggering the emergence of the additional sense—gets condensed in the linguistic expression. Consequently, Lacan claims, following Roman Jacobson again, the above mentioned metonymy starts to bear the features of *metaphor* as well. It is for this reason that, eventually, the linguistic expression of desire is always accompanied by the "différance" (the difference and the deferring) between the subject of the utterance event and the subject of what is uttered: *sujet de l'énonciation* and *sujet de l'énoncé* can never catch up with each other.[114]

The shift in meaning that necessarily occurs in a diacritical system of the demand's signifiers results, at the same time, in the continuous transformation of the object of the desire as well. *Desire wanders from one object to the other.* As Bernet writes, interpreting Lacan: "Each pleasure that has been gained will undermine itself; each event of pleasure will make room for some further ones. Consequently, each satisfaction of desire is, at the same time, the experience of a lack as well [. . .]."[115]

Now we are in a position to understand why Lacan circumscribes the law of discourse—which, as we saw, is the source of a double self-split—as "the law of (symbolic) castration." This law, as it was observed, demands that the human being should give a linguistic representation to his or her desire; yet the mere fact of this demand will bring about—

to quote Bernet again—the "loss of [. . .] reality in the sense of a directly accessible and unlimited presence."[116]

The above considerations might create the impression that the *symbolic*—language, discourse, expression, "signifier"—dissociates the human being from the *real.* Yet in Lacan's lecture we read,

> the moral law, the moral command, the presence of the moral agency in our activity, insofar as it is structured by the symbolic, is that through which the real is actualised—the real as such, the weight of the real.[117]

How can the two—at least seemingly—contradictory ideas be reconciled? Is it possible that the *real,* which becomes a presence through the *symbolic,* differs from "directly accessible and unlimited presence"?

That this is a question of crucial importance again can be clearly seen from a further objection Lacan raises to the tradition of philosophical ethics. Alongside with each of the three fundamental trends—the Aristotelian, the Kantian, and the Benthamian—an *ideal* is prone to make its appearance: virtue, duty, and usefulness, respectively. Lacan protests against all ideals on the grounds that they *expel,* they *oust the "real" from the horizon of the agent.* This is why he tries, relying on Freud, to assign—as Gondek puts it—the role of "the par excellence normative basic notion" to the *real.*[118] We could also say that it is *the weight of the real* from which Lacan derives *the ethical weight of desire.* Yet how can the "real" and the "normative" overlap?

The *real* does not have its usual sense in Lacan's theory. It does *not* refer to the real as "directly accessible and unlimited presence," with which we could count on the basis of our previous experiences and from which we usually expect to justify what we foresee. In fact, Lacan reminds his reader again and again that the "real" is not the "possible" becoming "actualized" but it is precisely the "impossible" which is "real." *Impossible* is, of course, not to be taken here as the conceptual counterpart of the "necessary" but that which cannot be *mastered,* which withdraws itself from the region of our control, which thwarts our previous expectations, upsets our calculations, makes a mockery of our plans, and scoffs at the fruits of our foresight—so, everything that opposes our effort to usher it into the enclosure of possibilities. When we follow ideals like virtue, duty, or usefulness, we in fact wish to master the unmasterable; we wish to create the impression that the unmasterable realm can still be invaded; we act as if we could arrest what is beyond our mastery by covering it up, by forgetting, or even by suppressing it. Philosophical ethics chases ideals and thus avoids the challenge to which the ethical owes its existence.

Thus, the tension of—or even opposition between—the two statements proves to be an illusion. What becomes precisely clear is that *the real—the real as such, the weight of the real—never manifests itself in the course of our actions without the loss of the real as a directly accessible and unlimited presence.*

It is on the basis of this idea that Lacan wishes to bring Freud's "metapsychology" closer to understanding. The above concept of the *real* provides the key for the interpretation of the "primary" and "secondary" process on the one hand, and the "pleasure principle" and the "reality principle" on the other. The novelty of this interpretation can already be seen in Lacan's emphasis on the ethical implications of the just mentioned distinctions. As we read in the text of the seminar,

> Contrary to received opinion, I believe that the opposition between the pleasure principle and the reality principle or between the primary process and the secondary process concerns not so much the sphere of psychology as that of ethics properly speaking.[119]

And Lacan writes further, "If we always return to Freud, it is because he started out with an initial, central intuition, which is ethical in kind."[120] However, Lacan's interpretation undoubtedly goes well beyond the simple reformulation of the original doctrine and alters it at highly significant points.

Lacan maintains that the real does not coincide with the real "as directly accessible and unlimited presence." Could it be that Freud's "reality principle" would solely be concerned with processes

> which represent [. . .] the fortunate encounters of an organism faced with a world where it doubtless finds something to eat and of which he is capable of assimilating certain elements, but which is, in principle, made up of random events and chance meetings, chaotic?[121]

Lacan's answer is contained in what he calls the "secret" of the Freudian reality principle: the reality principle, Lacan claims, "functions, in fact, to isolate the subject from reality."[122] Lacan here detects a differentiation which has its origins in the works of Freud already: in a way, Freud separated the "real" from "external reality" himself.

It is in line with this argumentation that Lacan connects the real not with what the living organism can *put to use* but with the quest for "the good," for the "summum bonum," for "perfect happiness," as it is not only in focus in Aristotle but, although in a somewhat more subordinate position, it has a significant role in Kant as well. Yet this is by no means to imply that the "summum bonum" would be identical with the "real." Not at all: the pursuit of perfect happiness belongs, according to Lacan, to the dimension of the imaginary.

A curious concept also finds its place in this line of reasoning: the concept of the "thing," which has a central position in Lacan's ethical thinking. The connection between Heidegger's *Das Ding* and Lacan's approach has been pointed out several times and the similarity is especially striking in the famous analysis which reveals a whole world in the void enclosed by a jug; it is obvious, indeed, that for Lacan the "thing" is by no means *this* or *that* thing in the world but just the void itself, around which still a whole world is revolving. Yet, in what follows, another aspect of Lacan's argument is going to be discussed. At one point, Lacan takes the important notion of *finding again* from Freud's essay entitled *Negation* (*Die Verneinung*),[123] which will play a significant role in the circumscription of the concept of the "thing": As Lacan writes, "*Das Ding* has, in effect, to be identified with the *Wieder zu finden,* the impulse to find again that for Freud establishes the orientation of the human subject to the object."[124]

Thus, what is at the core of all impulses of the "human subject" to search for an object is nothing else but the impulse of finding the "thing." For Lacan, two reasons allow us to claim this. The first one is that the *symbolic* structure of the linguistically expressed desire brings about—as it was pointed out—the feeling of a lack that accompanies not only every satisfaction of a need but the satisfaction of all desires as well, and thus satisfaction as pleasure only makes room for further events of pleasure. The second reason is that the above mentioned "impulse" of "finding again" sets every search for a thing on a path which leads into the dimension of the imaginary. What is to be meant by this dimension becomes immediately clear if we consider that, according to Lacan, the search for the "thing" is nothing else than the search for a thing *to be found again.* Yet this is supplemented by a further noteworthy remark:

> Moreover, since it is a matter of finding it again, we might just as well characterise this object as lost object. But although it is essentially a question of finding it again, the object indeed has never been lost.[125]

A la recherche des paradis perdus (in quest of paradise lost): there is no better way to characterize what the search for the "thing" means. The dimension in which the search takes place is one that has been marked out by the impulses to find a thing that has never in fact been lost: this is the dimension of the *imaginary.* The "thing"—be it conceived as the libidinously occupied body of the mother or as any other paradise-like wholeness under the sun—will always remain similar to that *void* which the potter encloses with the wall of the jug. Still, the search for it requires a perspective which looks at the *whole* and aims at *totality*. Besides, Lacan points out, this search decidedly goes on "according to the particular law of the pleasure principle."[126] Thus, we may take the thing to be a *total object of pleasure,*[127] with the important proviso that there is only one experience to be gained about it: *the experience of its lack.*

On the basis of the previous considerations, the experience of the lack can be characterized by a further basic feature. The lack is experienced among the conditions of a search which aims at *finding a lost object again,* yet, as we saw, what is to *be found again has never, in fact, been lost.* The paradoxical formulation prompts the following conclusion: what is expressed in the search for the total object of pleasure is nothing else but a "constraint of repetition," a *Widerholungszwang.* At this point, the pleasure principle enters into the service of the *death instinct.* The search for the "thing," Lacan says, conjures up the picture of such conditions before us in which we think we may "*realize our desires*"—an illusion in which Lacan discerns the "trespassing of death on life."[128]

In contrast with that, the law of symbolic representation is nothing else for Lacan than the true—the real—*principle of reality.* Yet this is a principle of reality which—contrary to what Freud suggested—cannot simply be assigned to consciousness (or to the preconscious), since it has its roots, as Lacan insists, in the *unconscious.* It is true that Lacan's notion of the *unconscious* is not the same as Freud's. It cannot be, if for nothing else than for the fact that it is no longer solely dominated by the *pleasure principle,* which directs—as we saw—the search for *imaginary happiness.* According to one of Lacan's most well known theses—which can be found in the lecture on *The Ethics of Psychoanalysis* just as much as in his other pieces—"the unconscious itself has in the end no other structure than the structure of language":[129] Lacan attributes a *symbolic* character to the unconscious.

It is precisely in its relation to the "thing" that the law of discourse, demanding the linguistic expression of desire from the human being, proves to be a law in the *ethical* sense as well. Considered now from this aspect, what it requires from the human is to never give his or her desire up; one should not budge an inch from desire: *ne pas céder sur son désir.*[130]

What does this new "slogan" of ethics mean, after ethics has been refigured according to the requirements of psychoanalysis? Should this slogan be taken as the "ethics of the right desire," which avoids the extremes of "both ethical absolutism ('only a single object is worthy of desire') and ethical relativism ('all objects are equally worthy of desire')," as Rudolf Bernet claims?[131] Or should we take it as announcing a "tragic form of being," "an ethical model with a heroic stance," as Gondek seems to believe?[132] Instead of taking a position here, I will try to follow a third route which, in a way, avoids the dilemma. As it has already been pointed out, Lacan tries to derive the ethical weight of desire from the weight of the *real.* Would it be possible to interpret the slogan above as an expression of this very effort?

If we try to approach the demand of *ne pas céder sur son désir* from this side, we have to remind ourselves that desire—in opposition to bare necessities—always already presupposes some linguistic mediation and, consequently, it belongs to the dimension of the *symbolic.* Not to budge an inch from desire therefore means the abandonment of the search for the total object of pleasure, for the "summum bonum," i.e., for *imaginary* happiness. It has already been pointed out that the *real*—the real as such, the weight of the real—will never manifest itself amidst our dealings without the loss of reality in the sense of a directly accessible and unlimited presence, or to put it more precisely, without giving up the *imagination* of such a reality. *Not to budge an inch from desire:* this slogan, then, seems to require nothing more and nothing less than to conquer, in ourselves, the instinct of finding again. This already contains the warning that we simply *cannot allow* ourselves to be dazzled by the illusion of a completely realized desire; it is *our task* to stand by the law of the linguistic expression of desire; we *must* thus stick to both the law and the *self-split* which is given in it. Otherwise, the *real*—the real as such, the weight of the real—cannot manifest itself. A further warning is also in place: that the real does not manifest itself does not mean that it is reduced to nothing, that it vanishes in thin air. Even if it does *not* manifest itself, it will *have its effect* all the same, yet this effect will be a *traumatic* one.

The requirement of *ne pas céder sur son désir* is, nevertheless, not without ambiguities in Lacan. The ultimate source of this ambiguity is that according to Lacan, every realization of desire is—as we saw—an experience of a lack. Although for Lacan this "lack-conception" of desire—as it might be called—has its basis in the diacritical system of the signifiers, and, thus in the *symbolic dimension,* it still remains open whether this conception can really be separated from the "instinct to find again" and from the *imaginary dimension* of the search for the total object of pleasure. Do we not drift toward this dimension because of the very idea that every pleasure is there just to make room for more events of pleasure? It is perhaps for this ambiguity that in Lacan the persistence in the self-split in desire assumes the shape of a "tragic form of being" indeed, which takes the original "lack of being" in human existence upon itself as *fate;* and it might be the result of the same ambiguity that no serious position is able to contest this "ethical model of heroism" in the lecture called *The Ethics of Psychoanalysis* than that of the "clever equilibrist," who, as Bernet wittily remarks, very well knows "how the required distance from the thing is to be taken."[133]

2. Desire and Wild Responsibility in Levinas

If in the tradition of moral philosophy one wishes to find a figure to whom Levinas—despite the striking novelty of his approach—is still in close proximity, then it is Kant who is the most likely to be mentioned. Yet, the differences are also obvious: as opposed to Kant, for Levinas the basic event of the ethical is not the hearing, and the listening to, the lawgiving "voice" of reason but is rather in the response to the alien appeal which has a claim on, and is directed to, us. With this move, Levinas—similarly to Nabert, Ricoeur, and Lacan—commits himself to the reevaluation of the ethical role of *desire.* This follows from the very stance Levinas takes: in an ethics taking the sense relationship between appeal and response as its starting point, desire should have a weightier function than in a law-based ethics. It is not difficult to see why. If someone has a *right* to (do) something, then this, for me an alien and law-based right, will *restrict* my desire in the name of an order, whereas an alien appeal, which has its origins precisely in desire, will not restrict my desire but will—almost literally—*appeal to* it: the appeal will turn to, and count on, it. Thus the response we may give as a reaction to an alien appeal grows necessarily out of desire. For Levinas, too, the crucial question becomes how that desire which may be the adequate vehicle of the ethical behavior, gets separated, and delineates itself, from all the other desires. Levinas, too, wishes to put an *event of split* on display *within the desire.*

Levinas is looking for an answer in situations where the appeal which has a claim on us is not only without any legitimacy or right but without arousing any desire in us, as well. It is along these lines that a passage in *Otherwise Than Being or Beyond Essence* can be interpreted: here Levinas says that the *good* assigns the subject "to approach the other, the neighbor,"[134] and then adds, "This is an assignation to a non-erotic proximity, to a desire of the non-desirable, to a desire of the stranger in the neighbor."[135]

In order to understand Levinas's surprising suggestion, it has to be recalled that he draws a sharp line of division between *need* (*besoin*) and *desire* (*désir*). Here Levinas's position indicates some parallels with that of Lacan's, although there can hardly be any kind of direct influence between the two thinkers (although Levinas knew at least Anika Lemaire's thesis on Lacan defended as early as 1969 in Louvain). Yet, here "parallel" should by no means be understood as overlap, not even as a similarity. Lacan derives desire from a *lack of being* (from a *manque d'être* which is interpreted by him at the same time, in a somewhat Heideggerian way, as a *manque à être,* as a lack in Being), while Levinas, as early as in *Totality and Infinity,* talks about "a desire that cannot be satisfied" and which, as he claims, is not "the Desire that is a lack."[136] So, when, in *Otherwise Than Being or Beyond Essence,* he constructs the notion of "desire of the nondesirable," he gets even more displaced from what we may call the "lack-conception" of desire. In *Otherwise Than Being or Beyond Essence,* Levinas concentrates on a kind of restlessness in desire, which however, cannot be traced back to the lack of being; restlessness rather finds its explanation precisely in a peculiar *surplus formation.*

Ricoeur, interpreting Hegel, made us familiar with the idea of the *reduplication of desire,* yet he identified "the desire for the desire of the other"—on the basis of Hegel again—as "man's desire to be recognized by man." The connectedness of appeal and response in Levinas, however, opens up new vistas for further lines of interpretation. This possibility was first realized by Bernhard Waldenfels in his great work *Registers of Response* (*Antwortregister*). As opposed to Ricoeur, Waldenfels does not follow the Hegelian model of mutual recognition but locates a *responsive desire,* which, as he claims, "is aroused as a result of the appeal of an alien desire, i.e., it does not arise purely by itself."[137] The notion of responsive desire helps us understand what is to be meant by "the surplus formation of desire." Desire, it might be claimed, gets multiplied because it does not "arise purely by itself" but as a result of appeals coming from alien desires, or to put it more simply, *it arrives as a response to the desire of the other.*

What is it that gives the ethical weight and significance of the desire interpreted in the Levinasian way? A *methodological device* will help us to formulate this question more clearly. It is thus that the *event of split,* characterized by Levinas with the notion of the "desire of the nondesirable," may properly be assessed.

In the examples Kant brings up in his works of moral philosophy, he investigates extreme cases where duty is not coupled by an appropriate inclination. Let us, similarly, imagine an *extreme case* where the self stands face-to-face with the other without being able to detect even the least power in the encounter to arouse desire. Will it even in this extreme case be true that one's own desire is doubled as a result of the appeals of an alien desire?

By talking about the "desire of the nondesirable," Levinas already has answered this question in the affirmative. His approach leaves the conception which interprets desire as a lack without foundations, since it sounds incontestable that we cannot experience a lack in the satisfaction of the desire without encountering—almost bumping into—something which is nondesirable. Desire is always surrounded by expectations which we are unaware of and which are determined by a "chain of signifiers." Attraction to an "ocean blue" eye is partly of a linguistic nature: the simile included in the compound word may give rise to great expectations. Yet, language will always contain various connotations which may thwart these expectations. Besides the metaphor of the "ocean blue" of the eye, language contains other assumptions, too, for example that blue is "cold." Yet, whether or not desire, in its restlessness, will bump into such a statement will not solely depend on language. Rather, when we find ourselves face-to-face with others, the expectations we are unaware of will not be thwarted by associations of a linguistic origin but by experiences of real disappointment. It is not enough to know that blue is cold: we have to find, to *feel* that the *look* that goes with it is cold, too, and it is then that the magic spell of the object may be broken. This is not simply because our desires, constantly marking out the lack of complete satisfaction, keep shifting and transforming along the lines of associations of a linguistic origin, but also because here desire *bumps into something which is nondesirable.*

Here we find traces of an event of split in which *ethos* gets separated from *eros.* "Erotic proximity," which Levinas also referred to, is undoubtedly a source of bounteous inventiveness. It has the power of transforming the nondesirable (which, thus, stands *in the way* of desire) into something desirable: this desirability will be unique, irreproducible, and unmistakable. ("Blue is, no doubt, cold, yet, what makes other looks cold, lends to *her* look—and *only* to her look—dignity.") What happens when this inventiveness, nevertheless, dries out? Then the nondesirable will not get transformed into the desirable but remains what it is: *nondesirable.* There is no *enticement* in it, yet it still shines forth with an *appeal* which cannot be traced back to mere *entitlement.* It still does not count on our sense of justice, it still does not simply appeal to our sense of right and wrong, but it appeals still to our desire. This special expression, "the desire of the nondesirable," does not, to be sure, mean much more than that we are *touched also by what is alien to us.* The mark of our being touched, the sign of our involvement here is, in Levinas's formulation, not "concupiscence," but "responsibility"[138]—a responsibility which does not know any laws and does not conform to any rights: an "unlimited" but "wild" responsibility. It is clear that a desire which figures as being touched by the one who is alien to us, and which is imbued with responsibility for the alien, has a special ethical weight.

What is, then, the status of that *good* which gives rise to "the desire of the nondesirable"? This "good" is surely not the good Aristotle identifies as the ultimate goal of all our efforts, neither the good which, according to Kant, is determined by the moral law. The good Levinas talks about does not have a place either in a teleological or a deontological ethics. It is least connected with the greatest possible pleasure proceeds of the satisfaction of needs, which utilitarianism wishes to express by calculuses. It is easier to formulate what the Levinasian conception of the good is not than to formulate what it actually is. To make positive statements about this conception makes the interpreter face almost insurmountable difficulties. Yet it can be safely said that the good, in Levinas's sense, is a *gift*. And what is given with the good is a *proximity which knows neither possession, nor appropriation.*

IV. Guilt as a Refusal of Response

It was a common practice of Western philosophical tradition to reduce evil to "privation," "nullity" or "non-being." *Malum est privatio boni:* this was one of the fundamental tenets maintained in European metaphysics. This interpretation of evil originates in the Platonic tradition and received a full expression for the first time in Plotinus.[139]

However, this "privation thesis" (as it is often referred to) has been decidedly rejected by a number of more recent approaches. A first break with Plotinus's view was already marked by Augustine's attempt to find the ultimate source of evil in human will. Yet the seemingly new direction taken by him eventually led to nothing but a detour. Augustine finally returned to the privation thesis since he ultimately thought to discover the origin of evil in the finitude of human freedom.[140] In modern times the conception of evil has significantly changed. Since Descartes's *Fourth Meditation,* and even more since Kant's *Essay on Radical Evil* (which was later incorporated into his book *Religion within the Limits of Reason Alone*), philosophical thinking has shown a strong tendency to consider evil as a mere consequence of freedom, and to give an account of its factual existence in terms of guilt, vice, and human depravity.

Recent approaches to evil have especially been dominated by what Paul Ricoeur has called "the ethical worldview." This term alludes to the German expression "*moralische Weltanschauung,*" introduced by Hegel in a famous passage of his *Phenomenology of Spirit.* It is not without significance, however, that Ricoeur slightly alters the formula taken over from this work. For him, in contrast with Hegel, the formula does not only designate Kant's and Fichte's ethical theory. What Ricoeur has in mind is rather the very specific attempt to understand freedom and evil reciprocally from each other.[141]

Ricoeur distinguishes between two consecutive stages in the development of what he calls "the ethical worldview." In his opinion, the initiative taken by Kant in his doctrine of radical evil was completed in a second stage by Nabert, who, in his *Elements for an Ethic,* tried not only to reduce evil to freedom but, conversely, from this reduction he tried to draw all consequences concerning the very concept of freedom as well.[142]

Ricoeur examines the ethical worldview from a hermeneutical perspective. He builds his analyses on the general assumption that when philosophical reflection begins, everything in fact has already been said in symbols and myths. This conviction is expressed by the famous aphorism "*Le symbole donne à penser,*" which Ricoeur formulates alluding to Kant at the end of his *Finitude et culpabilité.* From this standpoint it is quite natural to consider different philosophical conceptions of evil as elaborations, or as it were, rationalizations of a knowledge which was first expressed in myths. Thus, for instance, the ethical worldview can be considered as the philosophical equivalent of the biblical narrative on Adam's fall.

This analogy makes it possible for Ricoeur to pave the way toward a critical examination of the ethical worldview. He begins with the remark that the mythical universe is a broken world.[143] In Western culture, as he points out, there are essentially different narratives on the beginning and the end of evil. At least three main cycles of myths can be opposed to the biblical narrative on the fall: the Babylonean myth of creation, the Orphic-Platonic idea of a banished soul, and Greek tragedy. The most striking contrast can undoubtedly be observed between Adam's myth and Greek tragedy: while the former obviously wishes to explain the origin of evil by specifying a human action which can be considered as original sin, the latter, as Ricoeur understands it, is based on the view that human culpability arises from existence itself.[144] It is even more important for Ricoeur, however, that not only different cycles of myths contain different interpretations of evil but in most cases one and the same narrative gives rise to divergent conceptions as well. This is true, in particular, of the biblical story of the fall. Although it seeks to uncover the ultimate root of evil in original sin, it contains the embarrassing element that the first human couple in fact falls victim to the temptation of the "serpent." The figure of the serpent marks here, paradoxically enough, a beginning before the first beginning: it represents, as Ricoeur puts it, "the other face of evil," its irreducibility to human action, its *being always already there.*[145]

It is not difficult to see that the idea of radical evil exhibits an analogous ambiguity. Kant defines it, on the one hand, as a "propensity" which "precedes all acts and which, therefore, is itself not an act" while, on the other hand, he explicitly declares that "such a propensity must spring from freedom" and must, therefore, be considered as our own act since "nothing is morally evil (i.e., capable of being imputed) but that which is our own act."[146] Although Kant himself resolves this contradiction by introducing the concept of intelligible action,[147] this exit remains so obviously an emergency device that we can only agree with Ricoeur in calling the above mentioned ambiguity the "greatest paradox of ethics":[148] it reveals indeed an antinomy in the very heart of freedom. This antinomy represents, once again, "the other face of evil," its irreducibility to human action, its being always already there.

Thus Ricoeur is led to a critical discussion of the ethical worldview by discovering correspondences between mythical interpretations and philosophical conceptions of evil. But he does not go further. However clearly he can see that the hermeneutics of myths can never take the place of systematic philosophy,[149] he never goes on to the level of elaborating an independent approach to the problem of guilt and evil. He contents himself with the negative achievement of proving how the ethical worldview comes necessarily to its limits. He adds that the antinomy disclosed by him in the concept of radical evil can be understood as an expression of the "resistance of the tragic to the ethical."[150] But he does not even raise the question of how we could give an adequate account of this "resistance."

It is the Levinasian conception of a wild region of unlimited responsibility which can lead us further. This approach transcends the limits of the ethical worldview from the start. Its contrast with this worldview is, however, all the more instructive because the extended notion of responsibility is just as much bound up in *Otherwise Than Being or Beyond Essence* with an idea of original culpability as the concept of freedom is in Kant's *Essay on Radical Evil,* or in Nabert's *Elements for an Ethic.* As Levinas writes, "The more I return to myself, [. . .] the more I discover myself to be responsible; the more just I am, the more guilty I am."[151] Or to quote an even more emphatic formulation, "The irremissible guilt with regard to the neighbor is like a Nessus tunic my skin would be."[152] Yet, as Levinas insists, this unrestricted view of responsibility and culpability has nothing to do with the assumption of a "state of original sin."[153] The "irremissible guilt," which has just been mentioned, can hardly be properly understood if it is simply taken to be nothing but a more or less idiosyncratic version of a *peccatum originarium.* In reality, the idea of wild responsibility opens a new way toward understanding the enigmatic experience of evil as being always already there.

In what follows, I shall contrast the Levinasian idea of wild responsibility with Kant and Nabert's ethical worldview. After an interpretation of Kant's doctrine of radical evil, I shall dwell especially on the relationship between Nabert and Levinas. Some passages in *Otherwise Than Being or Beyond Essence,* in which Nabert is explicitly mentioned and criticized, will serve as guidelines for the characterization of this relationship. But the chief aim of the following investigations is neither historical nor philological. What will be at stake is rather the question whether a phenomenological approach to the experience of wild responsibility can provide a basis for a philosophical analysis of a problem which, according to the traditional view, belongs to the most obscure regions of metaphysics. Even if evil is susceptible, as Kant seems to claim, of being treated "within the limits of reason alone," it is (like, at least in a certain sense of the term, guilt) commonly regarded as an inaccessible topic for a thinking which tries to remain in touch with experience. It is, however, precisely this conviction which is challenged by Levinas and, to some extent, also by Nabert. To be sure, it remains to be seen how the new way opened by them can be discerned from the route taken by traditional metaphysics. Isn't it true, one may be tempted to ask, that the upshot of both conceptions is that "evils are prior to us and those that take hold on men do not do so with their good will," as Plotinus claimed?[154] I shall argue that this is not true. The similarity with traditional metaphysics is, as I am trying to show, nothing but a deceptive appearance.

I will divide my discussion into five sections. First, I shall try to show that characteristic traits of the experience of guilt are mirrored by the antinomy of Kant's doctrine of radical evil. Second, I shall claim that the failure of the ethical worldview to cope with the problem of evil is largely due to the fact that it has been based upon a far too narrow conception of responsibility. Third, it will be considered how, in a Nabertian perspective, this difficulty may be surmounted by an attempt to extend the scope of responsibility and to replace the "privation thesis" of traditional metaphysics by what could be called the "contradiction thesis." Finally, the fourth and the fifth section will be dedicated to an analysis of the Levinasian approach to guilt and evil.

1. The Antinomy in the Experience of Guilt

Kant's teaching on radical evil can be viewed as a philosophical appropriation of the religious doctrine of original sin from the perspective of an ethic of responsibility. It is not by accident that in the late work *Religion within the Limits of Reason Alone* (hereafter *Religion*) two "laws of freedom" are discerned: that of obligation and that of accountability.[155] As a principle of accountability, freedom plays a crucial role in the construction of the theory of radical evil. Kant does not so much state that the origin of evil lies in fact in human freedom as he rather demands that we should assume the responsibility for it.

The antinomy which has been identified by Ricoeur in this doctrine can also be best understood as a collision between the two "laws of freedom" mentioned above. On the one hand, the ethic of responsibility worked out in *Religion* requires that man should consider himself as the author of evil. But, on the other hand, the analysis of moral obligation accomplished by Kant in his ethical writings does not allow for him to designate freedom as the ultimate source of evil. For it is a firm and unchanging conviction of the critical philosophy of morals that freedom and morality belong inseparably together. A "free will" and a "will under moral laws" are "identical," says Kant in the *Foundations of the Metaphysics of Morals.*[156] "Thus freedom and unconditional practical law reciprocally imply each other," he concludes in the *Critique of Practical Reason.*[157] He formulates this position even more sharply in *Religion* when he asserts,

> To conceive of oneself as a freely acting being and yet as exempt from the law which is appropriate to such a being (the moral law) would be tantamount to conceiving a cause operating without any laws whatsoever (for determination according to natural laws is excluded by the fact of freedom); this is a self-contradiction.[158]

As we can see, Kant maintains his conviction that freedom and morality belong inseparably together, even after he has already developed his theory of radical evil. This observation is confirmed by a passage in his last ethical piece, the *Metaphysics of Morals,* in which he, once again, claims that freedom can never be seen when "the intelligent subject can decide against his (legislative) reason."[159]

We may thus see that as far as freedom is interpreted only as a principle of obligation—as it so often happens in the critical philosophy—it will always appear as inseparably interlocked with morality. If, however, it is considered as a principle of accountability, it turns out to be bound together, astonishingly, just as inextricably with an original culpability as with morality. The theory of radical evil is notoriously tormented by this antinomy.

On the one hand, Kant insists on the inseparability of freedom and morality. That is why he maintains that the incentive of morality, the respect for the law, necessarily exerts its influence upon every action. On the other hand, however, he clearly sees that this influence never comes into operation without some hindrance. It usually encounters the resistance put up to it by the incentives of sensibility. Yet, in *Religion,* Kant is far from seeing the origin of evil in this resistance. He does not incriminate sensibility; rather, he considers its incentives as neutral.

How can he, then, account for the possibility of faults? He does not content himself with assuming a propensity for evil, he also tries to specify what, more precisely, this propensity consists in. He characterizes it as *a general attitude of subordinating the incentive of morality to the incentives of sensibility.* We know that, according to Kant, the moral law demands more than a simple conformity of actions to itself: it also prescribes a particular disposition of mind characterized by the predominance of the respect for the law over all sensible inclinations, determining, thereby, a morally required order of incentives. That is why Kant can describe the subordination of the incentive of morality to the incentives of sensibility as *a reversal of the moral order of incentives.* This is the formula he proposes in order to overcome the antinomy which threatens his doctrine of radical evil.

This formula is designed to specify the nature of the intelligible action which has already been mentioned. However, the assumption that there is such an action remains precarious. That is why Kant's position in *Religion* may be described as "a nest of tangles"; it must, however, be added that "they are instructive tangles."[160] They are instructive not because the difficulties Kant is grappling with are "the difficulties of his historical setting rather than of philosophical argumentation," as Gordon Michalson explains his own remark,[161] but precisely because these difficulties mirror characteristic traits of the experience of guilt and are, therefore, of philosophical relevance.

This can be made clear by recalling an observation of Kant's in *Religion.* As he says, each evil action "must be regarded as though the individual had fallen into it directly from a state of innocence."[162] Kant leaves no doubt about the fact that this statement can only be justified from what he calls in his *Foundations of the Metaphysics of Morals* the "standpoint" of freedom.[163] It is not intended as a description of what actually happens but it is meant as a prescription of how what actually happens ought to be interpreted from the perspective of an ethic of responsibility. Although, as Kant emphasizes in the *Critique of Practical Reason,* "at the time I act I am never free,"[164] a person ought to consider himself or herself, according to what the ethic of responsibility expounded in *Religion* requires, as "susceptible of, and subjected to, imputability in the very moment of that action, just as much as though [. . .] he had stepped out of a state of innocence into evil."[165] However paradoxical this requirement may sound, it obviously expresses a constant feature of the experience of guilt. There is no feeling of culpability without this spontaneous assumption of responsibility. But the very words used by Kant to specify this feature of the experience of guilt are apt to remind us that the moral situation in which the culprit necessarily finds himself or herself is more intricate than that. The expression "as though" that occurs twice in what has been quoted from *Religion* indicates an enigma which remains uncovered in Kant's description.[166]

A similar ambiguity can be encountered in Kierkegaard's essay on *The Concept of Dread.* Here we are told: "With the first sin came sin into the world. Exactly in the same way is this true of every subsequent first sin of man, that with it sin comes into the world."[167] Thus, the Danish thinker (whose positive debts to Kant are, by the way, much greater than usually admitted)[168] holds a thesis that resembles the above mentioned conception of the critical philosophy: the individual falls into evil directly from a state of innocence. Moreover, Kierkegaard seems to take it for granted that this thesis expresses a genuine feature of the experience of guilt. This is implied by the general conviction which he formulates as follows: "How sin came into the world every man understands by himself alone; if he would learn it from another, he eo ipso misunderstands it."[169] However, the very fact that Kierkegaard tries to shed some light on the doctrine of original sin from this strictly individual standpoint shows that there is a concealed enigma in his approach just as much as in that of Kant's.

Can this enigma be unraveled at all? Kant seems to give an answer in the negative to this question by taking the view that the origin of evil "remains inscrutable to us."[170] As with Kierkegaard, the situation is similar. Although he devotes a book-length inquiry to the doctrine of *peccatum originarium,* he holds it to be a mystery which discursive knowledge can only elucidate but never explain. As we are told, "Sin does not properly belong to any science. It is the theme with which the sermon deals, where the individual talks as an individual to the individual."[171]

Ricoeur takes a first step toward the philosophical approach to this enigma by describing the peculiar experience of evil as being always already there and by pointing out that this experience is a necessary element of any experience of guilt.[172] But as far as the method of his considerations, termed as "hermeneutic phenomenology,"[173] is concerned, we cannot avoid arriving at the conclusion that there are no adequate means at his disposal to exploit his insight. The enigma of evil seems to require a standpoint which has rightly been characterized, even if in a rather polemical vein, by D. Janicaud as a "*phénoménologie de l'inapparent,*"[174] i.e., as a phenomenology which, paradoxically enough, does not concern itself simply with what appears but is just as interested in describing, as Levinas puts it, what *manifests itself precisely by not manifesting itself.*[175]

Probably it is only the phenomenology also concerned with what does *not* appear which has a chance to master the difficulties which exposed themselves as controversial, antinomical, and resistant to any consistent explanation in Kant's theory of radical evil for the first time. The contradiction between the requirement to assume the responsibility for the origin of evil, and the discovery of an evil which has always already been there, might be further accounted for precisely through such a phenomenological method, especially by applying the conceptual network of "phenomenon" and "enigma," elaborated by Levinas. Following this line of interpretation, we may characterize the experience of an evil which is always already there as part and parcel of the experience of a past that has never been present.[176] As we shall see, this characterization makes it possible for us to overcome the ethical worldview, which tries to reduce evil to freedom, without at the same time relapsing into a traditional metaphysics which assumes, as Plotinus formulated it, that "evils are prior to us and those that take hold on men do not do so with their good will." In order to avoid both of these extremes of misinterpretation, first the relationship between freedom and responsibility should be clarified.

2. Freedom and Responsibility

The ethical worldview, as Ricoeur conceives of it, does not acknowledge any kind of responsibility which is not strictly bound up with our own acts. Evidently, this is why it claims, as Ricoeur puts it, that "to affirm freedom is to take upon oneself the origin of evil."[177] The underlying consideration can be explained as follows: freedom, as a principle of accountability, is inseparably connected with responsibility. But, as it seems, one is only responsible for acts of his or her own. Therefore, there is no possibility to assert the freedom of one's own without taking the origin of evil upon himself or herself. But this consideration, as I shall argue, is highly misleading; it is, in fact, based upon a misconstruction of our concept of responsibility.

This can easily be shown if we take a glance at a much too neglected passage in Kant's *Critique of Practical Reason.* The line of thought in question is dedicated to an analysis of conscience and remorse.

Repentance is, as it is described by Kant, "a painful feeling caused by the moral disposition, empty in a practical sense since it cannot undo that which has been done." But Kant adds that, as pain, it is, at the same time, "entirely legitimate, because reason [. . .] acknowledges no temporal distinctions and only asks whether the event belongs to me as my act, and then morally connects with it the same feeling, whether the event occurs now or is long since past."[178]

Reason acknowledges no temporal distinctions—this is why I remain responsible for all my actions in spite of the fact that, as it has already been quoted, "at the time I act I am never free"; this is, in other words, how freedom, as Kant puts it here to convey his meaning, can be "saved."[179]

Reason acknowledges no temporal distinctions—this is, at the same time, clearly a proposition that expresses a speculative turn in Kant's theory of freedom. We may best see this by contrasting the thesis of the *Critique of Practical Reason* with an apparently similar formulation of Jean Nabert's. In Nabert's view, the experience of guilt establishes "simultaneity" between the act of judgment and the action judged, without depriving, however, the past thus retrieved of its inherent irrevocability.[180] Kant's point of departure, by contrast, is that "the past is no longer in my power" even at the time I act and, therefore, "every action which I perform is necessary because of determining grounds which are not in my power."[181] But this starting point does not prevent him from ascribing a special power to the act of the assumption of responsibility for past actions, namely the power to recuperate these actions into the possession of freedom. It is not surprising, however, that no such power of recuperation can ever be found within the sphere of temporality. So Kant's above proposition does not allude to simultaneity but rather to extratemporaneity. This obviously speculative turn is called upon to explain why, in spite of a breachless determinism accepted by the critical philosophy, the feeling of repentance is "entirely legitimate," i.e., how, under these circumstances, one can be justified at all to consider oneself as responsible for the acts of one's own. But, in order to obtain this justification of conscience and remorse, Kant finds himself compelled to accept a rather peculiar interpretation of what responsibility consists in. He has to commit himself to the highly questionable view that by assuming the responsibility for our actions we take them upon ourselves *as if* they had been done freely, although, as the breachless determinism necessarily implies, they were performed in a strictly determined way. I will call this view the *recuperative view of responsibility.* I would once more like to direct the attention to the structural role assigned to the expression "as if" in this view.

It is not difficult to understand why this conception of freedom as a principle of accountability is seriously misleading. The recuperative view of responsibility seems to consider the case when somebody *deliberately* takes upon himself what, in fact, *somebody else* has committed as paradigmatic. It can, of course, hardly be denied that there are such cases but they are certainly far from being regular instances of what responsibility in general means.

It is among the merits of the critical philosophy of morals to have perceived the self-assertion of freedom in the act of the assumption of responsibility. But it is highly questionable whether responsibility can just be reduced to this act. It is, therefore, only natural that other views of responsibility have been developed since Kant. Heidegger seems to have been the first to argue for the thesis that we had *always already* been encumbered by the burden of responsibility *before* we came to assume it by a self-assertive act of freedom. Thus, the famous chapter on conscience and guilt in *Being and Time* opposed an ontological conception of responsibility to Kant's ethical worldview.[182]

But Heidegger is not the only thinker to be mentioned in this respect. One is no less justified to cite the name of Nabert here, in whose first great work on moral philosophy, *Elements for an Ethic* (1943), the ethical worldview—as Ricoeur has rightly observed—was in fact completed rather than overcome. Yet Nabert's next book, *Essay on Evil* (1955), already marks a decisive break with Kant's position. The later Nabert assumes that the radical evil specified by the critical philosophy as a reversal of the moral order of incentives is, in fact, bound up with "an original scission of consciousnesses," with which, at the same time, freedom cannot be charged. Nevertheless, the I "takes [it] as much upon itself as it endures it."[183] Thus, the concept of responsibility which emerges in Nabert's *Essay on Evil* surpasses the scope of our own acts in extension. Freedom as a principle of accountability proves to be more far-reaching than freedom as a principle of obligation and action.

It is in a similar sense that Levinas talks about the "antecedence" of responsibility to freedom.[184] As we have seen, Levinas tries to conceive of the self of one's own in terms of its elementary relationship with the other. This approach renders the recuperative view of responsibility obsolete, since it is based upon the insight that we are not only responsible for the acts of our own but, as Levinas formulates it in *Otherwise Than Being or Beyond Essence,* we are also responsible, even if not in the same sense of the word, "for the faults or the misfortune of others."[185]

Do these conceptions of responsibility make the enigma of evil accessible? In order to decide this question, I shall first examine an approach suggested by the later philosophy of Nabert.

3. The Contradiction in Evil

One of the main theses Nabert proposes in his *Essay on Evil* is that the experience of evil is the experience of a *contradiction with oneself.* Nabert adds that this experience is inseparable from the experience of guilt.

The observation that, therefore, there is no guilt without contradiction has been formulated by the French philosopher André Vergez as an objection to any theory that admits a culpability irreducible to ignorance. In his work *Faute et liberté* this objection has been exploited as an indirect proof of Socrates' view that guilt is nothing but an error. In recourse to this ancient view, Vergez rejects all modern conceptions of a free will being capable of choosing between the good and the evil.[186] In order to defend his position, he also undertakes to refute Nabert's theory of culpability.[187]

But there is an answer to be gathered from Nabert's *Essai sur le mal* to this objection. A passage in Nabert's work indicates very instructively what it is which is not accounted for in Socrates' view accepted by Vergez. Nabert's argument can be summarized as follows: If every choice between the good and the evil were accomplished in an isolated and, so to speak, atomic situation of decision, and the free will could preserve its full availability from one such situation to another, then Socrates would perhaps be right in holding that nobody does evil on purpose. But it is precisely this presupposition which does not seem to hold true in the case of human will. Finite freedom gets again and again entangled in contradictions with itself, and it would be difficult to deny that these contradictions do, in fact, encroach upon its availability, because freedom, as a principle of accountability, bears the responsibility "for itself and the contradiction" it gets involved in.[188] In other words: responsibility inserts itself into a unity of a life in which there are no atomic or isolated situations of decision but in which the past does not lose the grip of the present and the future.

Let me illustrate these considerations by the example of Shakespeare's *Richard III.* Here evil is certainly done on purpose. At the beginning of the play, Richard says,

> I am determined to prove a villain.
> (1.1.30)[189]

But in spite of this resoluteness he gets ultimately involved in a contradiction with himself. This might be seen if we consider how this briskly self-assertive utterance finds an echo at the end of the play:

> I am a villain—yet I lie, I am not!
> Fool, of thyself speak well! fool, do not flatter.
> (5.3.192–93)

Here a contradiction is explicit. I am: I have become what I have been determined "to prove" from the outset. I am not: it is impossible that this should be what I call "myself." Do not flatter: do not deceive yourself.

We can see here that even when evil is done on purpose it is irreducible to what has been intended. This experience—with which we might get confronted just as much as Richard—reveals, to borrow an expression from Levinas, a *monstrosity;* and, as we may add, this monstrosity is to be faced as the monstrosity of ourselves. This trace of an "enigma" on the "phenomenon" of guilt can be described as a radical contradiction in evil.

The first to discover the possibility of this interpretation was Schelling in his famous *Philosophical Investigations Concerning Human Freedom* written in 1809. After refusing the "privation thesis" of traditional metaphysics, he asserts,

> In evil there is that contradiction which devours and always negates itself, which just while striving to become a creature destroys the nexus of creation and, in its ambition to be everything, falls into non-being.[190]

But in Schelling's exposition this fundamental insight—which can be referred to as the "contradiction thesis" of the theory of evil—remains inseparable from a speculative metaphysics.

However, Schelling's idea can be extracted from its original context. The radical contradiction of evil mentioned above can be interpreted as an event of singular significance within the unity of a life. This line of interpretation finds support in the narrative view of personal identity. This view provides a clue to a restatement of Schelling's idea within a framework which tries to keep away from speculation. However enigmatic the experience of a radical contradiction in evil may prove to be, it can very well be *narrated* how finite freedom gets again and again ensnared in such contradictions in the course of a life. It may be claimed that, thus, narrative intelligibility can take the place of metaphysical speculation.

In this way, the "privation thesis" of traditional metaphysics can be replaced by what has been called the "contradiction thesis." This replacement is, however, not to be taken as a simple substitution: it rather goes together with a profound transformation. For although the radical contradiction in evil can, so to speak, receive a configuration in a narrative, it certainly cannot be resolved and, thereby, reduced to nullity or nonbeing. It has to remain an "enigma" within the boundaries of the "phenomenon" of guilt: an eternal enigma that has already been anticipated or even expressed by the mythical symbol of the serpent, in which Ricoeur so clearly perceived "the resistance of the tragic to the ethical."

That this line of interpretation has nevertheless its weak points becomes clear if it is contrasted with the approach to guilt and evil proposed by Levinas.

4. The Self-Accusation of Remorse and the Split of the Self

Levinas tries to dissever responsibility from all acts of freedom. He insists on an original indebtedness to the other. With this indebtedness one has always already been encumbered without ever having it incurred upon himself or herself by any manifest action. While describing, in temporal terms, this peculiar concept of an original culpability which does not involve any actual guilt, Levinas comes to the conclusion that the kind of responsibility he speaks of includes a relationship with a past that has never been present.[191] Since this expression can obviously not be taken as referring to the temporal attribute of any substance or entity in the world but can only be understood as revealing a characteristic trait of lived experience, Levinas here in fact offers a formula with which the "enigma" of an evil that has always already been there can be interpreted as an internal feature of the "phenomenon" of guilt. It is precisely this point where the metaphysical tradition went astray: it has always been inclined to take this enigmatic feature of the phenomenon of guilt to be the manifestation of the mysterious reality of an entity in the world. This entity was called "matter," whose particularity consisted, strangely enough, in its being, as it were, an incorporated nullity, a nonexisting entity, a palpable and quite efficacious shadow. We can find this enormous quid pro quo, this exteriorization of what is, in fact, an internal feature of lived experience, at the root of the privation thesis of traditional metaphysics.

But how about the thesis of a contradiction in evil? Does Levinas accept and maintain it? If we are searching for an answer to this question, we may stumble upon a short passage in *Otherwise Than Being or Beyond Essence* in which the "self-accusation of remorse" is analyzed. As Levinas says,

> The ipseity has become at odds with itself in its return to itself. The self-accusation of remorse gnaws away at the closed and firm core of consciousness, opening it, fissioning it.[192]

At first sight, this passage may suggest a certain affinity with the thesis of a contradiction in evil. What is, indeed, the *ipseity's* becoming at odds with itself, if not a contradiction it gets involved in? Yet, upon closer consideration, the words above turn out to imply a dissimilarity as well; they may even be said to make it clear that the position Levinas takes is opposed to Nabert's whole enterprise.

It is not difficult to see the most significant difference between the two thinkers: whereas Nabert's approach to guilt and evil is embedded into the framework of a philosophical reflection upon consciousness, Levinas discovers in the "self-accusation of remorse" an impetus apt to "open," or even to "fission," the "hard and firm core" of consciousness. It is in this sense that he speaks of a split—or, more precisely, of a "fissibility" and a "fission" of the self.[193]

Nabert, in turn, never tries to transcend the closed sphere of consciousness in his inquiries. It is strictly from the perspective of a reflection upon the sentiment of guilt that he interprets the phenomenon of a contradiction with oneself. That is why he contents himself with tracing it back to a general condition which is purely internal to the ego: he finds this condition in what he describes as an "inequality" of the ego with itself.[194] Considered from the standpoint of philosophical reflection upon the sentiment of guilt, however, the contradiction with oneself necessarily appears as an *alienation* of the ego from itself.[195]

It is the adoption of this purely internal perspective of philosophical reflection which provokes the discontent and the protest of Levinas, who also takes Nabert's position into account in *Otherwise Than Being or Beyond Essence*. We find a passage here in which Nabert is mentioned by name. Levinas remarks that, in Nabert, the inequality of the ego with itself signifies not only "an inadequation of the apparent being with the profound or sublime being" but also "a return to an original innocence."[196] Levinas leaves no doubt about the critical intention of his observations. He does speak of an inequality with oneself, too, but his meaning is not the same as Nabert's. He uses it—as well as the related notion of a noncoincidence with oneself—in order to emphasize the *openness* of the self to the *other*, which he takes to be synonymous with its "fissibility" or "fission." He makes his differences with Nabert's notion of the inequality with oneself quite explicit; he goes as far as to claim that Nabert "is perhaps faithful to the tradition in which noncoincidence is only privation."[197] If one recalls how resolutely Nabert rejected the privation-thesis of traditional metaphysics, one is likely to be astonished to encounter such an objection. Levinas seems, however, to have something *specific* in mind when accusing Nabert of considering the inequality with oneself as a privation. Here it is the task of the interpreter to clarify Levinas's point.

It may be helpful for this purpose to take a side glance upon another passage as well, which can be related to Nabert even if, this time, he is not mentioned by name. Here Levinas contrasts, once again, his own view of inequality with the way the philosophical reflection upon consciousness conceives of it. He points out that, in consciousness, equality "is always reestablished"—or at least it "is sought in reflection and its *figures,* although the possibility of total reflection and of the unity of Mind [*Esprit*], beyond the multiplicity of souls, is not effectively assured."[198] It is very likely that here the term *figures of reflection* is an allusion to Nabert's way of thinking. The sense of this allusion may be clarified by an attempt to understand the above quoted remark on "an original innocence."

Similarly to Kant and Kierkegaard, Nabert, in his *Essay on Evil,* characterizes guilt as a break with the state of innocence. He is, of course, as far from perceiving a factual event in this break as his great predecessors. Rather, he considers innocence as an ideal contrast which reflection has recourse to in passing judgment upon guilt. The same is true of confidence, which, in Nabert's *Essay on Evil,* counts as the expression of a—merely hypothetical—"unity of Mind" (*Esprit*), "beyond the multiplicity of souls," as Levinas puts it; trust is nothing but an ideal measure applied to the break of the ties with others, i.e., to that scission or separation which is described by Nabert as a *mal de sécession* (evil of secession).[199] Consequently, innocence and confidence are, in Nabert, inseparably bound up with a reflection upon guilt.[200] Therefore, they may indeed be rightly characterized as "figures of reflection." As ideal correlates of reflection, these figures are opposed to reality. Yet, they may be regarded as figures of thought reflection necessarily makes use of when grappling with evil. They are like "lost paradises," *paradis perdus,* which, as Nabert says, "are never known but in distress."[201]

The seemingly harmless recourse to such figures of reflection in ethical thought and judgment implies a danger which cannot be disregarded: it is, as one is here inclined to say, in the "light" of mere *idealizations* that effective deeds are seen and evaluated. It is a consequence of this dubious procedure that guilt and evil are often seen as *negative imprints* of an original innocence, or of an ideal unity of Mind (in the sense of a community beyond the "multiplicity of souls"). Once this view is adopted, ethics is marked by an eternal provisionality. Everything which belongs to it can then be resumed in a single phrase: *à la recherche des paradis perdus.* Nabert's *Essay on Evil* is imbued by this idea. That is why, in Nabert's *Essay,* the inequality with oneself takes indeed the sense of a "return to an original innocence," as Levinas rightly observes.

It is in this context that we can understand the objection according to which, in Nabert's eyes, noncoincidence is *privation.* As soon as evil is contrasted with figures of reflection like original innocence and primordial unity of Mind, it appears as the *negative counterpart* of these idealizations. As a negative counterpart, however, it necessarily assumes the character of a lack, of a deficiency, or of a privation.

It is clear from these considerations that however decidedly Nabert rejects the privation thesis as a thematically elaborated tenet, he does not come to discard it as an operative device, to which the very choice of his philosophical method commits him. For Levinas, by contrast, it is among the tasks to detect and to dismiss privation even as such an operative device. That is why he finds the self-accusation of remorse important: for him it serves as a counterbalance to the aspiration of the self into an equality with itself. Levinas claims that the self-accusation of remorse brings this aspiration to a halt. Thus, he envisages the inequality of the self with itself without the possibility to return to an original innocence.

At the same time, the break with the philosophy of reflection opens for Levinas a way to show that "an other can of itself be in the same without alienating it."[202] Relying upon this idea of an "alterity in the same without alienation,"[203] he can dismiss all assumption of a primordially united community between oneself and the others, "beyond the multiplicity of souls," by affirming that: "The Mind [*Esprit*] is a multiplicity of individuals."[204] This statement is obviously to be connected with the remark on the "figures of reflection" and the unity of the Mind. It is by this observation that the polemic against Nabert is closed in *Otherwise Than Being or Beyond Essence.*

Yet, it seems to be possible to put an argument forward in defense of the recourse to the figures of reflection. One might hold that the idea of an original innocence, just as well as that of a primordially united community between oneself and the others, is an inevitable consequence of what can be described, with expressions borrowed from Levinas, as "the attraction of the contraries" or as "the reciprocal summoning of the terms which negate each other."[205] Yet, Levinas cuts the ground from under this argument: he undertakes, quite surprisingly, to show that no such reciprocity can be assumed between good and evil.

5. The Lack of Reciprocity between Good and Evil

Good and *evil:* these notions seem to form a conceptual opposition; they seem to relate to each other like *light* and *shadow.* The traditional tenet according to which evil is the privation of the good confirms this inveterated view.

However, Levinas arrives at the conclusion that it takes a good deal of violent simplification to interpret the peculiar difference between *good* and *evil* as a *contrariety* or even as an *opposition.* This is a strange idea indeed, which, at first sight, cannot be considered as obvious. The diacritical method may help us, however, to elucidate this idea. In order to demonstrate this, I shall distinguish several notions of guilt, claiming that neither of them can be opposed as "the" evil to "the" good. At the same time, I shall also question the view according to which it is not so much *evil* but rather *misfortune,* or the *ill* in general, which may be considered as the counterpart of the good.

Our considerations may be built on the distinction between wild responsibility and ordering law. As we know, wild responsibility may be interpreted as a responsibility for the "faults" and "misfortunes" of others. We may add that this responsibility, as Levinas understands it, remains irreducible even to an extended version of a responsibility for *oneself.*

Our first task will be to extract the phenomenon of guilt from the perspective of a reflection upon oneself. For this purpose, we have to focus upon situations which give rise to wild responsibility: upon situations, in other words, in which one finds himself or herself confronted with the appeals—or claims of response—of others. We may take for our point of departure the observation that, in such a situation, one may remain indebted to *the other* even if the response one gives to his or her appeal complies with *the law.* This observation leads us to the insight that it is a one-sided and therefore unsatisfactory procedure to define *guilt* as *a break of the law.* Such a definition takes a moral order for granted, without accounting, at the same time, for the fact of wild responsibility. If we start with wild responsibility, we arrive at a highly significant, although in itself incomplete, notion of guilt. In the wild region, where responsibility is without limit, measure, and law, guilt takes the sense of a *refusal of response.*

However, this sense is only an initial one. It assumes a *modified* and *further developed* shape as soon as the appeal of the other is no longer considered as unique, but also the accessory appeal of the third party is taken into consideration. From that point onward, a whole multitude of mutually incompatible claims of response may be simultaneously addressed to us. This situation cries for a proper measure. It is this need of justice that gives rise to the law. The law is destined to settle the conflict of incompatible appeals: it is this feature of the law which provides a relative justification to the widely accepted view that guilt is a break of the law. However, if we recall the already mentioned figure of a "refuser of response," who, though he or she will not respond, still maintains his or her pure respect for the law, we easily come to see the limited validity of this justification. We may, therefore, rightly claim that the initial sense of guilt (*refusal of response*) is prior to the view of guilt as a break of the law.

Undoubtedly, the refusal of response out of a pure respect for the law is a rare, almost exceptional, phenomenon. In most cases, refusal of response and break of the law go hand in hand. Ordinarily, the respect for the law results from an endeavor to develop an expressly and deliberately responsive behavior. It remains, nevertheless, a fact that the two notions of guilt in question are the products of two divergent, or even conflicting, approaches to one and the same experience.

It is all the more important to realize this fact because the heterogeneity of the two notions is not entirely negligible even in ordinary cases. This has to do with the fact that even if we fully meet the requirements set by the law, we still remain, more or less, in the other's debt. Here we must not lose sight of the fundamental difference, or the shift, between that which a response consists *in,* and that which it is a response *to.* This shift, or descent, is due to the fact that the appeal of the other is seized by a spontaneous proliferation, an exuberant formation of surplus, which no responsive behavior is able to keep up with. Yet, from this it also follows that no responsive behavior, however resolute, considerate, and devoted it may be, is preserved from a touch of an (unintended) refusal of response. In addition, the apparition of the ordering law in the scene involves a newly emerging danger: the very fact of wild responsibility risks to fade into oblivion. The moral order that comes to prevail provides an opportunity to cover up the traces of the refusal of response which resides in all responsive behavior. It encourages one to adopt a basic attitude of subordinating wild responsibility to the ordering law. Yielding without reserve to this prompting, one undoubtedly incurs a fault. This fault is obviously not a break of the law, but it is not an actual refusal of response, either. Rather, one adopts a general attitude which paves the way for actual refusals of response—provided that they do not entail any break of the law.

Thus, the initial sense of a refusal of response leads, in its further development, to a second notion of guilt, which may remind us of Kant's conception of radical evil. However, this similarity should by no means be exaggerated. It is true that we have been led by our considerations to envisage a basic attitude of subordinating wild responsibility to the ordering law, and it is equally true that nothing seems to be more natural than to understand this subordination, following the model of Kant's theory of radical evil, as a reversal of a preestablished order. However, Levinas's idea of an alternating movement between wild responsibility and ordering law soon calls this analogy into question: it leaves the assumption of a "preestablished order" without foundation and, *a fortiori,* the conception of a "reversal" of such an order as well. What was taken by Kant or Nabert as a clue to the enigma of evil has been disclosed as having no footing: not only "reversal" but also "scission" and "contradiction" prove to be entirely out of place here.

Indeed, where no original unity can be taken for granted, there can be no question of an original scission, either. However, it is not difficult to see that the idea of an original unity of consciousnesses does not apply to the relationship between appeal and response. This relationship may rightly be characterized as an intertwinement, an *entrelacs,* that is, as a connection which, precisely, does not take away the heterogeneity of its elements. In addition, here the connection of the elements is made by *reply* and *correspondence* rather than by a *synthesis.* It is only afterward that appeal and response can be united in a single consciousness; at the moment when they arise, they are separated from each other by an unbridgeable gap.

Similarly, our second notion of guilt remains just as much irreducible to a contradiction one gets entangled in, again and again, during his or her life. On the one hand, the idea of a contradiction with oneself is inseparable from the perspective of a reflection upon guilt. Consequently, even if it presupposes a split of the self, it evokes by the attraction of the contraries the ideal of an equality with oneself. On the other hand, our second notion of guilt is bound up with a split of the self which is not even visible from the perspective of reflection. Since wild responsibility and ordering law are not to be grasped as moments of any unified totality, this split does not evoke the mirage of an unscathed whole. Consequently, it does not nurture the mythical idea of a "state of innocence," either. It rather involves, to use a Levinasian expression we already encountered, the assumption of an "irremissible guilt."

Thus, we have arrived at a third notion of guilt which must be sharply distinguished from the first two. The irremissible guilt Levinas has in mind results from the fact that our life is intermingled not only with the misfortunes but also with the faults of others. Alluding to the biblical "remission of guilts," Levinas calls this guilt "irremissible" not because it surpasses all human—or even divine—capacities of forgiveness, but rather because it cannot be considered either as one's own deed, or as a readily encountered evil which nevertheless might be recuperated by a responsibility for oneself (in an extended sense of the word). This irremissible guilt is rather the product of a responsibility for the other which, as Levinas claims, is prior to all responsibility for oneself, even in the widest possible sense of the word.

It would be seriously misleading to assimilate this third notion of guilt we are considering to the conception of radical evil. The irremissible guilt specified by Levinas cannot be considered as a *Grundlaster,* a fundamental vice or depravity of human nature. It is even doubtful whether this guilt is a *bad* thing at all. And even if it is held to be, we must add that, as Levinas shows, here the *bad* carries a trace of the *good.* It is true, however, that the *good* does not mean here anything other than the restlessness of the desire which does not shrink from what is undesirable in the other.

A certain significance has to be assigned also to the fact that our third notion of guilt is implied by our second one. It is clear from the connection between the two concepts that the subordination of wild responsibility to the ordering law is to be considered as guilt not only because it paves the way for actual refusals of response but also because it reduces the restlessness of desire, working, thereby, *against the good.*

Here one may get the impression that our second notion of guilt can be opposed as "the" evil to the good. This impression is, however, ill founded. Even if the subordination of wild responsibility to the ordering law works *against* the good, it cannot be considered as its *negative counterpart.* The two concepts cannot, in reality, be situated on the same plane. The good, with the *anarchy* characteristic of it, belongs to the wild region of a responsibility for the other. The attitude of subordinating wild responsibility to the ordering law rather presupposes an external view of the wild region where the anarchy of the good takes place.

These considerations suggest that no concept of guilt can be opposed, as a unified and unequivocal notion of evil, to "the" good. The *bad* or the *ill* may be regarded as the counterpart of the *good* even less. What is commonly regarded as bad may, as we have seen, carry a trace of the good. The phenomenon of an irremissible guilt testifies to this interwovenness. Another example is the suffering engendered by a communication with the suffering of others. However, it does not follow from this that such an interwovenness can be detected in all cases. The relation of the good and the bad or the ill, just as well as the relation of good and evil, are characterized by a multiple, varied, and plurivocal alterity, which remains irreducible to such a regular figure of thought as the *opposition of negative counterparts.*

However divergent the directions we take in our inquiries may be, we arrive again and again at the conclusion formulated by Levinas, in a paradoxical way, as follows: good and evil differ from each other "with a difference more different than opposition."[206]

Notes

Prelude

1. T. Mann, *Der Zauberberg* (Berlin: Aufbau-Verlag, 1953), p. 767; in English: *The Magic Mountain,* trans. H. T. Lowe-Porter (London: Vintage, 1999), p. 541.

2. Ibid., p. 769; in English: p. 542.

3. Ibid., p. 768; in English: p. 542.

4. Ibid., p. 870; in English: p. 610.

5. T. Mann, *Doktor Faustus* (Berlin and Weimar: Aufbau-Verlag, 1965), p. 409; in English: *Doctor Faustus,* trans. H. T. Lowe-Porter (New York: Vintage Books, 1992), p. 301.

6. I. Kant, *Kritik der reinen Vernunft,* A 84 5 B 117; in English: *A Critique of Pure Reason,* trans. N. Kemp Smith (New York: St. Martin's Press, 1965), p. 120.

7. P. Ricoeur, *Soi-même comme un autre* (Paris: Seuil, 1990), p. 168. See also W. Dilthey, *Der Aufbau der geschichtlichen Welt in den Geisteswissenschaften,* vol. 7 of *Gesammelte Schriften* (Stuttgart and Göttingen: Teubner-Vandenhoeck and Ruprecht, 1965), pp. 191–204, 228–51.

8. Cf. W. Dilthey, *Der Aufbau der geschichtlichen Welt in den Geisteswissenschaften,* pp. 199, 203.

9. One of the most pregnant formulations of this requirement is to be found in Heidegger's *Being and Time.* Cf. M. Heidegger, *Sein und Zeit* (Tübingen: M. Niemeyer, 1979), p. 320: "die *Selbstheit des Ich qua Selbst*" versus "die *Selbigkeit und Beständigkeit eines immer schon Vorhandenen*"; in English: *Being and Time,* trans. J. Macquarrie and E. Robinson (Oxford: Basil Blackwell, 1962), p. 367.

10. Cf. E. Levinas, *Autrement qu'être ou au-delà de l'essence* (La Haye: M. Nijhoff, 1974). Quotation taken from (Paris: Livre de poche; Dordrecht, Boston, and London: Kluwer, 1990), p. 46: "*Intrigue de l'Autre dans le Même.*" Cf. ibid.: "*La subjectivité, c'est l'Autre dans le Même.*"

11. P. Ricoeur, "L'identité narrative," *Esprit,* nos. 7–8 (1988): 300.

12. A. MacIntyre, *After Virtue. A Study in Moral Theory* (London: Duckworth, 1987), p. 215.

13. On this controversial point see D. Carr's analysis in *Time, Narrative, and History* (Bloomington: Indiana University Press, 1986), especially pp. 7–17, 65–72.

14. P. Ricoeur, *Soi-même comme un autre,* p. 191.

15. P. Ricoeur, "Life in Quest of Narrative," in *On Paul Ricoeur. Narrative and Interpretation,* ed. D. Wood (London and New York: Routledge, 1991), p. 32. (Italics added.)

16. E. Husserl, *Cartesianische Meditationen,* ed. E. Ströker (Hamburg: F. Meiner, 1987), pp. 70, 78. See also *Cartesianische Meditationen,* vol. 1, *Husserliana,* ed. S. Strasser (Den Haag: M. Nijhoff, 1991 [1950]), pp. 103, 109. In English: *Cartesian Meditations,* trans. Dorion Cairns (The Hague: M. Nijhoff, 1969), pp. 68, 75.

17. See E. Husserl, *Zur Phänomenologie der Intersubjektivität III: 1929–35,* vol. 15, ed. I. Kern, *Husserliana* (Den Haag: M. Nijhoff, 1973), p. 419.

18. Cf. ibid., p. 359.

19. T. Mann, *Joseph und seine Brüder,* vol. 2 (Berlin and Weimar: Aufbau-Verlag, 1972), p. 342. In English: *Joseph and His Brothers,* trans. H. T. Lowe-Porter (London: Vintage, 1999), p. 667.

20. Ibid.

21. P. Ricoeur, *Temps et récit,* vol. 3 (Paris: Seuil, 1983–85), p. 356: "l'histoire d'une vie se constitue par une série de rectifications appliquées à des récits préalables [. . .]"

22. T. Mann, *Doktor Faustus,* p. 177; in English: p. 130.

23. T. Mann, *Die Entstehung des Doktor Faustus,* in *Doktor Faustus—Die Entstehung des Doktor Faustus* (Frankfurt am Main: Fischer, 1967), p. 749.

24. T. Mann, *Doktor Faustus,* p. 181; in English: p. 133.

25. Ibid.; in English: p. 134.

26. Ibid.

27. Ibid.

28. M. Proust, *Du côté de chez Swann,* in *A la recherche du temps perdu,* vol. I (Paris: Gallimard, 1987), p. 221. In English: M. Proust, *Swann's Way,* vol. 2, part 2 of *Remembrance of Things Past,* trans. C. K. Scott Moncrieff (London: Chatto and Windus, 1965), p. 8.

29. P. Ricoeur, *Temps et récit,* vol. 3, p. 356.

30. T. Mann, *Die Entstehung des Doktor Faustus,* in *Doktor Faustus—Die Entstehung des Doktor Faustus,* p. 749.

31. Cf. M. Merleau-Ponty, *Le visible et l'invisible* (Paris: Gallimard, 1964), p. 270. In English: M. Merleau-Ponty, *The Visible and the Invisible,* trans. A. Lingis (Evanston, Ill.: Northwestern University Press, 1969), p. 217: "the use of the diacritical."

32. Ibid., pp. 229, 267; in English: pp. 175, 213.

33. Ibid., p. 287: "*mon montage sur un système diacritique universel*"; in English: p. 233.

34. T. Mann, *Doktor Faustus,* p. 179; in English: p. 131.

35. Cf. M. Richir, *Méditations phénoménologiques* (Grenoble: Millon, 1992), p. 77: "le champ phénoménologique comme 'lieu' de foisonnement toujours inchoatifs de sens multiples, et relativement flous ou indéterminés."

36. Cf. M. Merleau-Ponty, *Le visible et l'invisible,* p. 203: "*sens sauvage*"; in English: p. 155: "wild meaning."

37. Cf. C. Lévi-Strauss, *La pensée sauvage* (Paris: Plon, Livre de poche "Agora," 1962), p. 297. M. Foucault, *Les mots et les choses* (Paris: Gallimard, 1966), p. 352.

Chapter 1

1. E. Husserl, *Ideen zu einer reinen Phänomenologie und phänomenologischen Philosophie,* vol. 3/1, Husserliana, ed. by K. Schuhmann (Den Haag: M. Nijhoff, 1976), p. 285. In English: *Ideas: General Introduction to Pure Phenomenology,* trans. W. R. Boyce Gibson (London and New York: Collier Macmillan Publishers, 1962 [1931]), p. 319.

2. Cf. M. Richir, *Méditations phénoménologiques,* p. 231.

3. E. Husserl, *Logische Untersuchungen,* vol. 2/2 (Tübingen: M. Niemeyer, 1980), p. 170. In English: *Logical Investigations,* vol. 2, trans. J. N. Findlay (London: Routledge and Kegan Paul, 1970), p. 807.

4. See E. Levinas, *Autrement qu'être ou au-delà de l'essence,* p. 62.

5. J.-F. Marquet, *Singularité et événement* (Grenoble: Millon, 1995), p. 75. D. Franck kindly reminded me in a letter of a similar passage in Heidegger's *Nietzsche* (Pfullingen: Neske, 1961, vol. II, p. 35f).

6. Cf. G. W. F. Hegel, *Phänomenologie des Geistes,* vol. 3 of *Werke in zwanzig Bänden,* ed. E. Moldenhauer and K.-M. Michel (Frankfurt am Main: Suhrkam p, 1970), pp. 60f.

7. M. Heidegger, "Hegels Begriff der Erfahrung," *Holzwege* (Frankfurt am Main: V. Klostermann, 1950), p. 169f. In English: M. Heidegger, *Hegel's Concept of Experience* (New York, Evanston, Ill., and London: Harper and Row, 1971), p. 119.

8. H.-G. Gadamer, *Wahrheit und Methode* (Tübingen: J. C. B. Mohr [Paul Siebeck], 1975 [1960]), p. 330.

9. Cf. G. W. F. Hegel, *Phänomenologie des Geistes,* p. 80.

10. H.-G. Gadamer, *Wahrheit und Methode,* p. 338.

11. See E. Husserl, *Logische Untersuchungen,* vol. 2/2, p. 42; in English: vol. 2, p. 702.

12. G. W. F. Hegel, *Phänomenologie des Geistes,* p. 78ff.

13. H. Putnam, *Reason, Truth, and History* (Cambridge: Cambridge University Press, 1981), especially pp. 51–54.

14. Putnam draws here upon David Wiggins. (Cf. D. Wiggins, *Substance and Sameness,* Oxford: Basil Blackwell, 1980.)

15. As a matter of fact, theory of reference and analysis of intentionality are closely related topics. Cf. R. McIntyre and D. W. Smith, *Husserl and Intentionality. A Study of Mind, Meaning, and Language* (Dordrecht, Boston, and Lancaster: D. Reidel, 1984), p. xvi: "there derive from Husserl's interlocking doctrines about mind and language important parallels between intentionality and reference."

16. E. Husserl, *Cartesianische Meditationen,* vol. 1, *Hua,* p. 115; in English: p. 82.

17. Ibid., p. 117; in English: p. 84.

18. The first to expressly formulate this idea was the young Schelling. See F. W. J. Schelling, *System des transzendentalen Idealismus,* vol. 1/3 of *Sämmtliche Werke,* ed. by K. F. A. Schelling (Stuttgart and Augsburg: Cotta, 1860), p. 331.

19. Cf. E. Husserl, *Logische Untersuchungen,* vol. 2/1, p. 379 n.; in English: vol. 2, p. 563 n.

20. H.-G. Gadamer, *Wahrheit und Methode,* p. 330.

21. Cf. R. McIntyre and D. W. Smith, *Husserl and Intentionality. A Study of Mind, Meaning, and Language*, p. 14: "*intentionality is the consciousness 'of' something 'as' conceived in a particular way.*"

22. E. Husserl, *Logische Untersuchungen*, vol. 2/2, p. 129; in English: vol. 2, p. 774.

23. E. Husserl, *Ideen zu einer reinen Phänomenologie und phänomenologischen Philosophie*, vol. 3/1, *Hua*, p. 284; in English: p. 318.

24. E. Husserl, *Logische Untersuchungen*, vol. 2/1, p. 372; in English: vol. 2, p. 558.

25. K. Twardowski, *Zur Lehre vom Inhalt und Gegenstand der Vorstellungen. Eine psychologische Untersuchung* (München and Wien: Philosophia Verlag, 1982 [1894]).

26. Cf. D. Føllesdal, "Husserl's Notion of Noema," *Journal of Philosophy* 66 (1969): 680–87. Reprinted in *Husserl, Intentionality, and Cognitive Science*, ed. H. Dreyfus (Cambridge and London: MIT Press, 1984), and R. McIntyre and D. W. Smith, *Husserl and Intentionality: A Study of Mind, Meaning, and Language*.

27. E. Husserl, *Ideen zu einer reinen Phänomenologie und phänomenologischen Philosophie*, vol. 3/1, p. 303; in English: p. 338.

28. J. J. Drummond, *Husserlian Intentionality and Non-Foundational Realism* (Dordrecht, Boston, and London: Kluwer, 1990), p. 125.

29. E. Husserl, *Ideen zu einer reinen Phänomenologie und phänomenologischen Philosophie*, vol. 3/1, p. 303; in English: p. 338.

30. Ibid., p. 297; in English: p. 333.

31. Ibid., p. 199; in English: p. 335.

32. E. Fink, "Die phänomenologische Philosophie Edmund Husserls in der gegenwärtigen Kritik," *Studien zur Phänomenologie* (Den Haag: M. Nijhoff, 1966), p. 130.

33. Ibid., p. 133.

34. J. Patočka, "Der Subjektivismus der Husserlschen und die Möglichkeit einer 'asubjektiven' Phänomenologie," *Die Bewegung der menschlichen Existenz, Phänomenologische Schriften*, vol. 2, ed. K. Nellen, J. Nemec, and I. Srubar (Stuttgart: Klett-Cotta, 1991), p. 277.

35. Ibid., p. 276.

36. Ibid., p. 276f.

37. Cf. E. Husserl, *Analysen zur passiven Synthesis*, vol. 11, *Hua*, pp. 154, 179.

38. *Edmund Husserls Vorlesungen zur Phänomenologie des inneren Zeitbewußtseins*, in *Jahrbuch für Philosophie und phänomenologische Forschung*, vol. 9, ed. M. Heidegger (Halle: M. Niemeyer, 1928), p. 451. (The pagination of this first edition has been included into the revised edition of the text which has been published by Rudolf Boehm in *Husserliana*, vol. 10.) In English: E. Husserl, *On the Phenomenology of the Consciousness of Internal Time (1893–1917)*, trans. J. B. Brough (Dordrecht, Boston, and London: Kluwer, 1991), p. 106.

39. Ibid.

40. Here *Sinn* (sense) is translated as "meaning."

41. E. Husserl, *Ideen zu einer reinen Phänomenologie und phänomenologischen Philosophie*, vol. 3/1, p. 286; in English: p. 320.

42. Ibid.

43. E. Husserl, *Logische Untersuchungen*, vol. 2/2, p. 129; in English: vol. p. 774.

44. Ibid., p. 134; in English: p. 778.

45. Ibid., p. 130; in English: p. 774.

46. Ibid.

47. Ibid., p. 131; in English: p. 775.

48. Ibid., p. 138f.; in English: p. 781f.

49. Ibid., p. 139; in English: p. 782.

50. Ibid., p. 142; in English: p. 784.

51. Ibid., p. 132; in English: p. 776.

52. Ibid., p. 131; in English: p. 775.

53. Ibid.

54. Ibid., p. 180; in English: p. 815.

55. Ibid., p. 137; in English: p. 780.

56. Ibid., p. 143; in English: p. 785.

57. Ibid., p. 139; in English: p. 782.

58. Cf. ibid., p. 141; in English: p. 783.

59. Ibid., p. 148ff.; in English: p. 789ff.

60. The term *Wahnehmungssinn* occurs in several passages of the *Logical Investigations*. The most important of these passages in the present context is to be found on p. 170 (in English: p. 807).

61. Ibid., p. 150; in English: p. 790.

62. Ibid., p. 149; in English: p. 790

63. Ibid.

64. Ibid., p. 148; in English: p. 789.

65. Ibid., p. 150; in English: p. 791.

66. Ibid., p. 150; in English: p. 790.

67. Ibid., p. 150; in English: p. 791.

68. See Merleau-Ponty, *Le visible et l'invisible*, p. 199; in English: p. 152.

69. D. Deleuze, *Différence et répétition* (Paris: P. U. F., 1968), p. 39f.; cf. p. 23.

70. M. Merleau-Ponty, *Le visible et l'invisible*, p. 203; in English: p. 155.

71. E. Husserl, *Cartesianische Meditationen*, vol. 1, *Hua*, p. 77; in English: p. 38f.: "Its beginning [the beginning of the descriptive theory of consciousness] is the pure—and, so to speak, still dumb—psychological experience, which now must be made to utter its own sense with no adulteration."

72. M. Merleau-Ponty, *Le visible et l'invisible*, p. 171.

73. E. Husserl, *Ideen zu einer reinen Phänomenologie und phänomenologischen Philosophie*, vol. 3/1, p. 287; in English: p. 321.

74. M. Merleau-Ponty, *Phénoménologie de la perception* (Paris: Gallimard, 1945), p. 448; in English: M. Merleau-Ponty, *Phenomenology of Perception*, trans. Colin Smith (London and New Jersey: Routledge, 1962), p. 391.

75. M. Merleau-Ponty, *Résumés de cours, Collège de France 1952–1960* (Paris: Gallimard, 1968), p. 41.

76. M. Merleau-Ponty, *Le visible et l'invisible,* p. 201; in English: p. 154.

77. Ibid., p. 167; in English: p. 126.

78. Ibid., p. 167; in English: p. 125.

79. Ibid., p. 201; in English: p. 153.

80. Ibid., p. 168; in English: p. 126.

81. Ibid., p. 165; in English: p. 124.

82. Ibid., p. 168; in English: p. 126.

83. M. Merleau-Ponty, *La prose du monde* (Paris: Gallimard, 1969), p. 34.

84. Cf. F. de Saussure, *Cours de linguistique générale,* ed. T. de Mauro (Paris: Payot, 1972), p. 166: "*dans la langue il n'y a que différences.*" Although Saussure himself does not use the expression "diacritical" for the designation of the differential relations between the elements of the linguistic system, Merleau-Ponty employs it as a well-known Saussurian term. See, for instance, M. Merleau-Ponty, "Sur la phénoménologie du langage," *Éloge de la philosophie et autres essais* (Paris: Gallimard, 1989), p. 80: "les signes, comme dit Saussure, sont essentiellement 'diacritiques'—[. . .] il n'y a dans la langue que des différences de significations."

85. M. Merleau-Ponty, *La prose du monde,* p. 145.

86. M. Merleau-Ponty, *Phénoménologie de la perception,* pp. 461–68, especially p. 462; in English: pp. 401–9, especially pp. 403–4.

87. M. Merleau-Ponty, *La prose du monde,* p. 26.

88. M. Merleau-Ponty, *Le visible et l'invisible,* p. 224; in English: p. 171.

89. J. Derrida, *La voix et le phénomène* (Paris: P. U. F., 1967), pp. 5, 111.

90. Cf. M. Merleau-Ponty, "Sur la phénoménologie du langage," *Eloge de la philosophie et autres essais,* p. 75f.

91. M. Merleau-Ponty, *La prose du monde,* p. 53.

92. M. Merleau-Ponty, "Sur la phénoménologie du langage," *Eloge de la philosophie et autres essais,* p. 75.

93. M. Merleau-Ponty, *La prose du monde,* p. 122. Cf. p. 20f.

94. Ibid., p. 19ff.

95. Cf. ibid., p. 68: "transmutation [. . .] du sens en signification."

96. The ready-made meanings of common language are described in the French original by variable terms. Merleau-Ponty speaks, for instance, of "*significations toutes faites,*" "*reçues,*" "*acquises,*" "*disponibles,*" "*instituées.*" The word "*sédimentation*" occurs also several times.

97. M. Merleau-Ponty, *La prose du monde,* p. 95.

98. M. Merleau-Ponty, "Le doute de Cézanne," *Sens et non-sens* (Paris: Gallimard, 1996), p. 19f.

99. M. Merleau-Ponty, *La prose du monde,* pp. 71–76.

100. M. Merleau-Ponty, *L'oeil et l'esprit* (Paris: Gallimard, 1964), pp. 48–51.

101. M. Merleau-Ponty, *La prose du monde,* p. 92f.

102. Ibid., p. 79.

103. J.-F. Marquet, "Proust, la fête inconcevable," *Miroirs de l'identité. La littérature hantée par la philosophie* (Paris: Hermann, 1996), p. 173.

104. Ibid.

105. M. Proust, *Du côté de chez Swann,* in *A la recherche du temps perdu,* vol. I, p. 357; in English: vol. 2, part 2, *Swann's Way,* p. 202.

106. This has been shown by Gilles Deleuze in *Proust et les signes* (Paris: Quadrige, P. U. F., 1996 [1964]).

107. M. Proust, *Du côté de chez Swann,* in *A la recherche du temps perdu,* vol. I, p. 207; in English: vol. 1, part 1, *Swann's Way,* p. 289f.

108. Ibid., p. 208; in English: vol. 1, p. 291.

109. Ibid., p. 207; in English: vol. 1, p. 290.

110. Ibid., p. 208; in English: vol. 1, p. 291.

111. Ibid., p. 215; in English: vol. 1, p. 302.

112. Ibid., p. 215; in English: vol. 1, p. 301.

113. M. Proust, *A la recherche du temps perdu,* vol. IV (Paris: Gallimard, 1954), p. 456. In English: M. Proust, *Time Regained,* vol. 6 of *In Search of Lost Time,* trans. C. K. Scott Moncrieff and Terence Kilmartin, rev. D. J. Enright (London: Vintage Books, 1996), p. 231.

114. *Du côté de chez Swann,* in *A la recherche du temps perdu,* vol. I, p. 342; in English: p. 180.

115. A. MacIntyre, *After Virtue: A Study in Moral Theory,* p. 211.

116. Ibid., p. 206.

117. Ibid.

118. Ibid.

119. Ibid., p. 208.

120. Ibid., p. 210.

121. W. Schapp, *In Geschichten verstrickt* (Wiesbaden: B. Heymann Verlag, 1976 [1953]), p. 100.

122. Ibid., p. 103ff.

123. S. Freud, "Abriß der Psychoanalyse," in *Abriß der Psychoanalyse—Das Unbehagen in der Kultur* (Frankfurt am Main: Fischer Taschenbuch Verlag, 1972), p. 57f.

Chapter 2

1. P. Ricoeur, *Temps et récit,* vol. 3, p. 45.

2. Ibid., vol. 3, p. 51.

3. Ibid., vol. 3, p. 50.

4. Ibid., vol. 3, p. 50f.

5. Ibid., p. 51.

6. See Aristotle, *Physics,* 219 a 2: "τί τῆς κινήσεώς ἐστιν."

7. Ibid., 219 b 1f.: "τοῦτο γάρ ἐστιν ὁ χρόνος, ἀριθμὸς κινήσεώς κατὰ τὸ πρότερον καὶ ὕστερον."

8. See Augustinus, *Confessiones,* XI, 26, 33: "*inde mihi visum est nihil esse aliud tempus quam distentionem; sed cuius rei, nescio, si non ipsius animi.*" Cf. XI. 29, 39: "*ecce distentio est vita mea.*"

9. P. Ricoeur, *Temps et récit,* vol. 3, p. 22.

10. R. Bernet, Einleitung to Husserl's *Texte zur Phänomenologie des inneren Zeitbewußtseins (1893–1917)* (Hamburg: Meiner, 1985), p. xiv.

11. See on this difference Rudolf Bernet's excellent study "Husserl and Heidegger on Intentionality and Being" in *Journal of the British Society of Phenomenology* 21 (1990): 136–52. The study has been reprinted in a French version under the title "Intentionnalité et transcendance (Husserl et Heidegger)" in Bernet's book *La vie du sujet* (Paris: P. U. F., 1994), pp. 39–64.

12. M. Heidegger, *Die Grundprobleme der Phänomenologie,* vol. 24 of *Gesamtausgabe,* ed. F.-W. von Herrmann (Frankfurt am Main: V. Klostermann, 1975), p. 443.

13. R. Bernet, Einleitung to Husserl's *Texte zur Phänomenologie des inneren Zeitbewußtseins (1893–1917)* (Hamburg: Meiner, 1985), p. lxii.

14. Even Merleau-Ponty says in a working note: "The I, really, is nobody, is the anonymous [. . .]." (M. Merleau-Ponty, *Le visible et l'invisible,* p. 299; in English: p. 246).

15. *Edmund Husserls Vorlesungen zur Phänomenologie des inneren Zeitbewußtseins,* in *Jahrbuch für Philosophie und phänomenologische Forschung,* ed. M. Heidegger (see chapter 1, note 38). As it has been pointed out, references to the same page numbers can be found in vol. 10, *Hua,* ed. R. Boehm published by M. Nijhoff. The English version of the text is to be found in E. Husserl, *On the Phenomenology of the Consciousness of Internal Time (1893–1917),* trans. J. B. Brough.

16. R. Bernet, "Die ungegenwärtige Gegenwart. Anwesenheit und Abwesenheit in Husserls Analyse des Zeitbewußtseins," in vol. 14, *Phänomenologische Forschungen* (Freiburg and München: K. Alber, 1983), p. 47.

17. Cf. R. Bernet, Einleitung to Husserl's *Texte zur Phänomenologie des inneren Zeitbewußtseins (1893–1917),* p. lxiiif.

18. E. Levinas, *Autrement qu'être ou au-delà de l'essence,* pp. 55–60; in English: pp. 31–34.

19. M. Henry, *Phénoménologie matérielle* (Paris: P. U. F., 1990), especially pp. 32–59.

20. Cf. F.-D. Sebbah, "Aux limites de l'intentionnalité: M. Henry et E. Levinas lecteurs des *Leçons sur la conscience intime du temps,*" in *Alter,* no. 2 (1994): 256: "E. Levinas et M. Henry décrivent le même processus: l'intentionnalité domestique l'*Urimpression.*"

21. E. Levinas, *Autrement qu'être ou au-delà de l'essence,* p. 58; in English: p. 33.

22. Ibid., p. 56; in English: p. 31f.

23. R. Bernet, "Die ungegenwärtige Gegenwart. Anwesenheit und Abwesenheit in Husserls Analyse des Zeitbewußtseins," in *Phänomenologische Forschungen,* vol. 14, p. 33.

24. Cf. *Edmund Husserls Vorlesungen zur Phänomenologie des inneren Zeitbewußtseins,* p. 482 (Appendix XII, 1911/12, according to Bernet); in English: p. 131.

25. *Edmund Husserls Vorlesungen zur Phänomenologie des inneren Zeitbewußtseins,* 1 (1905), p. 372; in English: p. 8.

26. Ibid., 8, p. 385; in English: p. 25 (cf. *Hua,* vol. 10, Nr. 53, 1911).

27. Ibid., Appendix XI, p. 478; in English: p. 127 (1907, according to Bernet).

28. Ibid., 39, p. 436; in English: p. 87 (cf. *Hua*, vol. 10, Nr. 54, the end of 1911).

29. Ibid., Appendix XI, p. 478; in English: p. 128 (1907, according to Bernet).

30. Ibid., Appendix I, p. 451; in English: p. 106 (1916, according to Bernet).

31. Ibid., 31, p. 424; in English: p. 71 (1905).

32. Ibid., Appendix I, p. 451; in English: p. 106 (1916, according to Bernet).

33. Ibid., 31, p. 422; in English: p. 69 (1905).

34. Ibid., 16, p. 400; in English: p. 42 (1905).

35. Ibid., 31, p. 423; in English: p. 69f. (1905). The latter English term has been slightly modified: *ursprüngliche Zeitstellenimpression* can be rendered as "original impression of temporal position" rather than as "impression of the original temporal position."

36. R. Bernet, "Die ungegenwärtige Gegenwart: Anwesenheit und Abwesenheit in Husserls Analyse des Zeitbewußtseins," vol. 14, *Phänomenologische Forschungen*, p. 45.

37. *Edmund Husserls Vorlesungen zur Phänomenologie des inneren Zeitbewußtseins*, section 31, p. 423; in English: p. 69 (1905).

38. Ibid., p. 423; in English: p. 70 (1905).

39. Ibid., Appendix VI, p. 467; in English: p. 118.

40. Ibid.

41. Ibid.

42. Ibid., Appendix XII, p. 482; in English: p. 131 (1911/12, according to Bernet).

43. R. Bernet, "Intentionnalité sans sujet ni objet?" in *La vie du sujet* (Paris: P. U. F., 1994), pp. 318–20.

44. F. Brentano, *Psychologie vom empirischen Standpunkt*, vol. 1, ed. O. Kraus (Hamburg: Meiner, 1973), p. 180. In English: *Psychology from an Empirical Standpoint*, trans. A. C. Rancurello, D. B. Terrell, and L. L. McAlister (London and New York: Routledge and Kegan Paul, Humanities Press, 1973), p. 128.

45. Ibid., pp. 180–82; in English: pp. 128–30.

46. Cf. J. B. Brough, "The Emergence of an Absolute Consciousness in Husserl's Early Writings on Time Consciousness," in *Husserl: Expositions and Appraisals*, ed. F. A. Elliston and P. McCormick (Notre Dame, Ind.: University of Notre Dame Press, 1977), pp. 83–100. Also by him, Translator's Introduction to Husserl's *On the Phenomenology of the Consciousness of Internal Time (1893–1917)*, pp. xlv–xlviii; R. Bernet, Einleitung to Husserl's *Texte zur Phänomenologie des inneren Zeitbewußtseins (1893–1917)*, pp. xxxiii–liii.

47. *Edmund Husserls Vorlesungen zur Phänomenologie des inneren Zeitbewußtseins*, 34, p. 428; in English: p. 77 (cf. *Hua*, vol. 10, Nr. 40).

48. Ibid., 36, p. 429; in English: p. 79 (cf. *Hua*, vol. 10, Nr. 54, at the end of 1911).

49. Ibid., Appendix IX, p. 472f.; in English: p. 123.

50. R. Bernet, Einleitung in E. Husserl's *Texte zur Phänomenologie des inneren Zeitbewußtseins (1893–1917)*, p. xlix.

51. Ibid., 39, p. 436; in English: p. 88 (cf. *Hua*, vol. 10, Nr. 54, at the end of 1911).

52. M. Heidegger, *Metaphysische Anfangsgründe der Logik im Ausgang von Leibniz, Gesamtausgabe,* vol. 26, ed. by Klaus Held (Frankfurt am Main: V. Klostermann, 1978), p. 264.

53. E. Levinas, "Intentionnalité et Sensation" (originally 1963), *En découvrant l'existence avec Husserl et Heidegger* (Paris: Vrin, 1974), p. 154; *Autrement qu'être ou au-delà de l'essence,* p. 57; in English: p. 32: "This specific intentionality is time itself."

54. *Edmund Husserls Vorlesungen zur Phänomenologie des inneren Zeitbewußtseins,* Appendix IX, p. 472; in English: p. 123.

55. Ibid.

56. Ibid., Appendix IX, p. 473; in English: p. 123.

57. Ibid., Appendix IX, p. 472; in English: p. 123.

58. Ibid., Appendix IX, p. 473; in English: p. 123.

59. Ibid.

60. F. Brentano, *Psychologie vom empirischen Standpunkt,* vol. 1, pp. 203–18; in English: pp. 143–54.

61. E. Husserl, *Logische Untersuchungen,* vol. 2/1, pp. 391–97; in English: vol. 2, pp. 572–76; cf. R. Bernet, "Intentionnalité sans sujet ni objet?" *La vie du sujet,* p. 310.

62. *Edmund Husserls Vorlesungen zur Phänomenologie des inneren Zeitbewußtseins,* Appendix III, p. 458; in English: p. 112 (1909/10, according to Bernet).

63. Ibid.

64. Ibid.

65. Ibid., p. 389; in English: p. 29.

66. Ibid., 16, p. 400; in English: p. 42 (1905).

67. M. Henry, *Phénoménologie matérielle,* p. 43.

68. E. Levinas, *Autrement qu'être ou au-delà de l'essence,* p. 59; in English: pp. 34, 33. The translation of these two passages has been modified. The English text renders *proto-impression,* by mistake, as "primal retention" (instead of "primal impression"). Furthermore, *impérieuse* is much stronger than "all-encompassing."

69. *Edmund Husserls Vorlesungen zur Phänomenologie des inneren Zeitbewußtseins,* Appendix I, p. 451; in English: p. 106 (1916, according to Bernet).

70. E. Levinas, "Réflexions sur la 'technique' phénoménologique" (originally 1959), *En découvrant l'existence avec Husserl et Heidegger,* p. 119.

71. Ibid.

72. Ibid., p. 118.

73. Ibid.

74. E. Levinas, "Intentionnalité et Sensation," in *En découvrant l'existence avec Husserl et Heidegger,* p. 152f.

75. Cf. ibid., pp. 152, 155.

76. Cf. ibid., pp. 154, 153.

77. Cf. ibid., p. 156.

78. Ibid.

79. Ibid., p. 153.

80. Ibid.

81. Ibid., p. 155.

82. E. Levinas, *Autrement qu'être ou au-delà de l'essence,* p. 58; in English: p. 33.

83. Ibid.

84. Ibid.

85. Ibid., p. 59; in English: p. 33.

86. M. Henry, *Phénoménologie matérielle,* p. 55.

87. E. Husserl, *Zur Phänomenologie der Intersubjektivität III: 1929–35,* vol. 15, *Hua,* ed. I. Kern (Den Haag: M. Nijhoff, 1973), p. 595.

88. M. Heidegger, *Metaphysische Anfangsgründe der Logik im Ausgang von Leibniz, Gesamtausgabe,* vol. 26, pp. 268, 271.

89. M. Merleau-Ponty, *Phénoménologie de la perception,* pp. 480–84; in English: pp. 419–23.

90. E. Husserl, *Zur Phänomenologie der Intersubjektivität III: 1929–35,* vol. 10, *Hua,* p. 540.

91. Cf. E. Husserl, *Phantasie, Zeitbewußtsein, Erinnerung. Zur Phänomenologie der anschaulichen Vergegenwärtigungen,* vol. 23, *Hua,* ed. E. Marbach (Den Haag, Boston, and London: M. Nijhoff, 1980), pp. 326, 316.

92. Cf. M. Henry, *La barbarie* (Paris: Grasset, 1987), pp. 20–23.

93. M. Henry, *Phénoménologie matérielle,* p. 42.

94. Ibid., p. 39.

95. Ibid., p. 46.

96. Ibid., pp. 30, 55.

97. Ibid., p. 53.

98. Cf. M. Richir, "Monadologie transcendantale et temporalisation" in *Husserl-Ausgabe und Husserl-Forschung,* ed. S. Ijsseling (Dordrecht, London, and Boston: Kluwer, 1990), p. 152; cf. also by him, *Méditations phénoménologiques,* p. 30.

99. Cf. R. Bernet, "Intentionnalité sans sujet ni objet?" in *La vie du sujet,* p. 322.

100. *Edmund Husserls Vorlesungen zur Phänomenologie des inneren Zeitbewußtseins,* Appendix I, p. 451; in English: p. 106 (1916, according to Bernet).

101. Cf. M. Merleau-Ponty, *Le visible et l'invisible,* p. 149; in English: p. 110; M. Richir, *Méditations phénoménologique,* esp. pp. 215–31 and pp. 345–50.

102. M. Richir, *Méditations phénoménologique,* pp. 76–85.

103. Ibid., p. 58: "The sublime in the phenomenological sense—this is nothing else but the phenomenological encounter with the phenomenological *apeiron* or boundlessness." Cf. ibid., p. 81: "The phenomenological sublime is that 'moment' in which the 'I' is engulfed by the endlessly nascent and rudimentary character of phenomena—so the 'I'. is submerged in what Kant calls the *shapeless*—and is forced to die, having lost all the symbolic footing which hitherto lent it its self- identity [. . .]. Yet this is still nothing more than the negative momentum of the sublime, which carries, in turn, its 'positive' counterpart as well and this is nothing else but the mysterious self-apprehension of ourselves as ourselves, which, getting over death, regains itself again in the mystery of its own corporeal reality [. . .]."

104. These investigations, to some extent, are already related to Richir's interpretation of time, which will be the topic of the next section. Here I exclusively concentrate on defining the reality unfolding as a destinal event in the

mode of a *presence* that *has never been future.* This concept cannot be found in Richir.

105. Op cit., p. 157: "the present is not on display as a commencement of a now-moment enveloped by protentions and retentions (Husserl)—this is a mere abstraction—but as a commencement, a process of a formation (sense formation), which takes place *quicker* than itself in order to keep its promise still to be fulfilled and, at the same time, also slower than itself, in order to measure which it has created against the exigency assigned to it by the past" (cf. op cit., p. 199).

106. Cf. especially M. Richir, *La crise du sens et la phénoménologie,* pp. 180–87 ("the moment of the living present is nothing else than *porte-à-faux en movement* [. . .]," p. 180; "*distortion originaire* between the sense projected and the sense retained," p. 182).

107. "[*P*] *henomenological time* (*time and space*) can, thus, not be taken either as linear, or as continuous, or as homogeneous: it is, in fact, *originally manifold and discontinuous, and falls into the splinters of originally manifold phases of the present from the very beginning,*" p. 187; cf. Merleau-Ponty, *Le visible et l'invisible,* p. 165.

108. Cf. E. Husserl, *Analysen zur passiven Synthesis,* vol. 11, section 46, *Hua,* p. 211: "evident ist doch, daß das Neue aller Erwartung ins Gesicht schlagen kann."

Chapter 3

1. It is by no means an accident that Vincent Descombes gave to his early survey of recent French thought the title *The Same and the Other* (*Le Même et l'Autre: Quarante-cinq ans de philosophie française 1933–1978* [Paris: Minuit, 1979]).

2. P. Ricoeur, *Soi-même comme un autre,* pp. 34, 350; in English: pp. 22, 302.

3. P. Ricoeur, *De l'interprétation. Essai sur Freud* (Paris: Seuil, 1965), p. 425. In English: *Freud and Philosophy. An Essay on Interpretation,* trans. Denis Savage (New Haven and London: Yale University Press, 1970), p. 439.

4. P. Ricoeur, *Soi-même comme un autre,* p. 22; in English: p. 11.

5. Ibid., p. 348; in English: p. 300.

6. Ibid., p. 350; in English: p. 301.

7. Ibid., p. 380; in English: p. 329.

8. Ibid., p. 350; in English: p. 301.

9. See D. Franck, *Chair et corps. Sur la phénomenologie de Husserl* (Paris: Minuit, 1981).

10. P. Ricoeur, *Soi-même comme un autre,* p. 375; in English: p. 324.

11. Ibid.

12. Ibid., p. 374; in English: p. 323.

13. Ibid., p. 369; in English: p. 318.

14. Ibid., p. 377; in English: p. 326.

15. Ibid.

16. Ibid., p. 14; in English: p. 3: "To 'as' I should like to attach a strong meaning, not only that of a comparison (oneself similar to another) but indeed that of an implication (oneself inasmuch as being other)."

17. Ibid., p. 211; in English: p. 337.

18. E. Levinas, "Réflexions sur la 'technique' phénoménologique" (1959), in *En découvrant l'existence avec Husserl et Heidegger*, p. 119.

19. E. Husserl, *Cartesianische Meditationen*, vol. 1, *Hua*, p. 126; in English: p. 95.

20. Ibid., pp. 97, 95; in English: pp. 62, 60.

21. Ibid., p. 148; in English: p. 116.

22. K. Held, "Das Problem der Intersubjektivität und die Idee einer phänomenologischen Transzendentalphilosophie," in *Perspektiven transzendental-phänomenologischer Forschung*, ed. U. Claesges and K. Held (Den Haag: M. Nijhoff, 1972), p. 35.

23. M. Merleau-Ponty, "De Mauss à Claude Lévi-Strauss," *Eloge de la philosophie et autres essais*, p. 134.

24. M. Merleau-Ponty, *Le visible et l'invisible*, p. 154; in English: p. 115.

25. B. Waldenfels, "Verschränkung von Heimwelt und Fremdwelt," in *Philosophische Grundlagen der Interkulturalität*, vol. 1 of *Studien zur interkulturellen Philosophie*, ed. R. A. Mall and D. Lohmar (Amsterdam and Atlanta: Rodopi, 1993), p. 60.

26. M. Merleau-Ponty, *Le visible et l'invisible*, p. 269; in English: p. 216.

27. Ibid., p. 204; in English: p. 155: "the reversibility which is the ultimate truth."

28. Ibid., p. 182; in English: p. 138: "reciprocal insertion and intertwining of one in the other."

29. M. Merleau-Ponty, *Le visible et l'invisible*, p. 228; in English: p. 174.

30. Cf. E. Husserl, *Zur Phänomenologie der Intersubjektivität III: 1929–35*, vol. 15, *Hua*, p. 603.

31. M. Merleau-Ponty, *Le visible et l'invisible*, pp. 269, 216.

32. Ibid., p. 185; in English: p. 141.

33. Ibid., pp. 183, 187, 299; in English: pp. 139, 142, 246.

34. Cf. ibid., p. 322; in English: p. 269.

35. Ibid., p. 231; in English: p. 177.

36. Ibid., p. 162; in English: p. 121.

37. Ibid., p. 306f.; in English: p. 253.

38. Ibid., p. 236; in English: p. 182.

39. Ibid., p. 229; in English: p. 175.

40. Ibid., p. 263; in English: p. 209.

41. Ibid., p. 263; in English: p. 209f.

42. Ibid., p. 229; in English: p. 175.

43. Ibid., p. 167; in English: p. 125.

44. Ibid., p. 229; in English: p. 175. Rudolf Bernet shows that it is precisely the idea of a "*système ouvert de différences diacritiques*" which connects the notion of a savage mind with the concept of nature exposed in the *Phenomenology of Perception*. See R. Bernet, "Le sujet dans la nature: Réflexions sur la phénoménologie de la perception chez Merleau-Ponty," in *Merleau-Ponty, phénoménologie et expérience*, ed. M. Richir and E. Tassin (Grenoble: Millon, 1992), esp. p. 76f. Reprinted in R. Bernet, *La vie du sujet* (Paris: P. U. F., 1994).

45. Ibid., p. 269; in English: p. 215.

46. Ibid., p. 201; in English: p. 154.

47. Ibid., p. 198; in English: p. 151.

48. Ibid., p. 230; in English: p. 176.

49. Ibid.

50. It is a merit of Marc Richir's to have pointed this out. See his paper "Communeauté, société et Histoire chez le dernier Merleau-Ponty," in *Merleau-Ponty, phénoménologie et expérience,* ed. M. Richir and E. Tassin, esp. pp. 17–19.

51. M. Merleau-Ponty, "De Mauss à Claude Lévi-Strauss," in *Eloge de la philosophie et autres essais,* p. 133.

52. Ibid.

53. Cf. M. Richir, *Phénoménologie et institution symbolique* (Grenoble: Millon, 1988), p. 377: "Nous avons la chance de demeurer toujours, peu ou prou, des étrangers [. . .]."

54. Husserl comes close to admitting this failure in one of his later working notes. See E. Husserl, *Zur Phänomenologie der Intersubjektivität III: 1929–35,* p. 450: "ich verbaliere, ganz äußerlicherweise auch selbstverständlich, daß ich nicht der Andere bin und daß ich [. . .] gleichsam miterfahre, mitdenke, mittue, dabei aber doch ich bin und nicht der Andere bin. Aber wie ist dieser Unterschied zu verstehen [. . .]?"

55. Such a concrete comparison has been made by Rudolf Bernet in a forthcoming paper with the title "La totalité détotalisée et l'infini: Sartre et Levinas sur la rencontre avec l'autre." (The paper was read on May 31, 2000, in the Philosophical Institute of the Eötvös Loránd University of Budapest.)

56. Cf. D. M. Levin, *The Philosopher's Gaze: Modernity in the Shadows of Enlightment* (Berkeley, Los Angeles, and London: University of California Press, 1999), p. 274: "Levinas can alter the phenomenology he inherited in many ways, can question some of its principal assumptions, even radically change its 'approach' to the subject and introduce new normative concepts to guide this approach; but he cannot renounce it entirely. Because phenomenology is the only method [. . .] that is uncompromisingly committed to *respecting* the articulation of experience just as it is actually lived [. . .]."

57. E. Levinas, *Totalité et Infini. Essai sur l'extériorité* (La Haye: M. Nijhoff, 1961); quoted in the Editions Livre de Poche (Dordrecht, Boston, and London: Kluwer, 1994), p. 342. In English: *Totality and Infinity,* trans. A. Lingis (Pittsburgh: Dusquesne University Press, 1969), p. 306.

58. Ibid., p. 329; in English: p. 295.

59. Ibid., pp. 281, 236–38; in English: pp. 251, 215f.

60. Ibid., p. 211; in English: p. 194.

61. Ibid., p. 281f.; in English: p. 215.

62. J. Derrida, *L'écriture et la différence* (Paris: Seuil, 1967), p. 180. In English: *Writing and Difference,* trans., A. Bass (London, Melbourne, and Henley: Routledge and Kegan Paul, 1978), p. 123.

63. E. Levinas, *Totalité et Infini. Essai sur l'extériorité,* p. 218; in English: p. 200.

64. Ibid.

65. Ibid., p. 293; in English: p. 262.

66. Ibid.

67. Ibid., p. 226f.; in English: p. 206.

68. Ibid., p. 293; in English: p. 262.

69. Ibid., p. 327; in English: p. 294.

70. Ibid., p. 330; in English: p. 296.

71. Ibid., p. 187; in English: p. 172.

72. Cf. E. Levinas, *Autrement qu'être ou au-delà de l'essence,* p. 81; in English: p. 47. Here Levinas affirms that the relationship with the other requires a "quasi-hagiographic style" that, however, "wishes to be neither a sermon nor the confession of a 'beautiful soul.'"

73. Ibid., p. 79; in English: p. 47: "'a signifyingness dealt' to the other."

74. Ibid., p. 111; in English: p. 69.

75. Ibid., p. 273; in English: p. 178.

76. Ibid., p. 205; in English: p. 129.

77. E. Levinas, *Totalité et Infini. Essai sur l'extériorité,* p. if. ("Préface à l'édition allemande" from 1987, not contained in the English version of the book.)

78. Ibid., p. 334; in English: p. 299.

79. Ibid., p. 25; in English: p. 36.

80. Ibid., p. 29; in English: p. 40.

81. Ibid., p. 301; in English: p. 269.

82. Ibid., p. 336; in English: p. 301.

83. Ibid., p. 212; in English: p. 194.

84. Ibid., p. 215; in English: p. 197.

85. Ibid., p. 24f.; in English: p. 35.

86. Ibid., p. 212; in English: p. 195.

87. Ibid.

88. Ibid.

89. Ibid., p. 243; in English: p. 220.

90. Ibid., p. 334; in English: p. 299f.

91. Ibid., p. 27; in English: p. 38.

92. Ibid., p. 115; in English: p. 112.

93. Ibid.

94. Ibid.

95. Ibid., p. 54; in English: p. 60.

96. Ibid., p. 125; in English: p. 120.

97. Ibid., p. 125f.; in English: p. 121.

98. Ibid., p. 281; in English: p. 251.

99. Ibid., p. 126; in English: p. 121.

100. E. Levinas, *Autrement qu'être ou au-delà de l'essence,* p. 46; in English: p. 25.

101. Ibid., p.120; in English: p. 75.

102. Ibid., p. 203f.; in English: p. 128.

103. Ibid., p. 172; in English: p. 109 (here the expression *non-lieu* is translated as "no grounds").

104. Ibid., p. 160, n.; in English: p. 194 (n. 3 to p. 101).

105. Ibid., p. 248f.; in English: p. 159f. (The translation has been slightly modified.)

106. S. Critchley, *The Ethics of Deconstruction: Derrida and Levinas* (London and Cambridge, Mass.: Basil Blackwell, 1992), p. 221.

107. Ibid., p. 222.

108. Ibid., p. 223.

109. E. Levinas, *Autrement qu'être ou au-delà de l'essence,* p. 256; in English: p. 165.

110. B. Waldenfels, *Antwortregister* (Frankfurt am Main: Suhrkamp, 1994), p. 357.

111. B. Waldenfels, *Antwortregister,* p. 355f.

112. Ibid., p. 359.

113. For an interpretation of this expression properly required in the present context, see T. W. Adorno, *Negative Dialektik* (Frankfurt am Main: Suhrkamp, 1994 [1966]), pp. 222–25.

114. See I. Kant, *Über ein vermeintes Recht, aus Menschenliebe zu lügen,* vol. 8, Academy Edition (Berlin and Leipzig: W. de Gruyter, 1923), pp. 425–30.

Chapter 4

1. B. Waldenfels, "Singularität im Plural," *Deutsch-Französische Gedankengänge* (Frankfurt am Main: Suhrkamp, 1995), p. 320f.

2. I. Kant, *Kritik der praktischen Vernunft,* vol. 5, Academy Edition, p. 98. In English: *Critique of Practical Reason and Other Writings in Moral Philosophy,* trans. L. White Beck (Chicago: University of Chicago Press, 1949 [repr. 1976]). In this English edition the page numbers of the German Academy Edition are indicated.

3. M. Heidegger, *Sein und Zeit,* p. 271; in English: p. 316.

4. Ibid., p. 283; in English: p. 329.

5. Cf. P. Ricoeur, *Soi-même comme un autre,* p. 405; in English: p. 351.

6. E. Levinas, *Autrement qu'être ou au-delà de l'essence,* p. 191; in English: p. 120.

7. Ibid., p. 192; in English: p. 120.

8. Ibid.

9. Cf. B. Waldenfels, *Antwortregister,* p. 357.

10. Cf. J.-P. Sartre, *L'être et le néant* (Paris: Gallimard, 1943), p. 126. In English: *Being and Nothingness,* trans. H. E. Barnes (London: Methuen, 1958), p. 84. It is worth being noted that, in § 46 of *Ideas I,* already Husserl attributed to the Cogito the "necessity of a fact."

11. Cf. S. Critchley, *The Ethics of Deconstruction. Derrida and Levinas,* p. 53f., n. 26.

12. E. Levinas, *Autrement qu'être ou au-delà de l'essence,* p. 84; in English: p. 49.

13. P. Ricoeur, *Autrement. Lecture d'Autrement qu'être ou au-delà de l'essence de Levinas* (Paris: P. U. F., 1997), p. 2.

14. S. Critchley, *The Ethics of Deconstruction. Derrida and Levinas,* p. 7.

15. E. Levinas, *Autrement qu'être ou au-delà de l'essence,* p. 85; in English: p. 50.

16. E. Levinas, *Totalité et Infini,* p. 219; in English: p. 200.

17. Ibid., p. 227; in English: p. 206.

18. Cf. J.-L. Marion, *Étant donné. Essai d'une phénoménologie de la donation* (Paris: P. U. F., 1997), pp. 408–13.

19. Cf. E. Levinas, *Autrement qu'être ou au-delà de l'essence,* p. 245; in English: p. 157.

20. Cf. B. Waldenfels, *Antwortregister,* p. 355f.

21. Cf. E. Levinas, *Autrement qu'être ou au-delà de l'essence,* p. 259; p. 166.

22. Ibid., p. 260; in English: p. 167.

23. See R. Bernasconi, "Skepticism in the Face of Philosophy," in *Re-Reading Levinas,* ed. R. Bernasconi and S. Critchley (London: Athlone, 1991), p. 150.

24. E. Levinas, *Autrement qu'être ou au-delà de l'essence,* p. 245; in English: p. 157.

25. Ibid., p. 261; in English: p. 168.

26. Ibid.

27. Ibid., p. 260; in English: p. 167.

28. P. Ricoeur, *Soi-même comme un autre,* p. 405; in English: p. 351.

29. Ibid., p. 409; in English: p. 355.

30. E. Levinas, *Totalité et Infini,* p. 5; in English: p. 21.

31. I. Kant, *Kritik der praktischen Vernunft,* vol. 5, Academy Edition, p. 98f.

32. A. MacIntyre, *After Virtue: A Study in Moral Theory,* pp. 52, 54.

33. Ibid., p. 54.

34. Ibid., p. 55.

35. P. Ricoeur, *Soi-même comme un autre,* p. 200; in English: p. 170. Cf. B. Williams, *Ethics and the Limits of Philosophy* (Glasgow: Collins, Fontana Press, 1985), p. 6.

36. P. Ricoeur, *Soi-même comme un autre,* p. 201; in English: p. 170f.

37. C. Taylor, *Sources of the Self. The Making of the Modern Identity* (Cambridge: Cambridge University Press, 1989), p. 72.

38. Ibid.: "We are convinced that a certain view is superior because we have lived a transition which we understand as error-reducing [. . .]."

39. Ibid., p. 73.

40. Ibid., p. 72.

41. Ibid., p. 68.

42. P. Ricoeur, *Soi-même comme un autre,* p. 320; in English: p. 275. Cf. C. Taylor, *Sources of the Self,* p. 12.

43. A. MacIntyre, *After Virtue,* p. 219. Cf. P. Ricoeur, *Temps et récit,* vol. 1, p. 114; C. Taylor, *Sources of the Self,* pp. 17, 48.

44. See C. Taylor, *Sources of the Self,* pp. 44, 46f. Cf. P. Ricoeur, *Soi-même comme un autre,* p. 204; in English: p. 173f (on Aristotle's concept of βούλησις and pp. 365–67; in English: pp. 315–17 (on Spinoza's concept of *conatus*).

45. C. Taylor, *Sources of the Self,* p. 3.

46. Ibid.

47. Ibid., p. 4.

48. Ibid., p. 14.

49. Ibid., p. 15f.

50. I. Kant, *Grundlegung zur Metaphysik der Sitten,* vol. 4, Academy Edition (Berlin: G. Reimer, 1911), p. 463. In English: *Foundations of the Metaphysics of Morals,* in *Critique of Practical Reason and Other Writings in Moral Philosophy,* trans. L. White Beck (Chicago: University of Chicago Press, 1949 [repr. 1976]). In this

English edition the page numbers of the German Academy Edition are indicated.

51. I. Kant, *Kritik der praktischen Vernunft,* vol. 5, Academy Edition, p. 46.

52. Ibid., p. 47.

53. Ibid., p. 46f. Cf. also pp. 31, 42f., 55, 91. Kant scholars have formed different opinions on this concept of a "fact of pure reason." See, for instance, G. Krüger, *Philosophie und Moral in der Kantischen Kritik* (Tübingen: J. C. B. Mohr [P. Siebeck] 1967 [1931]), especially pp. 67–69; D. Henrich, "Das Problem der Grundlegung der Ethik bei Kant und im spekulativen Idealismus," in *Sein und Ethos,* ed. P. Engelhardt (Mainz: Mathias Grünewald Verlag, 1963), p. 370f. ("eine Folge von Kants Konsequenz"); G. Prauss, *Kant über Freiheit als Autonomie* (Frankfurt am Main: V. Klostermann, 1983), p. 68 ("ein Unding").

54. I. Kant, *Grundlegung zur Metaphysik der Sitten,* vol. 4, Academy Edition, p. 428.

55. Ibid., p. 450. (The latter translation stems from Abbot.)

56. Ibid., p. 428.

57. Ibid., p. 431: "allgemeiner Zweckvorzug"; p. 438: "Würde (Prärogativ) vor allen bloßen Naturwesen."

58. Ibid., p. 431.

59. On these circumstances see my paper "Eine Methode rekonstruktiver Analyse," in *Doxa,* 17 (1989): 47–54.

60. I. Kant, *Kritik der praktischen Vernunft,* vol. 5, Academy Edition (Berlin: G. Reimer, 1913) p. 87: "only man, and, with him, every rational creature, is an end in itself" (trans. L. White Beck).

61. Ibid., p. 86.

62. Ibid., p. 79.

63. Ibid., p. 86.

64. Ibid., p. 73.

65. A. MacIntyre, *After Virtue: A Study in Moral Theory,* p. 150.

66. Aristoteles, *Ethica Nicomachea,* II. 4, 1105 a 32: "προαιρούμενος δι' αὐτά."

67. J. Nabert, *Eléments pour une éthique* (Paris: P. U. F., 1943), p. 142: "l'épure d'une histoire concrète." In English: *Elements for an Ethic,* trans. W. J. Petrek (Evanston, Ill.: Northwestern University Press, 1969), p. 117.

68. Ibid.

69. Ibid.

70. Ibid., p. 143; in English: p. 118.

71. Ibid.

72. Ibid.

73. Ibid.

74. Ibid., p. 144; in English: p. 119.

75. Ibid.

76. Ibid.: "If one conceives of a reason not secretly sustained by an aspiration of the acting being, its intrusion into life will inevitably appear as constraint. It is better to say that reason itself is desire if one wants to understand the authority it acquires [. . .]."

77. Ibid., p. 119; in English: p. 120.

78. P. Ricoeur, *De l'interprétation. Essai sur Freud,* p. 333; in English: p. 341.

79. J. Nabert, *Eléments pour une éthique,* 2d ed. (Paris: Aubier, 1962), p. 8f. In English: *Elements for an Ethic,* p. xxi.

80. Ibid., p. 47.

81. Ibid., p. 49.

82. Ibid.

83. Cf. P. Ricoeur, *Le volontaire et l'involontaire,* in vol. 1 of *Philosophie de la volonté* (Paris: Aubier, 1950), p. 453ff.

84. P. Ricoeur, *De l'interprétation. Essai sur Freud,* p. 443; in English: p. 458.

85. Ibid., p. 426; in English: p. 439.

86. Ibid., p. 426; in English: p. 440.

87. Ibid., p. 210; in English: p. 213.

88. Ibid., p. 472; in English: p. 489.

89. Ibid.

90. Ibid.

91. G. W. F. Hegel, *Phänomenologie des Geistes,* p. 144.

92. Ibid., pp. 139, 144.

93. P. Ricoeur, *De l'interprétation. Essai sur Freud,* p. 450; in English: p. 466.

94. Ibid., p. 451; in English: p. 466.

95. Ibid.; p. 451; in English: p. 466.

96. Ibid., p. 505; in English: p. 526.

97. Ibid., p. 508; in English: p. 529.

98. Ibid., p. 526f.; in English: p. 549. Ricoeur quotes here Proposition 36 of part 5 of Spinoza's *Ethics.*

99. Ibid.

100. Cf. P. Ricoeur, "Herméneutique des symboles et réflexion philosophique (II)," *Le conflit des interprétations. Essai d'herméneutique* (Paris: Seuil, 1969), p. 324: "La philosophie est éthique, mais l'éthique n'est pas purement morale."

101. P. Ricoeur, *De l'interprétation. Essai sur Freud,* p. 527; in English: p. 549.

102. P. Ricoeur, "Démythiser l'accusation," *Le conflit des interprétations,* p. 334f.

103. J. Lacan, *L'éthique de la psychanalyse,* bk. 7, *Le séminaire* (Paris: Seuil, 1986), p. 361. In English: *The Ethics of Psychoanalysis 1959–1960,* bk. 7, *The Seminar of Jacques Lacan,* ed. J.-A. Miller, trans. D. Porter (London: Routledge, 1992), p. 313.

104. Ibid., p. 11; in English: p. 3.

105. Ibid., p. 14; in English: p. 6.

106. Ibid.

107. Lásd A. Juranville, *Lacan et la philosophie* (Paris: P. U. F., 1984), section 32, pp. 199–207.

108. R. Bernet, "Subjekt und Gesetz in der Ethik von Kant und Lacan," in *Ethik und Psychoanalyse. Vom kategorischen Imperativ zum Gesetz des Begehrens: Kant und Lacan,* ed. H.-D. Gondek and P. Widmer (Frankfurt am Main: Fischer, 1994), p. 45.

109. Ibid., p. 41.

110. Ibid., p. 39.

111. Ibid., p. 39f.

112. W. Shakespeare, *King Lear,* the Arden edition, ed. R. A. Foakes (Walton-on-Thames: Thomas Nelson and Sons Ltd., 1997).

113. J. Lacan, *L'éthique de la psychanalyse,* Le séminaire, bk. 7, p. 340; in English: p. 294.

114. Cf. R. Bernet, "Subjekt und Gesetz in der Ethik von Kant und Lacan," in *Ethik und Psychoanalyse. Vom kategorischen Imperativ zum Gesetz des Begehrens: Kant und Lacan,* ed. H.-D. Gondek and P. Widmer, p. 37: "uneinholbare Differenz."

115. Ibid., p. 40.

116. Ibid., p. 35.

117. J. Lacan, *L'éthique de la psychanalyse,* Le séminaire, bk. 7, p. 28.

118. H.-D. Gondek, "Lacan und die Ethik der Psychoanalyse," in *Ethik und Psychoanalyse. Vom kategorischen Imperativ zum Gesetz des Begehrens: Kant und Lacan,* ed. H.-D. Gondek and P. Widmer, p. 217f.

119. J. Lacan, *L'éthique de la psychanalyse, Le séminaire,* bk. 7, p. 45; in English: p. 35.

120. Ibid., p. 48; in English: p. 38.

121. Ibid., p. 60; in English: p. 47.

122. Ibid., p. 59; in English: p. 46.

123. See S. Freud, *Die Verneinung,* in *Studienausgabe,* vol. 3: *Zur Psychologie des Unbewußten* (Frankfurt am Main: Fischer, 1982), p. 375.

124. J. Lacan, *L'éthique de la psychanalyse, Le séminaire,* bk. 7, p. 72; in English: p. 58.

125. Ibid.

126. Ibid.

127. R. Bernet, "Subjekt und Gesetz in der Ethik von Kant und Lacan," in *Ethik und Psychoanalyse. Vom kategorischen Imperativ zum Gesetz des Begehrens: Kant und Lacan,* ed. H.-D. Gondek and P. Widmer, p. 40f.

128. J. Lacan, *L'éthique de la psychanalyse, Le séminaire,* bk. 7, p. 341; in English: p. 294.

129. Ibid., 42; in English: p. 32.

130. See ibid., pp. 368–70; in English: pp. 319–21.

131. R. Bernet, "Subjekt und Gesetz in der Ethik von Kant und Lacan," in *Ethik und Psychoanalyse. Vom kategorischen Imperativ zum Gesetz des Begehrens: Kant und Lacan,* ed. H.-D. Gondek and P. Widmer, p. 42.

132. Gondek, H.-D., "Lacan und die Ethik der Psychoanalyse," in *Ethik und Psychoanalyse. Vom kategorischen Imperativ zum Gesetz des Begehrens: Kant und Lacan,* ed. H.-D. Gondek and P. Widmer, pp. 222, 219f.

133. R. Bernet, "Subjekt und Gesetz in der Ethik von Kant und Lacan," in *Ethik und Psychoanalyse. Vom kategorischen Imperativ zum Gesetz des Begehrens: Kant und Lacan,* ed. H.-D. Gondek and P. Widmer, p. 43.

134. E. Levinas, *Autrement qu'être ou au-delà de l'essence,* p. 195; in English: p. 123.

135. Ibid.

136. E. Levinas, *Totalité et Infini*, pp. 23, 302; in English: pp. 34, 269.

137. B. Waldenfels, *Antwortregister*, p. 342.

138. E. Levinas, *Autrement qu'être ou au-delà de l'essence*, p. 196; in English: p. 123.

139. See Plotinus, *Enneads*, I, 8, 11.

140. See A. Vergez, *Faute et liberté* (Paris: Les belles letters, 1969), pp. 128–35. Cf. P. Ricoeur, "Le 'péché originel': étude de signification," *Le conflit des interprétations: Essai d'herméneutique* (Paris: Seuil, 1969), pp. 265–82, especially p. 271. In English: *The Conflict of Interpretations*, ed. D. Ihde (Evanston, Ill.: Northwestern University Press, 1974), pp. 269–86, especially p. 275f.

141. P. Ricoeur, *Finitude et culpabilité* (Paris: Seuil, 1988), p. 14. In English: *Fallible Man*, trans. C. A. Kelbley (New York: Fordham University Press, 1986), p. xlvi: "we may understand by the ethical vision of the world our continual effort to understand freedom and evil by each other."

142. Ibid., p. 15ff.

143. Ibid., p. 476.

144. Ibid., p. 363.

145. P. Ricoeur, *Le conflit des interprétations*, p. 291; in English: p. 295: "The serpent, at the very heart of the Adam myth, stands for evil's other face, which the other myths tried to recount: evil already there, pregiven evil, evil that attracts and seduces man. The serpent signifies that man does not begin evil. He finds it. For him, to begin is to continue." Cf. ibid., p. 304; in English: p. 308: "The serpent, I think, represents the 'always already there.'"

146. See I. Kant, *Die Religion innerhalb der Grenzen der bloßen Vernunft*, vol. 6, Academy Edition, p. 31. In English: *Religion within the Limits of Reason Alone*, trans. Theodore M. Greene and Hoyt H. Hudson (New York: Harper Torchbooks, 1960), p. 26.

147. Ibid.

148. P. Ricoeur, *Le conflit des interprétations*, p. 426; in English: p. 436.

149. P. Ricoeur, *Finitude et culpabilité*, p. 476; in English: *Symbolism of Evil*, trans. E. Buchanan (Boston: Beacon Press, 1967), p. 345.

150. P. Ricoeur, *Le conflit des interprétations*, p. 305; in English: p. 309: "Therefore, just as the figure of the serpent, at the center of the Adam myth, counters the demythologization of the Babylonean myths, so, too, original sin marks, within the ethical vision of the world, the resistance of the tragic to the ethical." Cf. Jean Nabert, *Essai sur le mal* (Paris: Aubier, 1970), p. 54: "le tragique nous éveille à la pensée de ce qui se dérobe invinciblement aux catégories du monde moral."

151. E. Levinas, *Autrement qu'être ou au-delà de l'essence*, p. 177f.; in English: p. 112.

152. Ibid., p. 173; in English: p. 109.

153. Ibid., p. 193; in English: p. 121.

154. See Plotinus, *Enneads*, I. 8, 5 (trans. A. H. Armstrong).

155. I. Kant, *Die Religion innerhalb der Grenzen der bloßen Vernunft*, vol. 6, Academy Edition (Berlin: G. Reimer, 1907), p. 35; in English: p. 31.

156. I. Kant, *Grundlegung zur Metaphysik der Sitten,* vol. 4, Academy Edition, p. 447.

157. I. Kant, *Kritik der praktischen Vernunft,* vol. 5, Academy Edition, p. 29.

158. I. Kant, *Die Religion innerhalb der Grenzen der bloßen Vernunft,* vol. 6, Academy Edition, p. 35; in English: p. 30.

159. I. Kant, *Metaphysik der Sitten,* vol. 6, Academy Edition, p. 226.

160. G. E. Michalson, Jr., *Fallen Freedom. Kant on Radical Evil and Moral Regeneration* (Cambridge: Cambridge University Press, 1990), p. 5.

161. Ibid., p. xi.

162. I. Kant, *Die Religion innerhalb der Grenzen der bloßen Vernunft,* vol. 6, Academy Edition, p. 41; in English: p. 36.

163. I. Kant, *Grundlegung zur Metaphysik der Sitten,* vol. 4, Academy Edition, p. 455.

164. I. Kant, *Kritik der praktischen Vernunft,* vol. 5, Academy Edition, p. 95.

165. I. Kant, *Die Religion innerhalb der Grenzen der bloßen Vernunft,* vol. 6, Academy Edition, p. 41; in English: p. 36.

166. Cf. P. Ricoeur, *Le conflit des interprétations,* p. 425; in English: p. 435: "Everything is in this 'as if'. It is the philosophical equivalent of the myth of the Fall; it is the rational myth of the coming-to-be of evil [. . .]."

167. S. Kierkegaard, *The Concept of Dread,* trans. Walter Lowrie (Princeton: Princeton University Press, 1957), p. 28.

168. This is shown by A. MacIntyre in *After Virtue,* p. 43ff.

169. S. Kierkegaard, *The Concept of Dread,* p. 46.

170. I. Kant, *Die Religion innerhalb der Grenzen der bloßen Vernunft,* vol. 6, Academy Edition, p. 43; in English: p. 38.

171. S. Kierkegaard, *The Concept of Dread,* p. 14.

172. Cf. P. Ricoeur, *Le conflit des interprétations,* especially p. 426; in English: p. 435f.

173. Cf. D. Ihde, *Hermeneutic Phenomenology. The Philosophy of Paul Ricoeur* (Evanston, Ill.: Northwestern University Press, 1971).

174. D. Janicaud, *Le tournant théologique de la phénoménologie française* (Combas: Editions de l'éclat, 1991), p. 17f.

175. E. Levinas, "Enigme et phénomène," *En découvrant l'existence avec Husserl et Heidegger,* p. 209. In English: "Phenomenon and Enigma," *Collected Philosophical Papers,* trans. A. Lingis (Dordrecht, Boston, and Lancaster: M. Nijhoff, 1987), p. 66.

176. Cf. ibid., p. 211. See also J. Derrida, "La différance," *Marges de la philosophie* (Paris: Minuit, 1972), p. 22; in English: p. 21: "A past that has never been present: this formula is the one that Emmanuel Levinas uses [. . .] to qualify the trace and enigma of absolute alterity: the Other."

177. P. Ricoeur, *Le conflit des interprétations,* p. 422; in English: p. 431.

178. I. Kant, *Kritik der praktischen Vernunft,* vol. 5, Academy Edition, p. 98f.

179. Ibid., vol. 5, p. 95; in English: p. 98.

180. J. Nabert, *Eléments pour une éthique,* p. 5; in English: p. 5: "Memory recreates unceasingly a simultaneity of the interior act by which consciousness judges itself and of the past act which is the matter for this memory."

181. I. Kant, *Kritik der praktischen Vernunft,* vol. 5, Academy Edition, p. 94.

182. I have devoted a more detailed analysis to this problem in an essay entitled "Verantwortlichkeitsethische und fundamentalontologische Schuldauslegung." See *Wege und Irrwege des neueren Umganges mit Heideggers Werk. Ein ungarisch-deutsches Symposium,* ed. by I. M. Feher (Berlin: Duncker and Humblot, 1991), pp. 151–74.

183. J. Nabert, *Essai sur le mal* (Paris: Aubier, 1970), p. 91: "le mal radical dans le sujet de l'action se relie à une scission originaire des consciences que le moi prend en charge autant qu'il la subit."

184. E. Levinas, *Autrement qu'être ou au-delà de l'essence,* p. 31; in English: p. 15.

185. Ibid., p. 24; in English: p. 10.

186. See A. Vergez, *Faute et liberté,* pp. 6f., 40.

187. Ibid., p. 6 n.

188. J. Nabert, *Essai sur le mal,* p. 126.

189. W. Shakespeare, *King Richard III,* Arden edition, ed. A. Hammond (London and New York: Methuen, 1981).

190. F. W. J. Schelling, *Philosophische Untersuchungen über das Wesen der menschlichen Freiheit und die damit zusammenhängenden Gegenstände,* in vol. 7, *Sämmtliche Werke,* p. 390f. In English: *Of Human Freedom,* trans. J. Gutmann (Chicago: Open Court, 1936), p. 69.

191. Cf. ibid., p. 24; in English: p. 10: "the relationship with a past that is on the hither side of every present and every re-presentable, for not belonging to the order of presence, is included in the extraordinary and everyday event of my responsibility that answers for the freedom of another [. . .]."

192. E. Levinas, *Autrement qu'être ou au-delà de l'essence,* p. 198f.; in English: p. 125.

193. Ibid., p. 277; in English: p. 180.

194. Cf. J. Nabert, *Essai sur le mal,* p. 56: "le moi discerne l'invincible contradiction inscrite dans l'être qui est le sien [. . .]"; p. 57: "le moi doit reconnaître [. . .] l'inégalité qui demeure entre ce qu'il est et ce qu'il fait."

195. In his posthumous work, which has been published under the title *Le désir de Dieu* (Paris: Aubier 1966), Nabert expressly uses the term "*aliénation fondamentale*" (p. 22).

196. E. Levinas, *Autrement qu'être ou au-delà de l'essence,* p. 182; in English: p. 115.

197. Ibid.

198. Ibid., p. 198f.; in English: p. 125.

199. J. Nabert, *Essai sur le mal,* p. 131.

200. Ibid., p. 121: "ni l'innocence, ni la confiance ne se connaissent autrement que par une réflexion sur le péché et sur la trahison."

201. Ibid., p. 123.

202. E. Levinas, *Autrement qu'être ou au-delà de l'essence,* p. 199; in English: p. 125.

203. Ibid., p. 181; in English: p. 114f.

204. Ibid., p. 200; in English: p. 126.

205. E. Levinas, "Transcendance et Mal," *De Dieu qui vient à l'idée,* Paris: Vrin, 1982, p. 200. In English: "Transcendence and Evil," in *Collected Philosophical Papers,* trans. A. Lingis (Dordrecht, Boston, and London: M. Nijhoff, 1987).

206. E. Levinas, "Transcendance et Mal," *De Dieu qui vient à l'idée,* p. 205; in English: p. 184.

Bibliography

In the case of authors like Aristotle, Plotinus, and Augustine, the usual way of referring to ancient Greek and Latin texts is followed, and no edition is specified. The German original of Kant's works is referred to in the Edition of the Royal Prussian (later German) Academy of Sciences (abridged as "Academy Edition"), the volumes of which have been published since 1902. The German original of Husserl's works is referred to in the edition called *Husserliana* the volumes of which have been published since 1950.

Adorno, T. W. *Negative Dialektik.* Frankfurt am Main: Suhrkamp, 1994 (1966).

Bernasconi, R. "Skepticism in the Face of Philosophy." In *Re-Reading Levinas,* edited by R. Bernasconi and S. Critchley. London: Athlone, 1991.

Bernet, R., "Die ungegenwärtige Gegenwart. Anwesenheit und Abwesenheit in Husserls Analyse des Zeitbewußtseins." In *Phänomenologische Forschungen.* Vol. 14. K. Freiburg and München: Alber, 1983.

———. Einleitung to *Texte zur Phänomenologie des inneren Zeitbewußtseins (1893–1917),* by E. Husserl. Hamburg: Meiner, 1985.

———. "Husserl and Heidegger on Intentionality and Being." *Journal of the British Society of Phenomenology* 21 (1990): 136–52.

———. "Le sujet dans la nature. Réflexions sur la phénoménologie de la perception chez Merleau-Ponty." In *Merleau-Ponty, phénoménologie et expérience,* edited by M. Richir and E. Tassin. Grenoble: Millon, 1992. Reprinted in *La vie du sujet.* Paris: P. U. F., 1994.

———. "Subjekt und Gesetz in der Ethik von Kant und Lacan." In *Ethik und Psychoanalyse: Vom kategorischen Imperativ zum Gesetz des Begehrens: Kant und Lacan,* edited by H.-D. Gondek and P. Widmer. Frankfurt am Main: Fischer, 1994.

———. "Intentionnalité et transcendance (Husserl et Heidegger)." In *La vie du sujet: Recherches sur l'interprétation de Husserl dans la phénoménologie.* Paris: P. U. F., 1994, pp. 39–64.

———. "Intentionnalité sans sujet ni objet?" In *La vie du sujet: Recherches sur l'interprétation de Husserl dans la phénoménologie.* Paris: P. U. F., 1994, pp. 318–20.

———. "La totalité détotalisée et l'infini. Sartre et Levinas sur la rencontre avec l'autre." Paper presented at the Philosophical Institute of the Eötvös Loránd University of Budapest, May 31, 2000.

Brentano, F. *Psychologie vom empirischen Standpunkt*. Edited by O. Kraus. Hamburg: Meiner, 1973. In English: *Psychology from an Empirical Standpoint*. Translated by A. C. Rancurello, D. B. Terrell, and L. L. McAlister. London: Routledge and Kegan Paul; New York: Humanities Press, 1973.

Brough, J. B. "The Emergence of an Absolute Consciousness in Husserl's Early Writings on Time Consciousness." In *Husserl: Expositions and Appraisals*. Edited by F. A. Elliston and P. McCormick. Notre Dame, Ind.: University of Notre Dame Press, 1977, pp. 83–100.

———. Translator's Introduction to *On the Phenomenology of the Consciousness of Internal Time (1893–1917)* by E. Husserl. Dordrecht, Boston, and London: Kluwer, 1991.

Carr, D. *Time, Narrative, and History*. Bloomington: Indiana University Press, 1986.

Critchley, S. *The Ethics of Deconstruction: Derrida and Levinas*. London and Cambridge, Mass.: B. Blackwell, 1992.

Deleuze, G. *Proust et les signes*. Paris: Quadrige / P. U. F., 1996 (1964).

———. *Différence et répétition*. Paris: P. U. F., 1968.

Derrida, J. *L'écriture et la différence*. Paris: Seuil, 1967, p. 180. In English: *Writing and Difference*. Translated by A. Bass. Chicago: University of Chicago Press; London: Routledge and Kegan Paul, 1978.

———. *La voix et le phénomène*. Paris: P. U. F., 1967.

———. "La différance." In *Marges de la philosophie*. Paris: Minuit, 1972.

Descombes, V. *Le Même et l'Autre: Quarante-cinq ans de philosophie française 1933–1978*. Paris: Minuit, 1979.

Dilthey, W. *Der Aufbau der geschichtlichen Welt in den Geisteswissenschaften*. In *Gesammelte Schriften*. Vol. 7. Stuttgart: Teubner; Göttingen: Vandenhoeck and Ruprecht, 1965.

Drummond, J. J. *Husserlian Intentionality and Non-Foundational Realism*. Dordrecht, Boston, and London: Kluwer, 1990.

Fink, E. "Die phänomenologische Philosophie Edmund Husserls in der gegenwärtigen Kritik." In *Studien zur Phänomenologie*. Den Haag: M. Nijhoff, 1966.

Føllesdal, D. "Husserl's Notion of Noema." *Journal of Philosophy* 66 (1969), pp. 680–87. Reprinted in *Husserl, Intentionality, and Cognitive Science*, H. Dreyfus, ed. Cambridge: MIT Press, 1984.

Foakes, R. A., ed. *King Lear: The Arden Edition of Shakespeare's Works*. Walton-on-Thames: Thomas Nelson and Sons Ltd., 1997.

Foucault, M. *Les mots et les choses*. Paris: Gallimard, 1966.

Franck, D. *Chair et corps: Sur la phénomenologie de Husserl*. Paris: Minuit, 1981.

Freud, S. "Abriß der Psychoanalyse." In *Abriß der Psychoanalyse—Das Unbehagen in der Kultur*. Frankfurt am Main: Fischer Taschenbuch Verlag, 1972.

———. *Das Ich und das Es*. In *Das Ich und das Es und andere metapsychologische Schriften*. Frankfurt am Main: Fischer Taschenbuch Verlag, 1980.

———. *Die Verneinung*. In *Zur Psychologie des Unbewußten*. Vol. 3 of *Studienausgabe*. Frankfurt am Main: Fischer Taschenbuch Verlag, 1982.

Gadamer, H.-G. *Wahrheit und Methode*. Tübingen: J. C. B. Mohr (Paul Siebeck), 1975 (1960).

Gondek, H.-D. "Lacan und die Ethik der Psychoanalyse." In *Ethik und Psychoanalyse. Vom kategorischen Imperativ zum Gesetz des Begehrens: Kant und Lacan,* Edited by H.-D. Gondek and P. Widmer. Frankfurt am Main: Fischer Taschenbuch Verlag, 1994.

Hammond, A., ed. *King Richard III. The Arden Edition of William Shakespeare.* London and New York: Methuen, 1981.

Hegel, G. W. F. *Phänomenologie des Geistes, Werke in zwanzig Bänden.* Edited by E. Moldenhauer and K.-M. Michel. Vol. 3. Frankfurt am Main: Suhrkamp, 1970.

Heidegger, M. *Sein und Zeit.* Tübingen: M. Niemeyer, 1979 (1927). In English: *Being and Time.* Translated by J. Macquarrie and E. Robinson. Oxford: Basil Blackwell, 1962.

———. *Die Grundprobleme der Phänomenologie.* Vol. 24 of *Gesamtausgabe,* edited by F.-W. von Herrmann. Frankfurt am Main: V. Klostermann, 1975.

———. *Metaphysische Anfangsgründe der Logik im Ausgang von Leibniz.* Vol. 26 of *Gesamtausgabe,* edited by Klaus Held. Frankfurt am Main: V. Klostermann, 1978.

———. "Hegels Begriff der Erfahrung." In *Holzwege.* Frankfurt am Main: V. Klostermann, 1950. In English: *Hegel's Concept of Experience.* Translated by J. Glenn Gray and Fred D. Wieck. New York: Harper and Row, 1970.

Held, K. "Das Problem der Intersubjektivität und die Idee einer phänomenologischen Transzendentalphilosophie." In *Perspektiven transzendentalphänomenologischer Forschung,* edited by U. Claesges and K. Held. Den Haag: M. Nijhoff, 1972.

Henrich, D. "Das Problem der Grundlegung der Ethik bei Kant und im spekulativen Idealismus." In *Sein und Ethos,* edited by P. Engelhardt. Mainz: Mathias Grünewald Verlag, 1963

Henry, M. *La barbarie.* Paris: Grasset, 1987.

———. *Phénoménologie matérielle.* Paris: P. U. F., 1990.

Husserl, E. *Logische Untersuchungen.* 3 vols. Tübingen: M. Niemeyer, 1980 (1900–1901). In English: *Logical Investigations.* Translated by J. N. Findlay. London: Routledge and Kegan Paul; New Jersey: Humanities Press, 1970.

———. *Vorlesungen zur Phänomenologie des inneren Zeitbewußtseins.* In *Jahrbuch für Philosophie und phänomenologische Forschung.* Vol. 9, edited by M. Heidegger. Halle a. d. S.: M. Niemeyer, 1928. *Vorlesungen zur Phänomenologie des inneren Zeitbewußtseins.* Vol. 10, edited by Rudolf Boehm. Husserliana. In English: E. Husserl, *On the Phenomenology of the Consciousness of Internal Time (1893–1917).* Translated by J. B. Brough. Dordrecht, Boston, and London: Kluwer, 1991.

———. *Ideen zu einer reinen Phänomenologie und phänomenologischen Philosophie.* Vol. 3/1, edited by K. Schuhmann. *Husserliana.* Den Haag: M. Nijhoff, 1976. In English: *Ideas. General Introduction to Pure Phenomenology.* Translated by W. R. Boyce Gibson. London and New York: Collier Macmillan Publishers, 1962 (1931).

———. *Cartesianische Meditationen.* Edited by E. Ströker. Hamburg: F. Meiner, 1987. *Cartesianische Meditationen.* Vol. 1, edited by S. Strasser. *Husserliana.*

Den Haag: M. Nijhoff, 1991 (1950). In English: *Cartesian Meditations.* Translated by Dorion Cairns. The Hague: M. Nijhoff, 1969.

———. *Zur Phänomenologie der Intersubjektivität III: 1929–35.* Vol. 15, edited by I. Kern. *Husserliana.* Den Haag: M. Nijhoff, 1973.

———. *Phantasie, Bildbewußtsein, Erinnerung. Zur Phänomenologie der anschaulichen Vergegenwärtigungen.* Vol. 23, edited by E. Marbach. *Husserliana.* Den Haag: M. Nijhoff, 1980.

Ihde, D. *Hermeneutic Phenomenology: The Philosophy of Paul Ricoeur.* Evanston, Ill.: Northwestern University Press, 1971.

Janicaud, D. *Le tournant théologique de la phénoménologie française.* Combas: Editions de l'éclat, 1991.

Juranville, A. *Lacan et la philosophie.* Paris: P. U. F., 1984.

Kant, I. *Kritik der reinen Vernunft.* Vols. 3–4. Academy Edition. In English: *A Critique of Pure Reason.* Translated by N. Kemp Smith. New York: St. Martin's Press, 1965.

———. *Grundlegung zur Metaphysik der Sitten.* Vol. 4. Academy Edition. In English: *Foundations of the Metaphysics of Morals.* In *Critique of Practical Reason and Other Writings in Moral Philosophy.* Translated by L. White Beck. Chicago: University of Chicago Press, 1976.

———. *Kritik der praktischen Vernunft.* Vol. 5. Academy Edition. In English: *Foundations of the Metaphysics of Morals.* In *Critique of Practical Reason and Other Writings in Moral Philosophy.* Translated by L. White Beck. Chicago: University of Chicago Press, 1976.

———. *Die Religion innerhalb der Grenzen der bloßen Vernunft.* Vol. 6. Academy Edition. In English: *Religion within the Limits of Reason Alone.* Translated by Theodore M. Greene and Hoyt H. Hudson. New York: Harper Torchbooks, 1960.

———. *Metaphysik der Sitten.* Vol. 6. Academy Edition.

Kierkegaard, S. *The Concept of Dread.* Translated by Walter Lowrie. Princeton, N.J.: Princeton University Press, 1957.

Krüger, G. *Philosophie und Moral in der Kantischen Kritik.* Tübingen: J. C. B. Mohr [P. Siebeck], 1967 [1931].

Lacan, J. *L'éthique de la psychanalyse, Le séminaire.* Bk. 7. Paris: Seuil, 1986. In English: J.-A. Miller, ed., *The Ethics of Psychoanalysis 1959–1960, The Seminar of Jacques Lacan.* Bk. 7. Translated by D. Porter. London: Routledge, 1992.

Levin, D. M. *The Philosopher's Gaze. Modernity in the Shadows of Enlightenment.* Berkeley: University of California Press, 1999.

Levinas, E. *Totalité et Infini: Essai sur l'extériorité.* La Haye: M. Nijhoff, 1961. Quotations are taken from *Totalité et Infini.* Paris: Editions Livre de Poche; Dordrecht, Boston, and London: Kluwer, 1994. In English: *Totality and Infinity.* Translated by A. Lingis. Pittsburgh: Dusquesne University Press, 1969.

———. "Réflexions sur la 'technique' phénoménologique." In *En découvrant l'existence avec Husserl et Heidegger.* Paris: Vrin, 1974.

———. "Intentionnalité et Sensation." In *En découvrant l'existence avec Husserl et Heidegger.* Paris: Vrin, 1974.

———. "Enigme et phénomène." In *En découvrant l'existence avec Husserl et Heidegger.* Paris: Vrin, 1974. In English: "Phenomenon and Enigma." In *Collected Philosophical Papers.* Translated by A. Lingis. Dordrecht, Boston, and Lancaster: M. Nijhoff, 1987.

———. *Autrement qu'être ou au-delà de l'essence.* La Haye: M. Nijhoff, 1974. Quotations are taken from *Autrement qu'être ou au-delà de l'essence.* Paris: Editions Livre de Poche; Dordrecht, Boston, and London: Kluwer, 1990. In English: *Otherwise Than Being or Beyond Essence.* Translated by A. Lingis. The Hague: M. Nijhoff, 1981.

———. "Transcendance et Mal." In *De Dieu qui vient à l'idée.* Paris: Vrin, 1982. In English: "Transcendence and Evil." In *Collected Philosophical Papers.* Translated by A. Lingis. Dordrecht, Boston, and London: M. Nijhoff, 1987.

Lévi-Strauss, C. *La pensée sauvage.* Paris: Plon, Livre de poche, Agora, 1962.

MacIntyre, A. *After Virtue: A Study in Moral Theory.* London: Duckworth, 1987.

Mann, T. *Der Zauberberg.* Berlin: Aufbau-Verlag, 1953. In English: *The Magic Mountain.* Translated by H. T. Lowe-Porter. London: Vintage, 1999.

———. Joseph und seine Brüder. 3 vols. Berlin: Aufbau-Verlag, 1972. In English: *Joseph and His Brothers.* Translated by H. T. Lowe-Porter. London: Vintage, 1999.

———. *Doktor Faustus.* Berlin: Aufbau-Verlag, 1965. In English: *Doctor Faustus.* Translated by H. T. Lowe-Porter. New York: Vintage Books, 1992.

———. *Die Entstehung des Doktor Faustus.* In *Doktor Faustus—Die Entstehung des Doktor Faustus.* Frankfurt am Main: Fischer, 1967.

Marion, J.-L. *Etant donné. Essai d'une phénoménologie de la donation.* Paris: P. U. F., 1997.

Marquet, J.-F. *Singularité et événement.* Grenoble: Millon, 1995.

———. "Proust, la fête inconceivable." In *Miroirs de l'identité. La littérature hantée par la philosophie.* Paris: Hermann, 1996.

McIntyre, R. and D. W. Smith. *Husserl and Intentionality: A Study of Mind, Meaning, and Language.* Dordrecht: D. Reidel, 1984.

Merleau-Ponty, M. *Phénoménologie de la perception.* Paris: Gallimard, 1945. In English: *Phenomenology of Perception.* Translated by Colin Smith. London: Routledge, 1962.

———. "Le doute de Cézanne." In *Sens et non-sens.* Paris: Gallimard, 1996.

———. "Sur la phénoménologie du langage." In *Eloge de la philosophie et autres essays.* Paris: Gallimard, 1989.

———. "De Mauss à Claude Lévi-Strauss." In *Eloge de la philosophie et autres essays.* Paris: Gallimard, 1989.

———. *La prose du monde.* Paris: Gallimard, 1969.

———. *Le visible et l'invisible.* Paris: Gallimard, 1964. In English: *The Visible and the Invisible.* Translated by A. Lingis. Evanston, Ill.: Northwestern University Press, 1969.

———. *L'oeil et l'esprit.* Paris: Gallimard, 1964.

———. *Résumés de cours, Collège de France 1952–1960.* Paris: Gallimard, 1968.

Michalson, G. E., Jr. *Fallen Freedom: Kant on Radical Evil and Moral Regeneration.* Cambridge: Cambridge University Press, 1990.

Nabert, J. *Éléments pour une éthique.* Paris: P. U. F., 1943. In English: *Elements for an Ethic.* Translated by W. J. Petrek. Evanston, Ill.: Northwestern University Press, 1969.

———. Préface to édition d'*Eléments pour une éthique.* 2d ed. Paris: Aubier, 1962. In English: *Elements for an Ethic.* Translated by W. J. Petrek. Evanston, Ill.: Northwestern University Press, 1969.

———. *Essai sur le mal.* Paris: Aubier, 1970 (1955).

———. *Désir de Dieu.* Paris: Aubier, 1966.

Parfit, D. *Reasons and Persons.* Oxford: Clarendon Press, 1984.

Patočka, J. "Der Subjektivismus der Husserlschen und die Möglichkeit einer 'asubjektiven' Phänomenologie." In *Die Bewegung der menschlichen Existenz, Phänomenologische Schriften.* Vol. 2. Edited by K. Nellen, J. Nemec, and I. Srubar. Stuttgart: Klett-Cotta, 1991.

Prauss, G. *Kant über Freiheit als Autonomie.* Frankfurt am Main: V. Klostermann, 1983.

Proust, M. *Du côté de chez Swann,* in *A la recherche du temps perdu.* Vol. I. Paris: Gallimard, 1987. In English: *Swann's Way.* Vol. 2, part 2 of *Remembrance of Things Past.* Translated by C. K. Scott Moncrieff. London: Chatto and Windus, 1965.

———. *Temps retrouvé.* In *A la recherche du temps perdu.* Vol. IV. Paris: Gallimard, 1989. In English: M. Proust, *In Search of Time.* Vol. 6 of *Time Regained.* Translated by C. K. Scott Moncreiff and Terence Kilmartin. Revisions by D. J. Enright. London: Vintage Books, 1996.

Putnam, H. *Reason, Truth, and History.* Cambridge: Cambridge University Press, 1981.

Richir, M. *Phénoménologie et institution symbolique.* Grenoble: Millon, 1988.

———. "Monadologie transcendantale et temporalisation." In *Husserl-Ausgabe und Husserl-Forschung,* edited by S. Ijsseling. Dordrecht, Boston, and London: Kluwer, 1990.

———. "Communauté, société et histoire chez le dernier Merleau-Ponty." In *Merleau-Ponty, phénoménologie et expérience.* Edited by M. Richir and E. Tassin. Grenoble: Millon, 1992.

———. *Méditations phénoménologiques.* Grenoble: Millon, 1992.

Ricoeur, P. *Le volontaire et l'involontaire.* Vol. 1 of *Philosophie de la volonté.* Paris: Aubier, 1950.

———. *Finitude et culpabilité.* Paris: Seuil, 1988. In English the first part in separate volume with the title *Fallible Man.* Translated by C. A. Kelbley. New York: Fordham University Press, 1986.

———. *Finitude et culpabilité.* Paris: Seuil, 1988. In English the second part in separate volume with the title *Symbolism of Evil.* Translated by E. Buchanan. Boston: Beacon Press, 1967.

———. *De l'interprétation: Essai sur Freud.* Paris: Seuil, 1965. In English: *Freud and Philosophy. An Essay on Interpretation.* Translated by Denis Savage. New Haven and London: Yale University Press, 1970.

———. "Démythiser l'accusation." In *Le conflit des interprétations: Essai d'herméneutique.* Paris: Seuil, 1969. In English: *The Conflict of Interpretations.* Edited by D. Ihde. Evanston, Ill.: Northwestern University Press, 1974.

———. "Herméneutique des symboles et réflexion philosophique (II)." In *Le conflit des interprétations: Essai d'herméneutique.* Paris: Seuil, 1969. In English: *The Conflict of Interpretations.* Edited by D. Ihde. Evanston, Ill.: Northwestern University Press, 1974.

———. "Le 'péché originel': étude de signification." In *Le conflit des interprétations: Essai d'herméneutique.* Paris: Seuil, 1969. In English: *The Conflict of Interpretations.* Edited by D. Ihde. Evanston, Ill.: Northwestern University Press, 1974.

———. *Temps et récit.* Paris: Seuil, 1983–85.

———. *Soi-même comme un autre.* Paris: Seuil, 1990.

———. "L'identité narrative." *Esprit* 7–8 (1988).

———. "Life in Quest of Narrative." In *On Paul Ricoeur. Narrative and Interpretation.* Edited by D. Wood. London and New York: Routledge, 1991.

———. *Autrement: Lecture d'*Autrement qu'être au au-delà de l'essence *de Levinas.* Paris: P. U. F., 1997.

Sartre, J.-P. *L'être et le néant.* Paris: Gallimard, 1943. In English: *Being and Nothingness.* Translated by H. E. Barnes. London: Methuen, 1958.

Saussure, F. de. *Cours de linguistique générale.* Translated by T. de Mauro. Paris: Payot, 1972.

Schapp, W. *In Geschichten verstrickt.* Weisbaden: B. Heymann Verlag, 1976 (1953).

Schelling, F. W. J. *System des transzendentalen Idealismus.* In *Sämmtliche Werke.* Edited by K. F. A. Schelling. Stuttgart and Augsburg: Cotta, 1860.

———. *Philosophische Untersuchungen über das Wesen der menschlichen Freiheit und die damit zusammenhängenden Gegenstände.* In *Sämmtliche Werke.* Vol. 7. In English: *Of Human Freedom.* Translated by J. Gutmann. Chicago: Open Court, 1936.

Sebbah, F.-D. "Aux limites de l'intentionnalité: M. Henry et E. Levinas lecteurs des *Leçons sur la conscience intime du temps.*" *Alter* 2 (1994).

Taylor, C. *Sources of the Self: The Making of the Modern Identity.* Cambridge: Cambridge University Press, 1989.

Tengelyi, L. "Eine Methode rekonstruktiver Analyse." *Doxa* 17 (1989): 47–54.

———. "Verantwortlichkeitsethische und fundamentalontologische Schuldauslegung." See *Wege und Irrwege des neueren Umganges mit Heideggers Werk: Ein ungarisch-deutsches Symposium.* Edited by I. M. Feher. Berlin: Duncker and Humblot, 1991, pp. 151–74.

Twardowski, K. *Zur Lehre vom Inhalt und Gegenstand der Vorstellungen: Eine psychologische Untersuchung.* München and Wien: Philosophia Verlag, 1982 (1894).

Vergez, A. *Faute et liberté*. Paris: Les belles lettres, 1969.

Waldenfels, B. "Singularität im Plural." In *Deutsch-Französische Gedankengänge*. Frankfurt am Main: Suhrkamp, 1995.

———. "Verschränkung von Heimwelt und Fremdwelt." In *Philosophische Grundlagen der Interkulturalität*. Vol. 1 of *Studien zur interkulturellen Philosophie*. Edited by R. A. Mall and D. Lohmar. Amsterdam and Atlanta: Rodopi, 1993.

———. *Antwortregister.* Frankfurt am Main: Suhrkamp, 1994.

Wiggins, D. *Substance and Sameness*. Oxford: B. Blackwell, 1980.

Williams, B. *Ethics and the Limits of Philosophy*. Glasgow: Collins, Fontana Press, 1985.

———. *Problems of the Self.* Cambridge: Cambridge University Press, 1973.

Index of Names

Index of Subject Matter

About the Author

László Tengelyi is a professor of philosophy at Bergische Universität Wuppertal in Germany and serves on the editorial board for the journal *Husserl Studies*. He was recently elected president of the German Society of Phenomenological Research. He has published numerous articles in international journals as well as several books in Hungarian and one book in German.

Géza Kállay is the head of the School of English and American Studies at Eötvös Loránd University in Hungary.

Consulting Editors